ADVERTISEMENT.

The following Papers first appeared in *Bentley's Miscellany*, and are now collected at the suggestion of the many admirers of their gifted Author.

LONDON,
SEPTEMBER 1859.

SHAKSPEARE PAPERS:

PICTURES, GRAVE AND GAY.

BIOGRAPHICAL SKETCH OF DR. MAGINN.

WILLIAM MAGINN is no more! The bright spirit whose wit was the delight of thousands, — whose learning was the admiration of a quarter of a century, — whose poetry could win the applause of Byron himself,—and whose guileless simplicity and modesty were the charm of all who knew him, has now some years passed the portals of death, and his place knoweth him no longer! The drama is over—the last scene of his eventful history has descended, and the picturesque little village of Walton-on-Thames now contains all that was mortal of one of the most distinguished critics and scholars of the age. He died in his forty-ninth year, August 1842, leaving a wife and family to lament their irreparable loss.

Born in July 1794, the precocity of his talents astonished all who knew him, and gave a cheering presage of his future eminence. He entered college in his tenth year, and passed through it with distinction, winning all the honours that dignify and adorn an University career. For a few years he assisted his father in conducting a large and celebrated academy in Cork; but on the first appearance of *Blackwood's Magazine* he quitted Ireland, and edited that journal in Edinburgh. His papers are eminently original and fine; they attracted considerable attention, and would do honour to the loftiest name in our literature. Having by his connection with this periodical, and his contributions to the *Quarterly Review*, fully established his name as a writer of first-rate ability, he came to London, and was soon appointed to the joint-editorship of the *Standard* with the amiable and learned Dr. Giffard. On the establishment of *Bentley's Miscellany*, Dr. Maginn became a contributor to its pages. To him the public are indebted for the able series of articles entitled *The Shakspeare Papers*, (contained in this volume,) which have been so justly admired.

The following sketches of him, as he appeared about this period, have been drawn by a man of no slight talent, and with great powers of observation—the late Dr. Macnish, better known by his assumed signature of the Modern Pythagorean.

"I dined to-day at the Salopian with Dr. Maginn. He is a most remarkable fellow. His flow of ideas is incredibly quick, and his articulation so rapid, that it is difficult to follow him. He is altogether a person of vast acuteness, celerity of apprehension, and indefatigable activity both of body and mind. He is about my own height; but I could allow him an inch round the chest. His forehead is very finely developed, his organ of language and ideality large, and his reasoning faculties excellent. His hair is quite grey, although he does not look more than forty. I imagined he was much older-looking, and that he wore a wig. While conversing, his eye is never a moment at rest; in fact his whole body is in motion, and he keeps scrawling grotesque figures upon the paper before him, and rubbing them out again as fast as he draws them. He and Giffard are, as you know, joint editors of the *Standard*.

"I had some queer chat with O'Doherty. I did not measure Maginn's chest, but I examined his head.

He has a very fine development of the intellectual powers, especially ideality and wit, which are both unusually large. His language is also large, and he has much firmness and destructiveness, which latter accounts for the satirical bent of his genius. That beautiful tale, *The City of the Demons*, he informed me, he wrote quite off-hand. He writes with vast rapidity, and can do so at any time. He speaks French, Italian, and German fluently; these, together with a first-rate knowledge of Latin, Greek, and English, make him master of six languages, so that you can allow him one. He is altogether a very remarkable man. Indeed, I consider him quite equal to Swift; and had his genius, like Swift's, been concentrated in separate works, instead of being squandered with wasteful prodigality in newspapers, magazines, &c., I have no doubt it would have been considered equally original and wonderful. He was much tickled with the apotheosis which I recited to him. I told him you were master of seven languages. Had you been present, I would have confined your abilities to a smaller number, lest he had taken it into his head to try you with the others. The letter-press of the *Gallery of Literary Portraits* he hit off at a moment's notice, and in the course of a few minutes."

Scarcely less flattering is the following picture, drawn by the elegant pen of Dr. Moir of Musselburgh, a distinguished poet, and a good man, of whom Maginn always spoke, as he deserved, in the highest terms:

"To a portion, and no inconsiderable one, of the literary world, Dr. Maginn is known *par excellence* as *the Doctor;* in the same way as Professor Wilson is recognized as *the Professor.* Nearly twenty years, *eheu! fugaces, Posthume, labuntur anni!* have glided over since the Doctor and I were *co-litterateurs;* and yet, strange to say, we have never chanced to meet. By every one capable of judging, the powers of Dr. Maginn are acknowledged to be of the highest order. Has he given the world assurance of this in the way he might have done? We doubt much; but from *The City of the Demons,* *The Man in the Bill,* *Colonel Pride,* *The Shakspeare Papers,* and many other things, posterity will be able to appreciate him. *Ex pede Herc.*"

Such was William Maginn as he appeared to these two eminent men. And truly can it be said that the portrait is not overdrawn; or that if in any way unlike, it is because it scarcely does justice to the merits of its original. It is, to be sure, enviable praise to be associated with so brilliant a name as Swift; but, much as we admire the writings of the Dean, we must in justice say that they are far short of those of Maginn. For Swift was morose, and cynical, and austere,—Maginn was kind, and gentle, and child-like. Swift's whole conversation was irony or sarcasm; Maginn's was entirely genial and anecdotical, and free from bitterness. Like the lives of all literary men, that of Dr. Maginn will be best found in the series of his publications. We do not know a single individual to whom the praise of Parr on Fox more perfectly applies, and never do we peruse it that we do not almost fancy it was written expressly for Maginn.*

Can anything more exquisitely portray the kindliness of his heart, and his devotion to his children, than

---

* If you had been called upon to select a friend from the whole human race, where could you have found one endowed as he was with the guileless playfulness of a child, and the most correct and comprehensive knowledge of the world; or, distinguished as he was by an elegant taste in the dead and living languages, by a thorough acquaintance with the most important events of past and present times, by a profound skill in the history, and by a well-founded and well-directed reverence for the constitution of his country, and by the keenest penetration into all the nearer and all the remoter consequences of public measures?—PARR. *Character of Fox.*

the following verses, inlaid in this place like pieces of rich mosaic? They are simple and homely; but it is the spirit they breathe for which we love them.

"TO MY DAUGHTERS.

" O my darling little daughters!
    O my daughters, lov'd so well!
Who by Brighton's breezy waters
    For a time have gone to dwell.
Here I come with spirit yearning,
    With your sight my eyes to cheer,
When this sunny day returning
    Brings my forty-second year.

" Knit to me in love and duty
    Have you been, sweet pets of mine!
Long in health, and joy, and beauty,
    May it be your lot to shine!
And at last, when God commanding,
    I shall leave you both behind,
May I feel with soul expanding
    I shall leave you good and kind!

"May I leave my Nan and Pigeon*
   Mild of faith, of purpose true,
Full of faith and meek religion,
   With many joys, and sorrows few!
Now I part, with fond caressing,
   Part you now, my daughters dear—
Take, then take your father's blessing,
   In his forty-second year!
                  W. M."

We hope it will not be found that the young and interesting family of the great man, whose genius reflects credit on our country,—whose single-heartedness and benevolence were immediately observed by all who approached him,—who, in the course of as diversified a life as ever literary man led, never had but one foe,—whose political principles swerved not from their original path, but continued steady and firm to the last,—whose intellect adorned every theme that he touched, and whose only fault was to be too careless of the morrow (that prime failing in men of the loftiest minds),—we hope that this man's children will be provided for by the resources of such a country as ours. Literary men too rarely leave fortunes to their

---

* A pet name for his youngest daughter.

children; but the present is, perhaps, the most distressing instance that has happened for many years in England.—*August* 1842.

The following literary retrospect of Dr. Maginn will be read with interest:

BEFORE I close my desk, as I sit in my moonlit chamber this fine summer evening, let me recall one sufferer, now at rest,—slightly known to me, indeed, but remembered with a fearful distinctness—*so* slightly, that if you were to ask me his Christian name I could not tell it. A clear remembrance of his blanched cheek and wandering eye dwells in my memory. Who when I add the faltering voice, the symmetrical features, the grey hair, even in comparative youth,—the slashing reply, the sweet, good-natured smile,—who will not recall the name of Dr. Maginn?

I saw him one evening—how well I remember it, and with what throes and throbs the remembrance is even now recalled!—yes, even now. It was in an evening-party where;—but what has the world to do with our private reminiscences? And what am *I*, a stupid old man, (to night in one of my low-spirited seasons,) that I should aim at exciting the interest of the bright-eyed, blooming creatures who will bend over this page next month, perhaps as the travelling-carriage carries them far from London and distraction, to read the newspaper to papa, maybe, in some country parsonage, or to listen to the recital of Brother Tom's first essay in hunting and shooting, or to be the hand-maiden of mamma's charities, or the happy representative of Aunt Bountiful at the Sunday-school.

Let me return to Dr. Maginn; and for an instant mingle with the thoughts of him the recollections still dear to this elderly heart.

It was a low, long, narrow room through which I made my way into the throng of a party. That gentle confusion prevailed which shows that all is " going off " well. That Trophonius's-cave look which we sometimes see on the faces of those who are coming out as you go in, and which appears to proclaim that they are never to smile again, was not to be observed. And yet there was no singing, no dancing, no charades—and yet,— it was that hateful assemblage known by the name of a literary coterie.

I made my way into the very thick of the throng; elbowed a poetess to the right, trod upon the slipper of a lady historian, touched the saintly shoulder of some

Charlotte-Elizabeth of the day, and oh! more formidable than all, brushed, may be, the sacred dust off the sleeve of a Reviewer. All were standing, all were listening to some one who sat in the middle of a group; a low-seated man, short in stature, was uttering pleasantries, and scattering witticism about him, with the careless glee of his country—this was Maginn. His articulation was impeded by a stutter, yet the sentences that he stammered forth were brilliant repartees, uttered without sharpness, and edged rather with humour than with satire. His countenance was rather agreeable than striking; its expression sweet, rather than bright. The grey hair, coming straight over his forehead, gave a singular appearance to a face still bearing the attributes of youth. He was thirty or thereabouts, (yes, saucy niece of mine, thirty *is* still young;) but his thoughtful brow, his hair, the paleness of his complexion, gave him many of the attributes of age. I am, however, a firm believer in the axiom, that age can never be concealed upon a careful inspection,—we may look older than we are, but we rarely, alas! look younger. True, the first impression may deceive; but there is always some line, some tell-tale change somewhere, which betrays the ugly truth. I looked on for a moment, as the crew of authors, reviewers, playwrights, and novel-weavers paid homage to Dr. Maginn. He was then in the zenith of his glory—the glory which radiated from *John Bull* or sent forth a rich stream of light from the pages of *Fraser*. His conversation was careless and off-hand, and, but for the impediment of speech would have had the charm of a rich comedy. His choice of words was such as I have rarely met with in any of *my* contemporaries; for, indeed, in my day it has become the vogue to corrupt English in many ways, to bring down your subject by homely, if not coarse phrases, and to neglect all those adjuncts to reasoning and to wit which a true use of our language affords.

I passed on, the circle closed around Maginn, and that evening I saw him no more. Henceforth his career was a bright and perilous one, exercising a considerable, though ephemeral influence on the age in which he lived. No modern writer in periodicals has ever given to satire a less repulsive form of personality. No private venom seemed to direct the awful pen which spared not affectation, and lashed presumption till she bled to death. Why are not his essays collected? What holds them back from an expectant public? He wrote when our periodical literature was in its zenith; yet he bore away the palm; and his clear, firm hand might be discerned amid a host of inferior writers. There was no mistaking that emphatic, pure, and stately English of his—poor Maginn!

The next time I saw this ill-starred son of genius was in a friend's house, very early one morning, as Dr. Maginn was going away to France. He and I were for some minutes alone in a room together. It was a dingy, London morning, and the room corresponded to the day—a lodging-house room. It was not dirty, to speak individually; but a general air of antiquity, of long-established dustiness, of confirmed, ingrained, never-to-be-effaced uncleanliness sat upon every article in the apartment, even to the top of the bell-ropes. The fire was not lighted—it was September; the window was open sufficiently to chill the susceptible frame of the great Reviewer as he paced to and fro, never looking towards me, waiting for our common friend. I shut the window. He looked towards me for an instant, stammered out a "Thank you." His face was then of a leaden, ashy hue; his grey hair had become thin; his dress—but why expatiate upon *that;*—yet it looked sorrowful, and shattered like its wearer, and *I* fancied it meant much.

Our friend came into the room. I heard Maginn say, " I am going out of town;" and even those few words sounded ominous in my presaging mind—going out of town! Alas! how many reasons are there for which one may go out of town. Sorrow, sickness, weariness of spirit, embarrassed circumstances, and a long and mournful list of etceteras. I ran down the dingy stairs with a mournful conviction that Adversity, with her rapid strides had overtaken poor Maginn—and I was not wrong; perhaps he provoked the beldam (whom Gray chooses to apostrophize as a nurse) to follow him; and follow him she did—to his grave.

I got into the street—what a sensible difference in the atmosphere. How well De Balzac, in his *Père Goriot*, describes the atmosphere of a boarding-house—that ineffable, unventilated atmosphere. After enumerating all its compound attributes, how admirably he finishes the description, by saying it is impossible to sum it up!—it is—it is, in fact, the boarding-house atmosphere, and he cannot say more.

The lodging-house left much the same conviction on my mind—that no one could describe the sensations which are produced by its peculiar atmosphere. By the way, how is it that in this great metropolis there are no good lodgings to be had? Nothing on a good system—everything so dirty, so faded, so dear—everybody so imposing, such wretched lodging-house looks, such infamous little boys to wait at the street door, such drabs of housemaids, beds which one loathes, sofas which soil one's pantaloons, carpets old in the sin of dirt, and windows which you may look through if you can. In winter a tea-spoonful of coal in your fire-place; in summer a baking hot atmosphere; no ventilation, no good cleanings to refresh the apartments; suffocating nights and days; if you are a lover of cleanliness, you are wretched. Why are we so far behind all other places for the season (for London is now little else than a great watering-place, without mineral springs) in these essential comforts? I beg pardon for flying away from Dr. Maginn into the unwholesome air of lodging-houses.

Says a friend to me one day, "Come and meet Maginn; there shall be none save him, our own family, and yourself. You will see him to advantage." It was now two years since I had seen Maginn. Time, which ambles withal to many, had galloped with him. His grey hair was now very thin, and scattered over an anxious brow; the sweet mildness of his eye was gone, his speech was more faltering than ever; many moments elapsed before he could begin a word, for natural defect was heightened by nervous debility, and the approach of his last fatal disease. Still, broken up, impaired as he was, there were genuine bursts of humour, a scholar-like nicety of expression; above all, a humbled, and perhaps chastened spirit was apparent. We had a day of talk of the sterling and standard writers of England; themes fitted for the Augustan age flowed freely. Swift was, perhaps, the model of Maginn, certainly he was the object of his adoration; and, as he aptly quoted him, true Irish humour played upon the features of the modern satirist.

It was not long since the town had rung with conversation respecting the famous article in *Fraser*—the demolition of a certain aristocratic author—the unmanly and brutal revenge upon the most amiable of booksellers—the trial—the duel between Maginn and the assailant—the slow and cruel death of the beaten and affrighted publisher — the immunity which the offender had enjoyed—for fashion had lent her shield to the votary. I did then consider, and I still do consider, Maginn's article on the work in question one of his strongest and his best: strong, because hatred of vice lent it power; good, because written from the impulse of a mind which, however sullied by excess, was originally high-toned and fearless. Of course I abstained scrupulously from the subject, and was surprised at the readiness with which Maginn entered into it. He gave me the whole history of the duel from first to last; spoke of the gentlemanly bearing of his antagonist, and seemed to me to take an absolute pleasure in recounting the whole. But when he touched upon the sufferings of the injured and innocent publisher, his lip quivered, his frame writhed, a tear dimmed his eye, he walked hastily to and fro, and, when he returned to his seat, spoke of the subject no more. I longed to glean more from him; to gather up his real opinions of men and things; to draw him forth from the mask which the periodical writer must needs wear; to enjoy the true sentiment which lay beneath the satire, like sweet, crushed water-plants beneath the ice. But the limits of a London party are all too short, and tea came, and eleven o'clock came, and I rushed into the street, thence to mingle among many who would repudiate me if they thought I had any of the contamination of literature about me.

I saw Maginn no more. I was not surprised when I learned that slow disease had wasted his limbs and brought him to the brink of the grave, but had left his intellect bright and clear to the last. That was a wonderful mind which could stand the wear and tear to which poor Maginn subjected it. His last thoughts, as they are recorded, were of literature and of Homer. May we not hope that the pure ray of reason thus spared, was ofttimes, perhaps in the silence of the sleepless night, employed in holy and hopeful reflections—that the things of *this* life had a fitful and partial influence over his spirit—that the solemn expectation of eternity had the noblest and the greatest share of that mind, so vigorous in its close?

When I review, in my own study, the different literary circles which I have seen, I admire at the contrast between my setting out and the end of my journey as a pedestrian through the walks of life. I marvel at the various phases which the polite world has assumed, as it has shone upon me; the various aspects which certain cliques of men, all following the same pursuits, have worn. How like a dream it now seems, to suppose Maginn the soul and centre of a certain circle, who hung upon his applause, and adulated his talents! And now, how the memory of his brief, feverish existence has passed away, revived only by the accents of compassion, or adduced to "point a moral." To "adorn a tale" he never was intended. How completely was his fame limited to a certain circle! how un-English was his reputation! how non-European his celebrity! The circle that surrounded him is gradually melting away; it is broken up; one by one the leaves of the book have been snatched out by death:

the ears that listened to him are even already dulled; the eyes which gazed on him are closed in death. The very bookseller who suffered for his aggression upon the literary merits of Mr. Grantley Berkeley has sunk, after slow disease, to an untimely grave. Men of letters in the present day, live fast: the words of the Psalmist, applicable to all, to them are peculiarly appropriate. As soon as they arrive at their zenith, so soon does the canker-worm of disease undermine the root, and poison the sap that nourishes the tree: they pass away, to borrow from the sublimest of all human writers, " even as a sleep; they fade away suddenly like grass."

When last I saw Maginn, there gazed upon his soft but restless eye, there hung upon his words, a pale young man, himself a genius of the purest ray, adulating the genius of another. I knew him not; his manner was unobtrusive; the circle who stood around Maginn had scarcely heard his name. He stood behind in a retired part of the room. Unseen, he went away—no one missed him. No one alluded to the young Irishman: the name of Gerald Griffin was not so much as uttered in that noisy chamber. As he passed me, the grave and melancholy aspect, the lean form, and anxious countenance arrested my attention.

Amid the heads which were bowed down to listen to the fancies of Maginn, was a face then fresh, and youthful, and beaming. A dark, quick searching eye—a smile full of sweetness—a brow on which sat the innocence of youth—a gentle deportment, and the universal love and sympathy of all around him, proclaimed the presence of Laman Blanchard. I dare not prolong the theme—I will not linger on a remembrance too recent to be recalled without intense regret, a sorrow too fresh for consolation. The biographer, and the subject of his pen, the reviewer and the reviewed, alike sleep in the tomb. How hurried was their destiny! how brief their summer's day! how few the years that were allotted them to delight or to instruct mankind. I return to my first proposition—men of letters live fast: it was not so of yore. Formerly they attained old age: their occupation was not a killing one. Let me throw aside my pen and muse on things that have been—and recall, like the sexagenarian of old, the different aspects of the lettered world:—the coteries of the published and the publisher.

We cannot close this sketch better than by appending the following exquisite lines, which illustrate the versatile genius of the late Dr. Maginn:

"THE MOCKINGS OF THE SOLDIERS.

"FROM ST. MATTHEW.

" Plant a crown upon his head,
   Royal robe around him spread;
   See that his imperial hand
   Grasps as fit the sceptral wand:
   Then before him bending low,
   As becomes his subjects, bow;
   Fenced within our armed ring,
   Hail him, hail him, as our King!

" Platted was of thorns the crown,
   Trooper's cloak was royal gown;
   If his passive hand, indeed,
   Grasp'd a sceptre, 'twas a reed.
   He was bound to feel and hear
   Deeds of shame, and words of jeer;
   For he whom king in jest they call
   Was a doomed captive scoff'd by all.

"But the brightest crown of gold,
 Or the robe of rarest fold,
 Or the sceptre which the mine
 Of Golconda makes to shine,
 Or the lowliest homage given
 By all mankind under heaven,
 Were prized by him no more than scorn,
 Sceptre of reed or crown of thorn.

"Of the stars his crown is made,
 In the sun he is array'd,
 He the lightning of the spheres
 As a flaming sceptre bears:
 Bend in rapture before him
 Ranks of glowing seraphim;
 And we, who spurn'd him, trembling stay
 The judgment of his coming day.

W. M.

SHAKSPEARE PAPERS.

I. Sir John Falstaff.

II. Jaques.

III. Romeo.

IV. Midsummer Night's Dream—Bottom the Weaver.

V. His Ladies—Lady Macbeth.

VI. Timon of Athens.

VII. Polonius.

VIII. Iago.

SIR JOHN FALSTAFF.

"For those who read aright are well aware
That Jaques, sighing in the forest green,
Oft on his heart felt less the load of care
Than Falstaff, revelling his rough mates between."
MS. penes me.

"JACK FALSTAFF to my familiars!"—By that name, therefore, must he be known by all persons, for all are now the familiars of Falstaff. The title of "Sir John Falstaff to all Europe" is but secondary and parochial. He has long since far exceeded the limit by which he bounded the knowledge of his knighthood; and in wide-spreading territories, which in the day of his creation were untrodden by human foot, and in teeming realms where the very name of England was then unheard of, Jack Falstaff is known as familiarly as he was to the wonderful court of princes, beggars, judges, swindlers, heroes, bullies, gentlemen, scoundrels, justices, thieves, knights, tapsters, and the rest whom he drew about him.

It is indeed *his* court. He is lord paramount, the *suzerain* to whom all pay homage. Prince Hal may delude himself into the notion that he, the heir of

England, with all the swelling emotions of soul that rendered him afterwards the conqueror of France, makes a butt of the ton of man that is his companion. The parts are exactly reversed. In the peculiar circle in which they live, the prince is the butt of the knight. He knows it not,—he would repel it with scorn if it were asserted; but it is nevertheless the fact that he is subdued. He calls the course of life which he leads, the unyoked humour of his idleness; but he mistakes. In all the paths where his journey lies with Falstaff, it is the hard-yoked servitude of his obedience. In the soliloquies put into his mouth he continually pleads that his present conduct is but that of the moment, that he is ashamed of his daily career, and that the time is ere long to come which will show him different from what he seems. As the dramatic character of Henry V. was conceived and executed by a man who knew how genius in any department of human intellect would work,—to say nothing of the fact that Shakspeare wrote with the whole of the prince's career before him,—we may consider this subjugation to Falstaff as intended to represent the transition state from spoiled youth to energetic manhood. It is useless to look for minute traces of the historical Henry in these dramas. Tradition and the chronicles had handed him down to Shakspeare's time as a prince dissipated in youth, and freely sharing in the rough debaucheries of the metropolis. The same vigour " that did affright the air at Agincourt," must have marked his conduct and bearing in any tumult in which he happened to be engaged. I do not know on what credible authority the story of his having given Gascoigne a box on the ear for committing one of his friends to prison may rest, and shall not at present take the trouble of inquiring. It is highly probable that the chief justice amply deserved the cuffing, and I shall always assume the liberty of doubting that he committed the prince. That, like a " sensible lord," he should have hastened to accept any apology which should have relieved him from a collision with the ruling powers at court, I have no doubt at all, from a long consideration of the conduct and history of chief justices in general.

More diligent searchers into the facts of that obscure time have seen reason to disbelieve the stories of any serious dissipations of Henry. Engaged as he was from his earliest youth in affairs of great importance, and with a mind trained to the prospect of powerfully acting in the most serious questions that could agitate his time,—a disputed succession, a rising hostility to the church, divided nobility, turbulent commons, an internecine war with France impossible of avoidance, a web of European diplomacy just then beginning to develope itself, in consequence of the spreading use of the pen and inkhorn so pathetically deplored by Jack Cade, and forerunning the felonious invention, "contrary to the king's crown and dignity," of the printing-press, denounced with no regard to chronology by that illustrious agitator: —in these circumstances, the heir of the house of Lancaster, the antagonist of the Lollards,—a matter of accident in his case, though contrary to the general principles of his family,— and at the same time suspected by the churchmen of dangerous designs against their property,— the pretender on dubious title, but not at the period appearing so decidedly defective as it seems in ours, to the throne of France, —the aspirant to be arbiter or master of all that he knew of Europe,—could not have wasted all his youth in riotous living. In fact, his historical character is stern and severe; but with that we have here nothing to do. It is not the Henry of battles, and treaties, and charters, and commissions, and parliaments, we are now dealing with;—we look to the Henry of Shakspeare.

That Henry, I repeat, is subject and vassal of Falstaff. He is bound by the necromancy of genius to the "white-bearded Satan," who he feels is leading him to perdition. It is in vain that he thinks it utterly unfitting that he should engage in such an enterprise as the robbery at Gadshill; for, in spite of all protestations to the contrary, he joins the expedition merely to see how his master will get through his difficulty. He struggles hard, but to no purpose. Go he must, and he goes accordingly. A sense of decorum keeps him from participating in the actual robbery; but he stands close by, that his resistless sword may aid the dubious valour of his master's associates. Joining with Poins in the jest of scattering them and seizing their booty, not only is no harm done to Falstaff, but a sense of remorse seizes on the prince for the almost treasonable deed—

> "Falstaff sweats to death,
> And lards the lean earth as he walks along;
> Wer't not for laughing, *I should pity him.*"

At their next meeting, after detecting and exposing

the stories related by the knight, how different is the result from what had been predicted by Poins when laying the plot! " The virtue of this jest will be, the incomprehensible lies that this same fat rogue will tell us when we meet at supper: how thirty, at least, he fought with; what wards, what blows, what extremities he endured; and in the reproof of this lies the jest." Reproof indeed! All is detected and confessed. Does Poins *reprove* him, interpret the word as we will? Poins indeed! That were *lèse-majesté*. Does the prince? Why, he tries a jest, but it breaks down; and Falstaff victoriously orders sack and merriment with an accent of command not to be disputed. In a moment after he is selected to meet Sir John Bracy, sent special with the villainous news of the insurrection of the Percies; and in another moment he is seated on his joint-stool, the mimic King of England, lecturing with a mixture of jest and earnest the real Prince of Wales.

Equally inevitable is the necessity of screening the master from the consequences of his delinquencies, even at the expense of a very close approximation to saying the thing that is not; and impossible does Hal find it not to stand rebuked when the conclusion of his joke of taking the tavern bills from the sleeper behind the arras is the enforced confession of being a pickpocket. Before the austere king his father, John his sober-blooded brother, and other persons of gravity or consideration, if Falstaff be in presence, the prince is constrained by his star to act in defence and protection of the knight. Conscious of the carelessness and corruption which mark all the acts of his guide, philosopher, and friend, it is yet impossible that he should not recommend him to a command in a civil war which jeopardied the very existence of his dynasty. In the heat of the battle and the exultation of victory he is obliged to yield to the fraud that represents Falstaff as the actual slayer of Hotspur. Prince John quietly remarks, that the tale of Falstaff is the strangest that he ever heard: his brother, who has won the victory, is content with saying that he who has told it is the strangest of fellows. Does he betray the cheat? Certainly not,—it would have been an act of disobedience; but in privy council he suggests to *his* prince in a whisper,

"Come, bring your luggage [the body of Hotspur] *nobly*—"

nobly—as becomes your rank in *our* court, so as to do the whole of your followers, myself included, honour by the appearance of their master—

> "Come, bring your luggage nobly on your back:
> For my part, if a lie may do thee grace,
> I'll gild it with the happiest terms I have."

Tribute, this, from the future Henry V.! Deeper tribute, however, is paid in the scene in which state necessity induces the renunciation of the fellow with the great belly who had misled him. Poins had prepared us for the issue. The prince had been grossly abused in the reputable hostelrie of the Boar's Head while he was thought to be out of hearing. When he comes forward with the intention of rebuking the impertinence, Poins, well knowing the command to which he was destined to submit, exclaims, " My lord, he will drive you out of your revenge, and turn all to merriment, if you take not the heat." Vain caution! The scene, again, ends by the total forgetfulness of Falstaff's offence, and his being sent for to court. When, therefore, the time had come that considerations of the highest importance required that Henry should assume a more dignified character, and shake off his dissolute companions, his own experience and the caution of Poins instruct him that if the thing be not done on the heat—if the old master-spirit be allowed one moment's ground of vantage—the game is up, the good resolutions dissipated into thin air, the grave rebuke turned all into laughter, and thoughts of anger or prudence put to flight by the restored supremacy of Falstaff. Unabashed and unterrified he has heard the severe rebuke of the king—" I know thee not, old man," &c., until an opportunity offers for a repartee:

> " Know, the grave doth gape
> For thee thrice wider than for other men."

Some joke on the oft-repeated theme of his unwieldy figure was twinkling in Falstaff's eye, and ready to leap from his tongue. The king saw his danger: had he allowed a word, he was undone. Hastily, therefore, does he check that word;

> " Reply not to me with a fool-born jest;"

forbidding, by an act of eager authority,—what he must also have felt to be an act of self-control,—the outpouring of those magic sounds which, if uttered, would, instead of a prison becoming the lot of Falstaff, have conducted him to the coronation dinner, and established him as chief depository of what in after-days was known by the name of backstairs influence.

In this we find the real justification of what has generally been stigmatized as the harshness of Henry.

D

Dr. Johnson, with some indignation, asks why should Falstaff be sent to the Fleet?—he had done nothing since the king's accession to deserve it. I answer, he was sent to the Fleet for the same reason that he was banished ten miles from court, on pain of death. Henry thought it necessary that the walls of a prison should separate him from the seducing influence of one than whom he knew many a better man, but none whom it was so hard to miss. He felt that he could not, in his speech of predetermined severity, pursue to the end the tone of harshness towards his old companion. He had the nerve to begin by rebuking him in angry terms as a surfeit-swelled, profane old man,—as one who, instead of employing in prayer the time which his hoary head indicated was not to be of long duration in this world, disgraced his declining years by assuming the unseemly occupations of fool and jester,—as one whom he had known in a dream, but had awakened to despise,—as one who, on the verge of the gaping grave, occupied himself in the pursuits of such low debauchery as excluded him from the society of those who had respect for themselves or their character. But he cannot so continue; and the last words he addresses to him whom he had intended to have cursed altogether, hold forth a promise of advancement, with an affectionate assurance that it will be such as is suitable to his "strength and qualities." If in public he could scarce master his speech, how could he hope in private to master his feelings? No. His only safety was in utter separation: it should be done, and he did it. He was emancipated by violent effort; did he never regret the ancient thraldom? Shakspeare is silent: but may we not imagine that he who sate crowned with the golden rigol of England, cast, amid all his splendours, many a sorrowful thought upon that old familiar face which he had sent to gaze upon the iron bars of the Fleet?

As for the chief justice, he never appears in Falstaff's presence, save as a butt. His grave lordship has many solemn admonitions, nay, serious threats to deliver; but he departs laughed at and baffled. Coming to demand explanation of the affair at Gadshill, the conversation ends with his being asked for the loan of a thousand pounds. Interposing to procure payment of the debt to Dame Quickly, he is told that she goes about the town saying that her eldest son resembles him. Fang and Snare, his lordship's officers, are not treated with less respect, or shaken off with less ceremony. As for the other followers of the knight,—Pistol, Nym, Bardolph,—they are, by office, his obsequious dependents. But it is impossible that they could long hang about him without contracting, unknown even to themselves, other feelings than those arising from the mere advantages they derived from his service. Death is the test of all; and when that of Falstaff approaches, the dogged Nym reproaches the king for having run bad humours on the knight; and Pistol in swelling tone, breathing a sigh over his heart " fracted and corroborate," hastens to condole with him. Bardolph wishes that he was with him wheresoever he has gone, whether to heaven or hell: he has followed him all his life,—why not follow him in death? The last jest has been at his own expense; but what matters it now? In other times Bardolph could resent the everlasting merriment at the expense of his nose—he might wish it in the belly of the jester; but that's past. The dying knight compares a flea upon his follower's nose to a black soul burning in hell-fire; and no remonstrance is now made. "Let him joke as he likes," says and thinks Bardolph with a sigh, "the fuel is gone that maintained that fire. He never will supply it more; nor will it, in return, supply fuel for his wit. I wish that it could." And Quickly, whom he had for nine and twenty years robbed and cheated,—pardon me, I must retract the words,—from whom he had, for the space of a generation, levied tax and tribute as matter of right and due,—she hovers anxiously over his dying bed, and, with a pathos and a piety well befitting her calling, soothes his departing moments by the consolatory assurance, when she hears him uttering the unaccustomed appeal to God, that he had no necessity for yet troubling himself with thoughts to which he had been unused during the whole length of their acquaintance. Blame her not for leaving unperformed the duty of a chaplain: it was not her vocation. She consoled him as she could,—and the kindest of us can do no more.

Of himself, the centre of the circle, I have, perhaps, delayed too long to speak; but the effect which he impresses upon all the visionary characters around, marks Shakspeare's idea that he was to make a similar impression on the real men to whom he was transmitting him. The temptation to represent the gross fat man upon the stage as a mere buffoon, and to turn the attention of the spectators to the corporal qualities and the practical jests of which he is the object, could hardly be resisted by the players; and the popular notion of the Falstaff of the stage is, that he is no better than an upper-class Scapin. A proper consideration, not merely of the character of his mind as displayed in the lavish abundance of ever ready wit, and the sound good sense of his searching observation, but of the position which he always held in society, should have freed the Falstaff of the cabinet from such an imputation. It has not generally done so. Nothing can be more false, nor, *pace tanti viri*, more unphilosophical, than Dr. Johnson's critique upon his character. According to him.

"Falstaff is a character loaded with faults, and with those faults which naturally produce contempt. He is a thief and a glutton, a coward and a boaster, always ready to cheat the weak, and prey upon the poor; to terrify the timorous, and insult the defenceless. At once obsequious and malignant, he satirizes in their absence those whom he lives by flattering. He is familiar with the prince only as an agent of vice, but of this familiarity he is so proud, as not only to be supercilious and haughty with common men, but to think his interest of importance to the Duke of Lancaster. Yet the man thus corrupt, thus despicable, makes himself necessary to the prince that despises him, by the most pleasing of all qualities, perpetual gaiety; by an unfailing power of exciting laughter, which is the more freely indulged, as his wit is not of the splendid or ambitious kind, but consists in easy scapes and sallies of levity, which make sport, but raise no envy. It must be observed, that he is stained with no enormous or sanguinary crimes, so that his licentiousness is not so offensive but that it may be borne for his mirth.

"The moral to be drawn from this representation is, that no man is more dangerous than he that, with a will to corrupt, hath the power to please; and that neither wit nor honesty ought to think themselves safe with such a companion, when they see Henry seduced by Falstaff."

What can be cheaper than the venting of moral apophthegms such as that which concludes the critique? Shakspeare, who had no notion of copybook ethics, well knew that Falstaffs are not as plenty as blackberries, and that the moral to be drawn from the representation is no more than that great powers of wit will fascinate, whether they be joined or not to qualities commanding grave esteem. In the commentary I have just quoted, the Doctor was thinking of such companions as Savage; but the interval is wide and deep.

How idle is the question as to the cowardice of Falstaff. Maurice Morgann wrote an essay to free his character from the allegation; and it became the subject of keen controversy. Deeply would the knight have derided the discussion. His retreat from before Prince Henry and Poins, and his imitating death when attacked by Douglas, are the points mainly dwelt upon by those who make him a coward. I shall not minutely go over what I conceive to be a silly dispute on both sides: but in the former case Shakspeare saves his honour by making him offer at least some resistance to two bold and vigorous men when abandoned by his companions; and, in the latter, what fitting antagonist was the fat and blown soldier of three-score for

> " That furious Scot,
> The bloody Douglas, whose well-labouring sword
> Had three times slain the appearance of the King?"

He did no more than what Douglas himself did in the conclusion of the fight: overmatched, the renowned warrior

> "'Can vail his stomach, and did grace the shame
> Of those that turned their backs; and, in his flight,
> Stumbling in fear, was took."

Why press cowardice on Falstaff more than upon Douglas? In an age when men of all ranks engaged in personal conflict, we find him chosen to a command in a slaughterous battle; he leads his men to posts of imminent peril; it is his sword which Henry wishes to borrow when about to engage Percy, and he refuses to lend it from its necessity to himself; he can jest coolly in the midst of danger; he is deemed worthy of employing the arm of Douglas at the time that Hotspur engages the prince; Sir John Coleville yields himself his prisoner; and, except in the jocular conversations among his own circle, no word is breathed that he has not performed, and is not ready to perform, the duties of a soldier. Even the attendant of the chief justice, with the assent of his hostile lordship, admits that he has done good service at Shrewsbury. All this, and much more, is urged in his behalf by Maurice Morgann; but it is far indeed from the root of the matter.

Of his being a thief and a glutton I shall say a few words anon; but where does he cheat the weak or prey upon the poor,—where terrify the timorous or insult the defenceless,—where is he obsequious, where malignant,—where is he supercilious and haughty with common men,—where does he think his interest of importance to the Duke of Lancaster? Of this last charge I see nothing whatever in the play. The "Duke" of Lancaster* is a slip of the Doctor's pen.

---

* He is once called so by Westmoreland, Second Part of *Henry IV.* Act iv. Sc. 1.

"Health and fair greeting from our general,
    The prince Lord John and Duke of Lancaster;"

but it occurs nowhere else, and we must not place much reliance

But Falstaff nowhere extends his patronage to Prince John; on the contrary, he asks from the prince the favour of his good report to the king, adding, when he is alone, that the sober-blooded boy did not love him. He is courteous of manner; but, so far from being obsequious, he assumes the command wherever he goes. He is jocularly satirical of speech: but he who has attached to him so many jesting companions for such a series of years, never could have been open to the reproach of malignity. If the sayings of Johnson himself about Goldsmith and Garrick, for example, were gathered, must he not have allowed them to be far more calculated to hurt their feelings than anything Falstaff ever said of Poins or Hal? and yet would he not recoil from the accusation of being actuated by malignant feelings towards men whom, in spite of wayward conversations, he honoured, admired, and loved?

Let us consider for a moment who and what Falstaff was. If you put him back to the actual era in which his date is fixed, and judge him by the manners of that

---

on the authenticity or the verbal accuracy of such verses. He was Prince John of Lancaster, and afterwards Duke of Bedford. The king was then, as the king is now, Duke of Lancaster.

time; a knight of the days perhaps of Edward III.—at all events of Henry IV.—was a man not to be confounded with the knights spawned in our times. A knight then was not far from the rank of peer; and with peers, merely by the virtue of his knighthood, he habitually associated as their equal. Even if we judge of him by the repute of knights in the days when his character was written,—and in dealing with Shakspeare it is always safe to consider him as giving himself small trouble to depart from the manners which he saw around him,—the knights of Elizabeth were men of the highest class. The queen conferred the honour with much difficulty, and insisted that it should not be disgraced. Sir John Falstaff, if his mirth and wit inclined him to lead a reckless life, held no less rank in the society of the day than the Earl of Rochester in the time of Charles II. Henry IV. disapproves of his son's mixing with the loose revellers of the town; but admits Falstaff unreproved to his presence. When he is anxious to break the acquaintance, he makes no objection to the station of Sir John, but sends him with Prince John of Lancaster against the archbishop and the Earl of Northumberland. His objection is not that the knight, by his rank, is no fitting companion for a son of his own, but that he can better trust him with the steadier than the more mercurial of the brothers.

We find by incidental notices that he was reared, when a boy, page to Thomas Mowbray, Duke of Norfolk, head of one of the greatest houses that ever was in England, and the personal antagonist of him who was afterwards Henry IV.; that he was in his youth on familiar terms with John of Gaunt, the first man of the land after the death of his father and brother; and that, through all his life, he had been familiar with the lofty and distinguished. We can, therefore, conjecture what had been his youth and his manhood; we see what he actually is in declining age. In this, if I mistake not, will be found the true solution of the character; here is what the French call the *mot d'énigme*. Conscious of powers and talents far surpassing those of the ordinary run of men, he finds himself outstripped in the race. He must have seen many a man whom he utterly despised rising over his head to honours and emoluments. The very persons upon whom, it would appear to Dr. Johnson, he was intruding, were many of them his early companions,— many more his juniors at court. He might have attended his old patron, the duke, at Coventry, upon St.

Lambert's day, when Richard II. flung down the warder amidst the greatest men of England. If he jested in the tilt-yard with John of Gaunt, could he feel that any material obstacle prevented him from mixing with those who composed the court of John of Gaunt's son?

In fact, he is a dissipated man of rank, with a thousand times more wit than ever fell to the lot of all the men of rank in the world. But he has ill played his cards in life. He grumbles not at the advancement of men of his own order; but the bitter drop of his soul overflows when he remembers how he and that cheeseparing Shallow began the world, and reflects that the starveling justice has land and beeves, while he, the wit and the gentleman, is penniless, and living from hand to mouth by the casual shifts of the day. He looks at the goodly dwelling and the riches of him whom he had once so thoroughly contemned, with an inward pang that he has scarcely a roof under which he can lay his head. The tragic Macbeth, in the agony of his last struggle, acknowledges with a deep despair that the things which should accompany old age,—as honour, love, obedience, troops of friends,—he must not look to have. The comic Falstaff says nothing on the subject; but, by the choice of such associates as Bardolph, Pistol, and the rest of that following, he tacitly declares that he too has lost the advantages which should be attendant on years. No curses loud or deep have accompanied his festive career,—its conclusion is not the less sad on that account: neglect, forgotten friendships, services overlooked, shared pleasures unremembered, and fair occasions gone for ever by, haunt him, no doubt, as sharply as the consciousness of deserving universal hatred galls the soul of Macbeth.

And we may pursue the analogy farther without any undue straining. All other hope lost, the confident tyrant shuts himself up in what he deems an impregnable fortress, and relies for very safety upon his interpretation of the dark sayings of riddling witches. Divested of the picturesque and supernatural horror of the tragedy, Macbeth is here represented as driven to his last resource, and dependent for life only upon chances, the dubiousness of which he can hardly conceal from himself. The Boar's Head in Eastcheap is not the castle of Dunsinane, any more than the conversation of Dame Quickly and Doll Tearsheet is that of the Weird Sisters; but in the comedy, too, we have the man, powerful in his own way, driven to his last " frank," and looking to the chance of the hour for the living of the hour. Hope after hope has broken down, as prophecy after prophecy has been discovered to be juggling and fallacious. He has trusted that *his* Birnam Wood would not come to Dunsinane, and yet it comes;—that no man not of woman born is to cross his path, and lo! the man is here. What then remains for wit or warrior when all is lost—when the last stake is gone—when no chance of another can be dreamt of—when the gleaming visions that danced before their eyes are found to be nothing but mist and mirage? What remains for them but to die?—And so they do.

With such feelings, what can Falstaff, after having gone through a life of adventure, care about the repute of courage or cowardice? To divert the prince, he engages in a wild enterprise,—nothing more than what would be called a "lark" now. When deer-stealing ranked as no higher offence than robbing orchards,— not indeed so high as the taking a slice off a loaf by a wandering beggar, which some weeks ago has sent the vagrant who committed the "crime" to seven years' transportation,—such robberies as those at Gadshill, especially as all parties well knew that the money taken there was surely to be repaid, as we find it is in the end,* were of a comparatively venial nature. Old father antic, the Law, had not yet established his undoubted supremacy; and taking purses, even in the

---

* *Henry IV.* Part 1. Act iii. Sc. 3.

"*Fal.* Now Hal, to the news at court: for the robbery, lad? How is that answered?

    P. Hen.   My sweet beef, I must Still be good angel to thee.
The money is paid back.

    Fal.   I do not like That paying back; it is a double labour.

    P. Hen. I am good-friends with my father, and may do anything.

    Fal. Rob me the exchequer, the first thing thou dost; And do't with unwashed hands too.

    Bard.   Do, my lord."

The quiet and business-like manner in which Bardolph enforces on the heir-apparent his master's reasonable proposition of robbing the exchequer, is worthy of that plain and straightforward character. I have always considered it a greater hardship that Bardolph should be hanged "for pix of little price" by an old companion at Gadshill, than that Falstaff should have been banished. But Shakspeare wanted to get rid of the party; and as, in fact, a soldier was hanged in the army of Henry V. for such a theft, the opportunity was afforded. The king is not concerned in the order for his execution however, which is left with the Duke of Exeter.

I have omitted a word or two from the ordinary editions in the above quotation, which are useless to the sense and spoil the metre. A careful consideration of Falstaff's speeches will show, that though they are sometimes printed as prose, they are in almost all cases metrical. Indeed, I do not think that there is much prose in any of Shakspeare's plays.

days of Queen Elizabeth, was not absolutely incompatible with gentility. The breaking up of the great households and families by the wars of the Roses, the suppression of the monasteries and the confiscation of church property by Henry VIII., added to the adventurous spirit generated throughout all Europe by the discovery of America, had thrown upon the world "men of action," as they called themselves, without any resources but what lay in their right hands. Younger members of broken houses, or aspirants for the newly lost honours or the ease of the cloister, did not well know what to do with themselves. They were too idle to dig; they were ashamed to beg;—and why not apply at home the admirable maxim,

> "That they should take who have the power,
> And they should keep who can,"

which was acted upon with so much success beyond the sea. The same causes which broke down the nobility, and crippled the resources of the church, deprived the retainers of the great baron, and the sharers of the dole of the monastery, of their accustomed mode of living; and robbery in these classes was considered the most venial of offences. To the system of poor laws,—a system worthy of being projected "in great Eliza's golden time" by the greatest philosopher of that day, or, with one exception, of any other day,—are we indebted for that general respect for property which renders the profession of a thief infamous, and consigns him to the hulks, or the tread-mill, without compassion. But I must not wander into historical disquisitions; though no subject would, in its proper place, be more interesting than a minute speculation upon the gradual working of the poor-law system on English society. It would form one of the most remarkable chapters in that great work yet to be written, "The History of the *Lowest* Order from the earliest times,"—a work of far more importance, of deeper philosophy, and more picturesque romance, than all the chronicles of what are called the great events of the earth. Elsewhere let me talk of this. I must now get back again to Falstaff.

His Gadshill adventure was a jest,—a jest, perhaps, repeated after too many precedents; but still, according to the fashion and the humour of the time, nothing more than a jest. His own view of such transactions is recorded; he considers Shallow as a fund of jesting to amuse the prince, remarking that it is easy to amuse "with a sad brow" (with a solemnity of appearance) "a fellow that never had the ache in his shoulders." What was to be accomplished by turning the foolish justice into ridicule, was also to be done by inducing the true prince to become for a moment a false thief. The serious face of robbery was assumed " to keep Prince Harry in perpetual laughter." That, in Falstaff's circumstances, the money obtained by the night's exploit would be highly acceptable, cannot be doubted; but the real object was to amuse the prince. He had no idea of making an exhibition of bravery on such an occasion; Poins well knew his man when he said beforehand, " As for the third, if he fight longer than he see reason, I'll forswear arms:" his end was as much obtained by the prince's jokes upon his cowardice. It was no matter whether he invented what tended to laughter, or whether it was invented upon him. The object was won so the laughter was in any manner excited. The exaggerated tale of the misbegotten knaves in Kendal-green, and his other lies, gross and mountainous, are told with no other purpose; and one is almost tempted to believe him when he says that he knew who were his assailants, and ran for their greater amusement. At all events, it is evident that he cares nothing on the subject. He offers a jocular defence; but immediately passes to matter of more importance than the question of his standing or running:

> "But, lads, I'm glad you have the money. Hostess!
> Clap to the doors; watch to-night, pray to-morrow.
> Gallants, lads, boys, hearts-o'-gold! All the titles of
> Good fellowship come to you!"

The money is had; the means of enjoying it are at hand. Why waste our time in inquiring how it has been brought here, or permit nonsensical discussions on my valour or cowardice to delay for a moment the jovial appearance of the bottle?

I see no traces of his being a glutton. His roundness of paunch is no proof of gormandizing propensities; in fact, the greatest eaters are generally thin and spare. When Henry is running over the bead-roll of his vices, we meet no charge of gluttony urged against him.

> "There is a devil
> Haunts thee i' the likeness of a fat old man;
> A ton of man is thy companion.
> Why dost thou cónverse with that trunk of humours,
> That bolting-hutch of beastliness, that swoln parcel of
> Dropsies, that huge bombard of sack, that stuffed
> Cloakbag of guts, that roasted Manningtree ox
> With the pudding in his belly, that reverend vice,

> That grey iniquity, that father ruffian,
> That vanity in years? Wherein is he good
> But to taste sack, and drink it? Wherein neat
> And cleanly, but to carve a capon, and eat it?"*

The sack and sugar Falstaff admits readily; of addiction to the grosser pleasure of the table neither he nor his accuser says a word. Capon is light eating; and his neatness in carving gives an impression of delicacy in the observances of the board. He appears to have been fond of capon; for it figures in the tavern-bill found in his pockets as the only eatable beside the stimulant anchovy for supper, and the halfpenny-worth of bread. Nor does his conversation ever turn upon gastronomical topics. The bottle supplies an endless succession of jests; the dish scarcely contributes one.

We must observe that Falstaff is never represented as drunk, or even affected by wine. The copious potations of sack do not cloud his intellect, or embarrass his tongue. He is always self-possessed, and ready to pour forth his floods of acute wit. In this

---

* This and the foregoing passage also are printed as prose: I have not altered a single letter, and the reader will see not only that they are dramatical blank-verse, but dramatical blank-verse of a very excellent kind. After all the editions of Shakspeare, another is sadly wanted. The text throughout requires a searching critical revision·

he forms a contrast to Sir Toby Belch. The discrimination between these two characters is very masterly. Both are knights, both convivial, both fond of loose or jocular society, both somewhat in advance of their youth—there are many outward points of similitude, and yet they are as distinct as Prospero and Polonius. The Illyrian knight is of a lower class of mind. His jests are mischievous; Falstaff never commits a practical joke. Sir Toby delights in brawling and tumult; Sir John prefers the ease of his own inn. Sir Toby sings songs, joins in catches, and rejoices in making a noise; Sir John knows too well his powers of wit and conversation to think it necessary to make any display, and he hates disturbance. Sir Toby is easily affected by liquor and roystering; Sir John rises from the board as cool as when he sate down. The knight of Illyria had nothing to cloud his mind; he never aspired to higher things than he has attained; he lives a jolly life in the houschold of his niece, feasting, drinking, singing, rioting, playing tricks from one end of the year to the other: his wishes are gratified, his hopes unblighted. I have endeavoured to show that Falstaff was the contrary of all this. And we must remark that the tumultuous Toby has some dash of romance in him, of which no trace can be found in the English knight. The wit and grace, the good-humour and good looks of Maria, conquer Toby's heart, and he is in love with her—love expressed in rough fashion, but love sincere. Could we see him some dozen years after his marriage, we should find him sobered down into a respectable, hospitable, and domestic country gentleman, surrounded by a happy family of curly-headed Illyrians, and much fonder of his wife than of his bottle. We can never so consider of Falstaff; he must always be a dweller in clubs and taverns, a perpetual diner-out at gentlemen's parties, or a frequenter of haunts where he will not be disturbed by the presence of ladies of condition or character. In the *Merry Wives of Windsor*,—I may remark, in passing, that the Falstaff of that play is a different conception from the Falstaff of *Henry IV.*, and an inferior one—his love is of a very practical and unromantic nature. The ladies whom he addresses are beyond a certain age; and his passion is inspired by his hopes of making them his East and West Indies,—by their tables and their purses. No; Falstaff never could have married, —he was better " accommodated than with a wife." He might have paid his court to old Mistress Ursula, and sworn to marry her weekly from the time when he perceived the first white hair on his chin; but the oath was never kept, and we see what was the motive of his love, when we find him sending her a letter by his page after he has been refused credit by Master Dombledon, unless he can offer something better than the rather unmarketable security of himself and Bardolph.

We must also observe that he never laughs. Others laugh with him, or at him; but no laughter from him who occasions or permits it. He jests with a sad brow. The wit which he profusely scatters about is from the head, not the heart. Its satire is slight, and never malignant or affronting; but still it is satirical, and seldom joyous. It is anything but *fun*. Original genius and long practice have rendered it easy and familiar to him, and he uses it as a matter of business. He has too much philosophy to show that he feels himself misplaced; we discover his feelings by slight indications, which are, however, quite sufficient. I fear that this conception of the character could never be rendered popular on the stage; but I have heard in private the part of Falstaff read with a perfectly grave, solemn, slow, deep, and sonorous voice, touched occasionally somewhat with the broken tone of age, from beginning to end, with admirable effect. But I can imagine him painted according to my idea. He is always caricatured. Not to refer to ordinary drawings, I remember one executed by the reverend and very clever author of the *Miseries of Human Life*, (an engraving of which, if I do not mistake, used to hang in Ambrose's parlour in Edinburgh, in the actual room which was the primary seat of the *Noctes Ambrosianæ*,) and the painter had exerted all his art in making the face seamed with the deep-drawn wrinkles and lines of a hard drinker and a constant laugher. Now, had jolly Bacchus

"Set the trace in his face that a toper will tell,"

should we not have it carefully noted by those who everlastingly joked upon his appearance? should we not have found his Malmsey nose, his whelks and bubukles, his exhalations and meteors, as duly described as those of Bardolph? A laughing countenance he certainly had not. Jests such as his are not, like Ralph's, "lost, unless you print the face." The leering wink in the eye introduced into this portraiture is also wrong, if intended to represent the habitual look of the man. The chief justice assures us that his eyes were moist like those of other men of his time of life; and, without his lordship's assurance, we may be certain that Falstaff seldom played tricks with them. He rises before me as an elderly and very corpulent gentleman, dressed like other military men of the time, [of Elizabeth, observe, not Henry,] yellow-cheeked, white-bearded, double chinned, with a good-humoured but grave expression of countenance, sensuality in the lower features of his face, high intellect in the upper.

Such is the idea I have formed of Falstaff, and perhaps some may think I am right. It required no ordinary genius to carry such a character through so great a variety of incidents with so perfect a consistency. It is not a difficult thing to depict a man corroded by care within, yet appearing gay and at ease without, if you every moment pull the machinery to pieces, as children do their toys, to show what is inside. But the true art is to let the attendant circumstances bespeak the character, without being obliged to label him: "*Here you may see the tyrant;*" or, "*Here is the man heavy of heart, light of manner.*" Your ever-melancholy and ostentatiously broken-hearted heroes are felt to be bores, endurable only on account of the occasional beauty of the poetry in which they figure. We grow tired of " the gloom the fabled

Hebrew wanderer wore," &c., and sympathize as little with perpetual lamentations over mental sufferings endured, or said to be endured, by active youth and manhood, as we should be with its ceaseless complaints of the physical pain of corns or toothache. The death-bed of Falstaff, told in the *patois* of Dame Quickly to her debauched and profligate auditory, is a thousand times more pathetic to those who have looked upon the world with reflective eye, than all the morbid mournings of Childe Harold and his poetical progeny.

At the table of Shallow, laid in his arbour, Falstaff is compelled by the eager hospitality of his host to sit, much against his will. The wit of the court endures the tipsy garrulity of the prattling justice, the drunken harmonies of Silence, whose tongue is loosed by the sack to chaunt butt-ends of old-fashioned ballads, the bustling awkwardness of Davy, and the long-known ale-house style of conversation of Bardolph, without uttering a word except some few phrases of commonplace courtesy. He feels that he is in mind and thought far above his company. Was that the only company in which the same accident had befallen him? Certainly not; it had befallen him in many a mansion more honoured than that of Shallow, and amid society loftier in name and prouder in place. His talent and the use to which he had turned it, had as completely disjoined him in heart from those among whom he mixed, or might have mixed, as it did from the pippin-and-caraway-eating party in Gloucestershire. The members of his court are about him, but not of him; they are all intended for use. From Shallow he borrows a thousand pounds; and, as the justice cannot appreciate his wit, he wastes it not upon him, but uses other methods of ingratiating himself. Henry delights in his conversation and manner, and therefore all his fascinations are exerted to win the favour of one from whom so many advantages might be expected. He lives in the world alone and apart, so far as true community of thought with others is concerned; and his main business in life is to get through the day. That —the day—is his real enemy; he rises to fight it in the morning; he gets through its various dangers as well as he can; some difficulties he meets, some he avoids; he shuns those who ask him for money, seeks those from whom he may obtain it; lounges here, bustles there; talks, drinks, jokes, schemes; and at last his foe is slain, when light and his troubles depart. "The day is gone — the night's our own." Courageously has he put an end to one of the three hundred and sixty-five tormentors which he has yearly to endure; and to-morrow—why—as was to-day, so to-morrow shall be. At all events I shall not leave the sweet of the night un-picked, to think anything more about it. Bring me a cup of sack! Let us be merry! Does he ever think of what were his hopes and prospects at the time, when was

> "Jack Falstaff, now Sir John, a boy,
> And page to Thomas Mowbray, duke of Norfolk?"

Perhaps!—— but he chases away the intrusive reflection by another cup of sack and a fresh sally of humour.

Dryden maintained that Shakspeare killed Mercutio, because, if he had not, Mercutio would have killed him. In spite of the authority of

> "All those prefaces of Dryden,
> For these our critics much confide in,"

Glorious John is here mistaken. Mercutio is killed precisely in the part of the drama where his death is requisite. Not an incident, scarcely a sentence, in this most skilfully managed play of *Romeo and Juliet*, can be omitted or misplaced. But I do think that Shakspeare was unwilling to hazard the reputation of

Falstaff by producing him again in connexion with his old companion, Hal, on the stage. The dancer in the epilogue of the Second part of *Henry IV.* promises the audience, that " if you be not too much cloyed with fat meat, our humble author will continue the story, with Sir John in it, and make you merry with fair Katherine of France: where for anything I know, Falstaff shall die of a sweat, unless already he be killed with your hard opinions."* The audience was not cloyed with fat meat, Sir John was not killed with their hard opinions; he was popular from the first hour of his appearance: but Shakspeare never kept his word. It was the dramatist, not the public, who

---

* I consider this Epilogue to be in blank-verse,—
 " First my fear, then my courtesy, then my speech," &c.
but some slight alterations should be made: the transposition of a couple of words will make the passage here quoted metrical.

> " One word more I beseech you. If you be not
> Too much cloyed with fat meat, our humble author
> *The story will continue* with Sir John in 't,
> And make you merry with fair *Kate* of France. Where
> (For any thing I know) Falstaff shall die of
> A sweat, unless already he be killed with
> Your hard opinions; Oldcastle died a martyr,
> And this is not the man.
> My tongue is weary, when my legs are too,
> I'll bid you good-night; and kneel down before you,
> But indeed to pray for the queen."

killed his hero in the opening scenes of *Henry V.*; for he knew not how to interlace him with the story of Agincourt. There Henry was to be lord of all; and it was matter of necessity that his old master should disappear from the scene. He parted therefore even just between twelve and one, e'en at turning of the tide, and we shall never see him again until the waters of some Avon, here or elsewhere,—it is a good Celtic name for rivers in general,—shall once more bathe the limbs of the like of him who was laid for his last earthly sleep under a grave-stone bearing a disregarded inscription, on the north side of the chancel in the great church at Stratford.

W. M.

JAQUES.

"As he passed through the fields, and saw the animals around him,—'Ye,' said he, 'are happy, and need not envy me that walk thus among you burthened with myself; nor do I, ye gentle beings, envy your felicity, for it is not the felicity of man. I have many distresses from which ye are free; I fear pain when I do not feel it; I sometimes shrink at evils recollected, and sometimes start at evils anticipated. Surely the equity of Providence has balanced peculiar sufferings with peculiar enjoyments.'

"With observations like these the prince amused himself as he returned, uttering them with a plaintive voice, yet with a look that discovered him to feel some complacence in his own perspicacity, and to receive some solace of the miseries of life from consciousness of the delicacy with which he felt, and the eloquence with which he bewailed them."—RASSELAS, chap. ii.

THIS remark of Dr. Johnson on the consolation derived by his hero from the eloquence with which he gave vent to his complaints is perfectly just, but just only in such cases as those of Rasselas. The misery that can be expressed in flowing periods cannot be of more importance than that experienced by the Abyssinian prince enclosed in the Happy Valley. His greatest calamity was no more than that he could not leave a place in which all the luxuries of life were at his command. But, as old Chremes says in the *Heautontimorumenos*,

"Miserum? quem minus credere 'st?
Quid reliqui 'st, quin habeat, quæ quidem in homine dicuntur bona?
Parentes, patriam incolumem, amicos, genu', cognatos, divitias:
Atque hæc perinde sunt ut illius animus qui ea possidet;
Qui uti scit, ei bona; illi, qui non utitur rectè, mala."*

On which, as

"Plain truth, dear Bentley, needs no parts of speech,"

I cannot do better than transcribe the commentary of Hickie, or some other grave expositor from whose pages he has transferred it to his own. "'Tis certain that the real enjoyment arising from external advantages depends wholly upon the situation of the mind of him who possesses them; for if he chance to labour under any secret anguish, this destroys all relish; or,

---

* It may be thus attempted in something like the metre of the original, which the learned know by the sounding name of Tetrameter Iambic Acatalectic:

"Does Clinia talk of misery? Believe his idle tale who can?
What hinders it that he should have whate'er is counted good for man,—
His father's home, his native land, with wealth, and friends, and kith and kin?
But all these blessings will be prized according to the mind within:
Well used, the owner finds them good; if badly used, he deems them ill.
  Cl. Nay, but his sire was always stern, and even now I fear him still," &c.

if he know not how to use them for valuable purposes, they are so far from being of any service to him, that they often turn to real misfortunes." It is of no consequence that this profound reflection is nothing to the purpose in the place where it appears, because Chremes is not talking of any secret anguish, but of the use or abuse made of advantages according to the disposition of the individual to whom they have been accorded; and the anguish of Clinia was by no means secret. He feared the perpetual displeasure of his father, and knew not whether absence might not have diminished or alienated the affections of the lady on whose account he had abandoned home and country; but the general proposition of the sentence cannot be denied. A " fatal remembrance"—to borrow a phrase from one of the most beautiful of Moore's melodies—may render a life, apparently abounding in prosperity, wretched and unhappy, as the vitiation of a single humour of the eye casts a sickly and unnatural hue over the gladsome meadow, or turns to a lurid light the brilliancy of the sunniest skies.

Rasselas and Jaques have no secret anguish to torment them, no real cares to disturb the even current of their tempers. To get rid of the prince first:—
His sorrow is no more than that of the starling in the

Sentimental Journey. He cannot get out. He is discontented, because he has not the patience of Wordsworth's nuns, who fret not in their narrow cells; or of Wordsworth's muse, which murmurs not at being cribbed and confined to a sonnet. He wants the philosophy of that most admirable of all jail-ditties, —and will not reflect that

> " Every island is a prison,
> Close surrounded by the sea;
> Kings and princes, for that reason,
> Prisoners are as well as we."

And as his calamity is, after all, very tolerable,—as many a sore heart or a wearied mind, buffeting about amid the billows and breakers of the external world, would feel but too happy to exchange conditions with him in his safe haven of rest,—it is no wonder that the weaving of sonorous sentences of easily soothed sorrow should be the extent of the mental afflictions of Rasselas, Prince of Abyssinia.

Who or what Jaques was before he makes his appearance in the forest, Shakspeare does not inform us,—any farther than that he had been a *roué* of considerable note, as the Duke tells him, when he proposes to

"Cleanse the foul body of the infected world,
  If they will patiently receive my medicine.
    Duke. Fie on thee! I can tell what thou wouldst do.
    Jaques. What, for a counter, would I do but good?
    Duke. Most mischievous foul sin, in chiding sin;
  For thou thyself hast been a libertine
  As sensual as the brutish sting itself;
  And all the embossed sores and headed evils
  That thou with licence of free foot hast caught,
  Wouldst thou disgorge into the general world."

This, and that he was one of the three or four loving lords who put themselves into voluntary exile with the old Duke, leaving their lands and revenues to enrich the new one, who therefore gave them good leave to wander, is all we know about him, until he is formally announced to us as the melancholy Jaques. The very announcement is a tolerable proof that he is not soul-stricken in any material degree. When Rosalind tells him that he is considered to be a melancholy fellow, he is hard put to it to describe in what his melancholy consists. "I have," he says,

"Neither the scholar's melancholy, which
  Is emulation; nor the musician's, which is
Fantastical; nor the courtier's, which is proud;
  Nor the soldier's,
Which is ambitious; nor the lawyer's, which
  Is politic; nor the lady's, which is nice;
  Nor the lover's, which is all these: but it is

> A melancholy of mine own, compounded
> Of many simples, extracted from many objects,
> And indeed
> The sundry contemplation of my travels,
> In which my often rumination wraps me
> In a most humorous sadness."*

He is nothing more than an idle gentleman given to musing, and making invectives against the affairs of the world, which are more remarkable for the poetry of their style and expression than the pungency of their satire. His famous description of the seven ages of man is that of a man who has seen but little to complain of in his career through life. The sorrows of his infant are of the slightest kind, and he notes that it is taken care of in a nurse's lap. The griefs of his schoolboy are confined to the necessity of going to school; and he, too, has had an anxious hand to attend to him. His shining morning face reflects the superintendence of one—probably a mother—interested in his

---

* This is printed as prose, but assuredly it is blank verse. The alteration of a syllable or two, which in the corrupt state of the text of these plays is the slightest of all possible critical licences, would make it run perfectly smooth. At all events, in the second line, "emulation" should be "emulative," to make it agree with the other clauses of the sentence. The courtier's melancholy is not *pride*, nor the soldier's *ambition*, &c. The adjective is used throughout,—*fantastical, proud, ambitious, politic, nice.*

welfare. The lover is tortured by no piercing pangs of love, his woes evaporating themselves musically in a ballad of his own composition, written not to his mistress, but fantastically addressed to her eyebrow. The soldier appears in all the pride and the swelling hopes of his spirit-stirring trade,

> "Jealous in honour, sudden and quick in quarrel,
> Seeking the bubble reputation
> Even in the cannon's mouth."

The fair round belly of the justice lined with good capon lets us know how he has passed his life. He is full of ease, magisterial authority, and squirely dignity. The lean and slippered pantaloon, and the dotard sunk into second childishness, have suffered only the common lot of humanity, without any of the calamities that embitter the unavoidable malady of old age.* All the characters in Jaques's sketch are well taken care of. The infant is nursed; the boy educated; the youth tormented with no greater cares than the necessity of hunting after rhymes to please the ear of a lady, whose love sits so lightly upon him as to set him upon nothing more serious than such

---

* "Senectus ipsa est morbus."—*Ter. Phorm.* iv. i. 9.

a self-amusing task; the man in prime of life is engaged in gallant deeds, brave in action, anxious for character, and ambitious of fame; the man in declining years has won the due honours of his rank, he enjoys the luxuries of the table and dispenses the terrors of the bench; the man of age still more advanced is well to do in the world. If his shank be shrunk, it is not without hose and slipper,—if his eyes be dim, they are spectacled,—if his years have made him lean, they have gathered for him wherewithal to fatten the pouch by his side. And when this strange eventful history is closed by the penalties paid by men who live too long, Jaques does not tell us that the helpless being,

" Sans teeth, sans eyes, sans taste, sans everything,"

is left unprotected in his helplessness.

Such pictures of life do not proceed from a man very heavy at heart. Nor can it be without design that they are introduced into this especial place. The moment before, the famished Orlando has burst in upon the sylvan meal of the Duke, brandishing a naked sword, demanding with furious threat food for himself and his helpless companion,

" Oppressed with two weak evils, age and hunger."

The Duke, struck with his earnest appeal, cannot refrain from comparing the real suffering which he witnesses in Orlando with that which is endured by himself and his " co-mates, and partners in exile." Addressing Jaques, he says,

> " Thou seest we are not all alone unhappy.
> This wide and universal theatre
> Presents more woeful pageants than the scene
> Wherein we play in."*

But the spectacle and the comment upon it lightly touch Jaques, and he starts off at once into a witty and poetic comparison of the real drama of the world with the mimic drama of the stage, in which, with the sight of well-nurtured youth driven to the savage desperation of periling his own life, and assailing that of others,—and of weakly old age lying down in the feeble but equally resolved desperation of dying by the wayside, driven to this extremity by sore fatigue and hunger,—he diverts himself and his audience, whether in the forest or theatre, on the stage or in the closet, with graphic descriptions of human life; not one of them, proceeding as they do from the lips of the *melancholy* Jaques, presenting a single point

---

* Query on? "Wherein we play *in*" is tautological. "Wherein we play *on*," *i. e.* "continue to play."

on which true melancholy can dwell. Mourning over what cannot be avoided must be in its essence commonplace: and nothing has been added to the lamentations over the ills brought by the flight of years since Moses, the man of God,* declared the concluding period of protracted life to be a period of labour and sorrow;—since Solomon, or whoever else writes under the name of the Preacher, in a passage which, whether it is inspired or not, is a passage of exquisite beauty, warned us to provide in youth, " while the evil days come not, nor the years draw nigh when thou shalt say, I have no pleasure in them; while the sun, or the light, or the moon, or the stars be not darkened, nor the clouds return after the rain: in the day when the keepers of the house shall tremble, and the strong men shall bow themselves, and the grinders cease because they are few, and those that look out of the windows be darkened, and the doors shall be shut in the streets, when the sound of the grinding is low, and he shall rise up at the voice of the bird, and all the daughters of music shall be brought low; also when they shall be afraid of that which is high, and fears shall be in the way,

---

* Psalm xc. "A prayer of Moses, the man of God," v. 10.

and the almond-tree shall flourish, and the grasshopper shall be a burthen, and desire shall fail: because man goeth to his long home, and the mourners go about the streets: or ever the silver cord be loosed, or the golden bowl be broken, or the pitcher be broken at the fountain, or the wheel broken at the cistern;"— or, to make a shorter quotation, since Homer summed up all these ills by applying to old age the epithet of λυγρος,—a word which cannot be translated, but the force of which must be felt. Abate these unavoidable misfortunes, and the catalogue of Jaques is that of happy conditions. In his visions there is no trace of the child doomed to wretchedness before its very birth; no hint that such a thing could occur as its being made an object of calculation, one part medical, three parts financial, to the starveling surgeon, whether by the floating of the lungs, or other test equally fallacious and fee-producing, the miserable mother may be convicted of doing that which, before she had attempted, all that is her soul of woman must have been torn from its uttermost roots, when in an agony of shame and dread the child that was to have made her forget her labour was committed to the cesspool. No hint that the days of infancy should be devoted to the damnation of a factory, or to the tender mercies of a parish beadle. No hint that philosophy should come forward armed with the panoply offensive and defensive of logic and eloquence, to prove that the inversion of all natural relations was just and wise,— that the toil of childhood was due to the support of manhood, —that those hours, the very labours of which even the etymologists give to recreation, should be devoted to those wretched drudgeries which seem to split the hearts of all but those who derive from them blood-stained money, or blood-bedabbled applause. Jaques sees not Greensmith squeezing his children by the throat until they die. He hears not the supplication of the hapless boy begging his still more hapless father for a moment's respite, ere the fatal handkerchief is twisted round his throat by the hand of him to whom he owed his being. Jaques thinks not of the baby deserted on the step of the inhospitable door, of the shame of the mother, of the disgrace of the parents, of the misery of the forsaken infant. His boy is at school, his soldier in the breach, his elder on the justice-seat. Are these the woes of life? Is there no neglected creature left to himself or to the worse nurture of others, whose trade it is to corrupt,—who will teach him what was taught to swaggering Jack Chance, found on Newgate steps, and educated at the venerable seminary of St. Giles's Pound, where

> "They taught him to drink, and to thieve, and fight,
> And everything else but to read and write."

Is there no stripling short of commons, but abundant in the supply of the strap or the cudgel?—no man fighting through the world in fortuneless struggles, and occupied by cares or oppressed by wants more stringent than those of love?—or in love itself does the current of that bitter passion never run less smooth than when sonnets to a lady's eyebrow are the prime objects of solicitude?—or may not even he who began with such sonneteering have found something more serious and sad, something more heart-throbbing and soul-rending, in the progress of his passion? Is the soldier melancholy in the storm and whirlwind of war? Is the gallant confronting of the cannon a matter to be complained of? The dolorous flight, the trampled battalion, the broken squadron, the lost battle, the lingering wound, the ill-furnished hospital, the unfed blockade, hunger and thirst, and pain, and fatigue, and mutilation, and cold, and rout, and scorn, and slight,—services neglected, unworthy claims preferred, life wasted, or honour tarnished,—are all passed by! In peaceful life we have no deeper misfortune placed before us than that it is not unusual that a justice of peace may be prosy in remark and trite in illustration. Are there no other evils to assail us through the agony of life? And when the conclusion comes, how far less tragic is the portraiture of mental imbecility, if considered as a state of misery than as one of comparative happiness, as escaping a still worse lot! Crabbe is sadder far than Jaques, when, after his appalling description of the inmates of a workhouse,—(what would Crabbe have written *now?*)—he winds up by showing to us amid its victims two persons as being

> "*happier* far than they,
> The moping idiot, and the madman gay."

If what he here sums up as the result of his life's observations on mankind be all that calls forth the melancholy of the witty and eloquent speaker, he had not much to complain of. Mr. Shandy lamenting in sweetly modulated periods, because his son has been christened Tristram instead of Trismegistus, is as much an object of condolence. Jaques has just seen the aspect of famine, and heard the words of despair; the Duke has pointed out to him the consideration that more woful and practical calamities exist than even the exile of princes and the downfall of lords; and he breaks off into a light strain of satire, fit only for jesting comedy. Trim might have rebuked him as he rebuked the prostrate Mr. Shandy, by reminding him that there are other things to make us melancholy in the world: and nobody knew it better, or could say it better, than he in whose brain was minted the hysteric passion of Lear choked by his button,—the farewell of victorious Othello to all the pomp, pride, and circumstance of glorious war,—the tears of Richard over the submission of roan Barbary to Bolingbroke,—the demand of Romeo that the Mantuan druggist should supply him with such soon-speeding gear that will rid him of hated life

> "As violently as hasty powder fired
> Doth hurry from the fatal cannon's womb,"—

the desolation of Antony,—the mourning of Henry over sire slain by son, and son by sire,—or the despair of Macbeth. I say nothing of the griefs of Constance, or Isabel, or Desdemona, or Juliet, or Ophelia, because in the sketches of Jaques he passes by all allusion to women: a fact which of itself is sufficient to prove that his melancholy was but in play,—was nothing more than what Arthur remembered when he was in France, where

> "Young gentlemen would be as sad as night,
> Only for wantonness."

Shakspeare well knew that there is no true pathetic, nothing that can permanently lacerate the heart, and embitter the speech, unless a woman be concerned. It is the legacy left us by Eve. The tenor of man's woe, says Milton, with a most ungallant and grisly pun, is still from *wo*-man to begin; and he who will give himself a few moments to reflect will find that the stern trigamist is right. On this, however, I shall not dilate. I may perhaps have something to say as we go on, of the ladies of Shakspeare. For the present purpose, it is enough to remark with Trim, that there are many real griefs to make a man lie down and cry, without troubling ourselves with those which are put forward by the poetic mourner in the forest of Arden.

Different indeed is the sight set before the eyes of Adam in the great poem just referred to, when he is told to look upon the miseries which the fall of man has entailed upon his descendants. Far other than the scenes that flit across this melancholy man by profession are those evoked by Michael in the visionary lazar-house. It would be ill-befitting, indeed, that the merry note of the sweet bird warbling freely in the glade should be marred by discordant sounds of woe, cataloguing the dreary list of disease,

> " All maladies
> Of ghastly spasm, or racking torture, qualms
> Of heartsick agony, all feverous kinds,
> Convulsions, epilepsies, fierce catarrhs,
> Intestine stone and ulcer, colic pangs,
> Demoniac frenzy, moping melancholy,
> Marasmus, and wide-wasting pestilence,
> Dropsies, and asthmas, and joint-racking rheums;"

while, amid the dire tossing and deep groans of the sufferers,

> " —— Despair
> Tended the sick, busiest from couch to couch:
> And over them triumphant Death his dart
> Shook, but delayed to strike."

And equally ill-befitting would be any serious allusion to those passions and feelings which in their violence or their anguish render the human bosom a lazar-house filled with maladies of the mind as racking and as wasting as those of the body, and call forth a supplication for the releasing blow of Death as the final hope, with an earnestness as desperate, and cry as loud as ever arose from the tenement, sad, noisome, and dark, which holds the joint-racked victims of physical disease. Such themes should not sadden the festive banquet in the forest. The Duke and his co-mates and partners in exile, reconciled to their present mode of life, ["I would not change it," says Amiens, speaking, we may suppose, the sentiments of all,] and successful in having plucked the precious jewel, content, from the head of ugly and venomous Adversity, are ready to bestow their woodland fare upon real suffering, but in no mood to listen to the heart-rending descriptions of sorrows graver than those which form a theme for the discourses which Jaques in mimic melancholy contributes to their amusement.

Shakspeare designed him to be a maker of fine sentences, — a dresser forth in sweet language of the ordinary common-places or the common-place mishaps of mankind, and he takes care to show us that he did not intend him for anything beside. With what admirable art he is confronted with Touchstone. He enters merrily laughing at the pointless philosophising of the fool in the forest. His lungs crow like chanticleer when he hears him moralizing over his dial, and making the deep discovery that ten o'clock has succeeded nine, and will be followed by eleven. When Touchstone himself appears, we do not find in his own discourse any touches of such deep contemplation. He is shrewd, sharp, worldly, witty, keen, gibing, observant. It is plain that he has been mocking Jaques; and, as is usual, the mocked thinks himself the mocker. If one has moralized the spectacle of a wounded deer into a thousand similes, comparing his weeping into the stream to the conduct of worldlings in giving in their testaments the sum of more to that which had too much,—his abandonment, to the parting of the flux of companions from misery,—the sweeping by of the careless herd full of the pasture, to the desertion of the poor and broken bankrupt by the fat and greasy citizens, —and so forth; if such have been the common-places of Jaques, are they not fitly matched by the commonplaces of Touchstone upon his watch? It is as high a stretch of fancy that brings the reflection how

> "—— from hour to hour we ripe and ripe,
> And then from hour to hour we rot and rot,
> And thereby hangs a tale,"

which is scoffed at by Jaques, as that which dictates his own moralizings on the death of the deer. The motley fool is as wise as the melancholy lord whom he is parodying. The shepherd Corin, who replies to the courtly quizzing of Touchstone by such apophthegms as that "it is the property of rain to wet, and of fire to burn," is unconsciously performing the same part to the clown, as *he* had been designedly performing to Jaques. Witty nonsense is answered by dull nonsense, as the emptiness of poetry had been answered by the emptiness of prose. There was nothing sincere in the lamentation over the wounded stag. It was only used as a peg on which to hang fine conceits. Had Falstaff seen the deer, his imagination would have called up visions of haunches and pasties, preluding an everlasting series of cups of sack among the revel riot of boon companions, and he would have instantly ordered its throat to be cut. If it had fallen in the way of Friar Lawrence, the mild-hearted man of herbs would have endeavoured to extract the arrow, heal the wound, and let the hart ungalled go free. Neither would have thought the hairy fool a subject for reflections, which neither relieved the wants of man nor the pains of beast. Jaques complains of the injustice and cruelty of killing deer, but unscrupulously sits down to dine upon venison, and sorrows over the sufferings of the native burghers of the forest city, without doing anything farther than amusing himself with rhetorical flourishes drawn from the contemplation of the pain which he witnesses with professional coolness and unconcern.

It is evident, in short, that the happiest days of his life are those which he is spending in the forest. His raking days are over, and he is tired of city dissipation. He has shaken hands with the world, finding, with Cowley, that "he and it would never agree." To use an expression somewhat vulgar, he has had his fun for his money; and he thinks the bargain so fair and conclusive on both sides, that he has no notion of opening another. His mind is relieved of a thousand anxieties which beset him in the court, and he breathes freely in the forest. The iron has not entered into his soul; nothing has occurred to chase sleep from his eyelids; and his fantastic reflections are, as he himself takes care to tell us, but general observations on the ordinary and outward manners and feelings of mankind,—a species of taxing which

> "—— like a wild-goose flies,
> Unclaim'd of any man."

Above all, in having abandoned station, and wealth, and country, to join the faithful few who have in evil report clung manfully to their prince, he knows that he has played a noble and an honourable part; and they to whose lot it may have fallen to experience the happiness of having done a generous, disinterested, or self-denying action,—or sacrificed temporary interests to undying principle,—or shown to the world without, that what are thought to be its great advantages can be flung aside, or laid aside, when they come in collision with the feelings and passions of the world within,—will be perfectly sure that Jaques, reft of land, and banished from court, felt himself exalted in his own eyes, and therefore easy of mind, whether he was mourning in melodious blank verse, or weaving jocular parodies on the canzonets of the good-humoured Amiens.

He was happy " under the greenwood tree." Addison I believe it is who says, that all mankind have an instinctive love of country and woodland scenery, and he traces it to a sort of dim recollection imprinted upon us of our original haunt, the garden of Eden. It is at all events certain, that, from the days when the cedars of Lebanon supplied images to the great poets of Jerusalem, to that in which the tall tree haunted Wordsworth " as a passion," the forest has caught a strong hold of the poetic mind. It is with reluctance that I refrain from quoting; but the passages of surpassing beauty which crowd upon me from all times and languages are too numerous. I know not which to exclude, and I have not room for all; let me then take a bit of prose from one who never indulged in poetry, and I think I shall make it a case in point.

In a little book called *Statistical Sketches of Upper Canada, for the use of Emigrants, by a Backwoodsman*, now lying before me, the author, after describing the field-sports in Canada with a precision and a *goût* to be derived only from practice and zeal, concludes a chapter, most appropriately introduced by a motto from *The Lady of the Lake*,

> " 'Tis merry, 'tis merry in good greenwood,
> When the mavis and merle are singing,
> When the deer sweep by, and the hounds are in cry,
> And the hunter's horn is ringing,"

by saying,

"It is only since writing the above that I fell in with the first volume of *Moore's Life of Lord Edward Fitzgerald;* and I cannot describe the pleasure I received from reading his vivid, spirited, and accurate description of the feelings he experienced on first taking on him the life of a hunter. At an earlier period of life than Lord Edward had then attained, I made my debut in the forest, and first assumed the blanket-cloak and the rifle, the moccasin and the snow-shoe; and the ecstatic feeling of Arab-like independence, and the utter contempt for the advantage and restrictions of civilization, which he describes, I then felt in its fullest power. And even now, when my way of life, like Macbeth's, is falling 'into the sere, the yellow leaf,' and when a tropical climate, privation, disease, and thankless toil are combining with advancing years to unstring a frame the strength of which once set hunger, cold, and fatigue at defiance, and to undermine a constitution that once appeared ironbound, still I cannot lie down by a fire in the woods without the elevating feeling which I experienced formerly returning, though in a diminished degree. This must be human nature;—for it is an undoubted fact, that no man who associates with and follows the pursuits of the Indian, for any length of time, ever voluntarily returns to civilized society.

"What a companion in the woods Lord Edward must have been! and how shocking to think that, with talents which would have made him at once the idol and the ornament of his profession, and affections which must have rendered him an object of adoration in all the relations of private life—with honour, with courage, with generosity, with every trait that can at once ennoble and endear,—he should never have been taught that there is a higher principle of action than the mere impulse of the passions, —that he should never have learned, before plunging is country into blood and disorder, to have weighed the means he possessed with the end he proposed, or the problematical good with the certain evil!—that he should have had Tom Paine for a tutor in religion and politics, and Tom Moore for a biographer, to hold up as a pattern, instead of warning, the errors and misfortunes of a being so noble,—to subserve the revolutionary purposes of a faction, who, like Samson, are pulling down a fabric which will bury both them and their enemies under it."

Never mind the aberrations of Lord Edward Fitzgerald, the religion or the politics of Tom Paine, or the biography of Tom Moore. On all these matters I may hold my own opinions, but they are not wanted now; but have we not here the feelings of Jaques? Here are the gloomy expressions of general sorrow over climate, privation, disease, thankless toil, advancing years, unstrung frame. But here also we have ecstatic emotions of Arab-like independence, generous reflections upon political adversaries, and high-minded adherence to the views and principles which in his honour and conscience he believed to be in all circumstances inflexibly right, coming from the heart of a forest. The Backwoodsman is Dunlop; and is he, in spite of this sad-sounding passage, melancholy? Not he, in good sooth. The very next page to that which I have quoted is a description of the pleasant mode of travelling in Canada, before the march of improvement had made it comfortable and convenient.*

Jaques was just as woe-begone as the Tyger, and no more. I remember when he—Dunlop I mean, not Jaques—used to laugh at the phrenologists of Edin-

* "Formerly, that is to say, previous to the peace of 1815, a journey between Quebec and Sandwich was an undertaking considerably more tedious and troublesome than the voyage from London to Quebec. In the first place, the commissariat of the expedition had to be cared for; and to that end every gentleman who was liable to travel had, as a part of his appointments, a provision basket, which held generally a cold round of beef, tin plates and drinking cups, tea, sugar, biscuits, and about a gallon of brandy. These, with your wardrobe and a camp-bed, were stowed away in a batteau, or flat-bottomed boat; and off you set with a crew of seven stout, light-hearted, jolly, lively Canadians, who sung their boat songs all the time they could spare from smoking their pipes. You were accompanied by a fleet of similar boats, called a brigade, the crews of which assisted each other up the rapids, and at night put into some creek, bay, or uninhabited island, where fires were lighted, tents made of the sails, and the song, the laugh, and the shout were heard, with little intermission, all the night through; and if you had the felicity to have among the party a fifer or a fiddler, the dance was sometimes kept up all night,—for, if a Frenchman has a fiddle, sleep ceases to be a necessary of life with him. This mode of travelling was far from being unpleasant, for there was something of romance and adventure in it; and the scenes you witnessed, both by night and day, were picturesque in the highest degree. But it was tedious: for you were in great luck if you arrived at your journey's end in a month; and if the

burgh for saying, after a careful admeasurement, that his skull in all points was exactly that of Shakspeare,— I suppose he will be equally inclined to laugh when he finds who is the double an old companion has selected for him. But no matter. His melancholy passes away not more rapidly than that of Jaques; and I venture to say that the latter, if he were existing in flesh and blood, would have no scruple in joining the doctor this moment over the bowl of punch which I am sure he is brewing, has brewed, or is about to brew, on the banks of Huron or Ontario.

Whether he would or not, he departs from the stage with the grace and easy elegance of a gentleman in heart and manners. He joins his old antagonist the usurping Duke in his fallen fortunes; he had spurned him in his prosperity: his restored friend he bequeaths to his former honour, deserved by his pa-

---

weather were boisterous, or the wind a-head, you might be an indefinite time longer.

"But your march of improvement is a sore destroyer of the romantic and picturesque. A gentleman about to take such a journey now-a-days, orders his servant to pack his portmanteau, and put it on board the *John Molson*, or any of his family; and at the stated hour he marches on board, the bell rings, the engine is put in motion, and away you go smoking, and splashing, and walloping along, at the rate of ten knots an hour, in the ugliest species of craft that ever disfigured a marine landscape."

tience and his virtue,—he compliments Oliver on his restoration to his land, and love, and great allies,—wishes Silvius joy of his long-sought and well-earned marriage,—cracks upon Touchstone one of those good-humoured jests to which men of the world on the eve of marriage must laughingly submit,—and makes his bow. Some sage critics have discovered as a great geographical fault in Shakspeare, that he introduces the tropical lion and serpent into Arden, which, it appears, they have ascertained to lie in some temperate zone. I wish them joy of their sagacity. Monsters more wonderful are to be found in that forest; for never yet, since water ran and tall tree bloomed, were there gathered together such a company as those who compose the *dramatis personæ* of *As You Like it*. All the prodigies spawned by Africa, "*leonum arida nutrix*," might well have teemed in a forest, wherever situate, that was inhabited by such creatures as Rosalind, Touchstone, and Jaques.

---

* As to the question which opened these Papers,—why, I must leave it to the jury. Is the jesting, revelling, rioting Falstaff, broken of fortunes, luckless in life, sunk in habits, buffeting with the discreditable part of the world, or the melancholy, mourning, com-

plaining Jaques, honourable of conduct, high in moral position, fearless of the future, and lying in the forest away from trouble,—which of them, I say, feels more the load of care? I think Shakspeare well knew, and depicted them accordingly. But I must leave it to my readers, *si qui sunt*. W. M.

ROMEO.

> "Of this unlucky sort our Romeus is one,
> For all his hap turns to mishap, and all his mirth to mone."
> *The Tragicall Historye of Romeus and Juliet.*

"NEVER," says Prince Escalus, in the concluding distich of *Romeo and Juliet*,

> "— was there story of more woe
> Than this of Juliet and her Romeo."

It is a story which, in the inartificial shape of a black-letter ballad, powerfully affected the imagination, and awakened the sensibilities of our ancestors, and in the hands of Shakspeare has become *the* love-story of the whole world. Who cares for the loves of Petrarch and Laura, or of Eloisa and Abelard, compared with those of Romeo and Juliet? The gallantries of Petrarch are conveyed in models of polished and ornate verse; but, in spite of their elegance, we feel that they are frosty as the Alps beneath which they were written. They are only the exercises of genius, not the ebullitions of feeling; and we can easily credit the story that Petrarch refused a dispensation to marry Laura, lest marriage might spoil his poetry. The muse, and not the lady, was his mistress. In the case of Abelard there are many associations which are not agreeable; and, after all, we can hardly help looking upon him as a fitter hero for *Bayle's Dictionary* than a romance. In *Romeo and Juliet* we have the poetry of Petrarch without its iciness, and the passion of Eloisa free from its coarse exhibition. We have, too, philosophy far more profound than ever was scattered over the syllogistic pages of Abelard, full of knowledge and acuteness as they undoubtedly are.

But I am not about to consider Romeo merely as a lover, or to use him as an illustration of Lysander's often-quoted line,

"The course of true love never did run smooth."

In that course the current has been as rough to others as to Romeo; who, in spite of all his misfortunes, has wooed and won the lady of his affections. That Lysander's line is often true, cannot be questioned; though it is no more than the exaggeration of an annoyed suitor to say that love has *never* run smoothly. The reason why it should be so generally true, is given in *Peveril of the Peak,* by Sir Walter Scott; a man who closely approached to the genius of Shakspeare in depicting character, and who, above all writers of imagination, most nearly resembled him in the possession of keen, shrewd, every-day common sense, rendered more remarkable by the contrast of the romantic, pathetic, and picturesque by which it is in all directions surrounded.

" This celebrated passage

['Ah me! for aught that ever I could read,' &c.]

which we have prefixed to this chapter, [chap. xii. vol. i. *Peveril of the Peak,*] has, like most observations of the same author, its foundation in real experience. The period at which love is felt most strongly is seldom that at which there is much prospect of its being brought to a happy issue. In fine, there are few men who do not look back in secret to some period of their youth at which a sincere and early affection was repulsed or betrayed, or became abortive under opposing circumstances. It is these little passages of secret history, which leave a tinge of romance in every bosom, scarce permitting us, even in the most busy or the most advanced period of life, to listen with total indifference to a tale of true love."*

These remarks, the justice of which cannot be questioned, scarcely apply to the case of Romeo. In no respect save that the families were at variance, was the match between him and Juliet such as not to afford a prospect of happy issue; and everything indicated the possibility of making their marriage a ground of reconciliation between their respective houses. Both are tired of the quarrel. Lady Capulet and Lady Montague are introduced in the very first scene of the play, endeavouring to pacify their husbands; and when the brawl is over, Paris laments to Juliet's father that it is a pity persons of such honourable reckoning should have lived so long at variance. For Romeo himself old Capulet expresses the highest respect, as being one of the ornaments of the city; and, after the death of Juliet, old Montague, touched by her truth and constancy, proposes to raise to her a statue of gold. With such sentiments and predispositions, the early passion

---

* Was Sir Walter thinking of his own case when he wrote this passage? See his Life by Lockhart, vol. i. p. 242. His family used to call Sir Walter *Old Peveril*, from some fancied resemblance of the character.

of the Veronese lovers does not come within the canon of Sir Walter Scott; and, as I have said, I do not think that Romeo is designed merely as an exhibition of a man unfortunate in love.

I consider him to be meant as the character of an *unlucky* man,—a man who, with the best views and fairest intentions, is perpetually so unfortunate as to fail in every aspiration, and, while exerting himself to the utmost in their behalf, to involve all whom he holds dearest in misery and ruin. At the commencement of the play an idle quarrel among some low retainers of the rival families produces a general riot, with which he has nothing to do. He is not present from beginning to end; the tumult has been so sudden and unexpected, that his father is obliged to ask

"What set this ancient quarrel new abroach?"

And yet it is this very quarrel which lays him prostrate in death by his own hand, outside Capulet's monument, before the tragedy concludes. While the fray was going on, he was nursing love-fancies, and endeavouring to persuade himself that his heart was breaking for Rosaline. How afflicting his passion must have been, we see by the conundrums he makes upon it:

> "Love is a smoke raised with the fume of sighs;
> Being purged, a fire sparkling in lovers' eyes;
> Being vex'd, a sea nourish'd with lovers' tears.*
> What is it else?—a madness most discreet,
> A choking gall, and a preserving sweet."—

And so forth. The sorrows which we can balance in such trim antitheses do not lie very deep. The time is rapidly advancing when his sentences will be less sounding.

> "It is my lady; oh, it is my love!
> O that she knew she were!"

speaks more touchingly the state of his engrossed soul than all the fine metaphors ever vented. The supercilious Spartans in the days of their success prided themselves upon the laconic brevity of their despatches to states in hostility or alliance with them. When they were sinking before the Macedonians, another style was adopted; and Philip observed that he had taught them to lengthen their monosyllables. Real love has had a contrary effect upon Romeo. It has abridged his swelling passages, and brought him to the language of prose. The reason of the alteration is the same in both cases. The brevity of the Spartans was the result of studied affectation. They sought, by the insolence of

---

* Is there not a line missing?

threats obscurely insinuated in a sort of demi-oracular language, to impose upon others,—perhaps they imposed upon themselves,—an extravagant opinion of their mysterious power. The secret was found out at last, and their anger bubbled over in big words and lengthened sentences. The love of Rosaline is as much affected on the part of Romeo, and it explodes in wire-drawn conceits.

> " When the devout religion of mine eye
>   Maintains such falsehood, then turn tears to fires;
> And those who often drown'd could never die,
>   Transparent heretics, be burnt for liars.
> One fairer than my love!—the all-seeing sun
> Ne'er saw her match since first the world begun."

It is no wonder that a gentleman who is so clever as to be able to say such extremely fine things, forgets, in the next scene, the devout religion of his eye, without any apprehension of the transparent heretic being burnt for a liar by the transmutation of tears into the flames of an *auto da fe*. He is doomed to discover that love in his case is not a madness most discreet when he defies the stars; there are then no lines of magnificent declamation.

> " Is it even so? then I defy you, stars!
> Thou knowest my lodging: get me ink and paper,
> And hire post-horses; I will hence to-night."

Nothing can be plainer prose than these verses. But how were they delivered? Balthazar will tell us.

> " Pardon me, sir; I dare not leave you thus:
> Your looks are pale and wild, and do import
> Some misadventure."

Again, nothing can be more quiet than his final determination:

> " Well, Juliet, I will lie with thee to-night."

It is plain Juliet,—unattended by any romantic epithet of love. There is nothing about "Cupid's arrow," or "Dian's wit;" no honeyed word escapes his lips,—nor again does any accent of despair. His mind is so made up,—the whole course of the short remainder of his life so unalterably fixed, that it is perfectly useless to think more about it. He has full leisure to reflect without disturbance upon the details of the squalid penury which made him set down the poor apothecary as a fit instrument for what now had become his " need ; " and he offers his proposition of purchasing that soon-speeding gear which is to hurry him out of life, with the same business-like tone as if he were purchasing a pennyworth of sugar-candy. When the apothecary suggests the danger of selling such drugs, Romeo can reflect on the folly of scrupling to sacrifice life when the holder of it is so poor and unfortunate. Gallant and gay of appearance himself, he tells his new-found acquaintance that bareness, famine, oppression, ragged misery, the hollow cheek and the hungry eye, are fitting reasons why death should be desired, not avoided; and with a cool philosophy assures him that gold is worse poison than the compound which hurries the life-weary taker out of the world. The language of desperation cannot be more dismally determined. What did the apothecary think of his customer as he pocketed the forty ducats? There you go, lad,—there you go, he might have said,—there you go with that in your girdle that, if you had the strength of twenty men, would straight despatch you. Well do I know the use for which you intend it. To-morrow's sun sees not you alive. And you philosophise to me on the necessity of buying food and getting into flesh. You taunt my poverty,—you laugh at my rags,—you bid me defy the law,—you tell me the world is my enemy. It may be so, lad,—it may be so; but less tattered is my garment than your heart,—less harassed by law of one kind or another my pursuit than yours. What ails that lad? I know not, neither do I care. But that he should moralize to me on the hard lot which I experience,—that he, with those looks and those accents, should fancy that I, amid my beggarly account of empty boxes, am less happy than he,—ha! ha! ha!—it is something to make one laugh. Ride your way, boy: I have your forty ducats in my purse, and you my drug in your pocket. And the law! Well! What can the executioner do worse to me in my penury and my age than you have doomed for yourself in your youth and splendour. I carry not my hangman in my saddle as I ride along. And the curses which the rabble may pour upon my dying moments,—what are they to the howling gurgle which, now rising from your heart, is deafening your ears? Adieu, boy,—adieu!—and keep your philosophy for yourself. Ho! ho! ho!

But had any other passion or pursuit occupied Romeo, he would have been equally unlucky as in his love. Ill fortune has marked him for her own. From beginning to end he intends the best; but his interfering is ever for the worst. It is evident that he has not taken any part in the family feud which divides Verona, and his first attachment is to a lady of the antagonist house.* To see that lady,—perhaps

---

* Rosaline was niece of Capulet. The list of persons invited to the ball is
"Signior Martino, and his wife and daughters;
County Anselm[o], and his beauteous sisters;

to mark that he has had no share in the tumult of the morning,—he goes to a ball given by Capulet, at which the suitor accepted by the family is to be introduced to Juliet as her intended husband. Paris is in every way an eligible match.

"Verona's summer hath not such a flower."

He who has slain him addresses his corse as that of the "noble County Paris," with a kindly remembrance that he was kinsman of a friend slain in Romeo's own cause. Nothing can be more fervent, more honourable, or more delicate than his devoted and considerate wooing. His grief at the loss of Juliet is expressed in few words; but its sincerity is told by his midnight and secret visit to the tomb of her whom living he had honoured, and on whom, when dead, he could not restrain himself from lavish-

> The lady widow of Vetruvio;
> Signior Placentio, and his lovely nieces;
> Mercutio, and his brother Valentine;
> Mine uncle Capulet, his wife and daughters;
> *My fair niece Rosaline;* [and] Livia;
> Signior Valentio, and his cousin Tybalt;
> Lucio, and the lively Helena."

I have altered *Anselme* to the Italian form *Anselmo*, and in the seventh line inserted *and*. I think I may fairly claim this list as being in verse. It is always printed as prose.

ing funereal homage. Secure of the favour of her father, no serious objection could be anticipated from herself. When questioned by her mother, she readily promises obedience to parental wishes, and goes to the ball determined to " look to like, if looking liking move." Everything glides on in smooth current till the appearance of him whose presence is deadly. Romeo himself is a most reluctant visitor. He apprehends that the consequences of the night's revels will be the vile forfeit of a despised life by an untimely death, but submits to his destiny. He foresees that it is no wit to go, but consoles himself with the reflection that he " means well in going to this mask." His intentions, as usual, are good; and, as usual, their consequences are ruinous.

He yields to his passion, and marries Juliet. For this hasty act he has the excuse that the match may put an end to the discord between the families. Friar Lawrence hopes that

> " this alliance may so happy prove
> To turn your households' rancour into love."

It certainly has that effect in the end of the play, but it is by the suicidal deaths of the flower and hope of both families. Capulet and Montague tender, in a gloomy peace, the hands of friendship, over the untimely grave of the poor sacrifices to their enmity. Had he met her elsewhere than in her father's house, he might have succeeded in a more prosperous love. But there his visit is looked upon by the professed duellist Tybalt, hot from the encounter of the morning, and enraged that he was baulked of a victim, as an intrusion and an insult. The fiery partisan is curbed with much difficulty by his uncle; and withdraws, his flesh trembling with wilful choler, determined to wreak vengeance at the first opportunity on the intruder. It is not long before the opportunity offers. Vainly does Romeo endeavour to pacify the bullying swordsman,—vainly does he protest that he loves the name of Capulet,—vainly does he decline the proffered duel. His good intentions are again doomed to be frustrated. There stands by his side as mad-blooded a spirit as Tybalt himself, and Mercutio, all unconscious of the reasons why Romeo refuses to fight, takes up the abandoned quarrel. The star of the unlucky man is ever in the ascendant. His ill-omened interference slays his friend. Had he kept quiet, the issue might have been different; but the power that had the steerage of his course had destined that the uplifting of his sword was to be the signal of death to his very friend. And when the dying Mercutio says, "Why the devil came you between us? I was hurt under your arm;" he can only offer the excuse, which is always true, and always unavailing, "I thought all for the best." All his visions of reconciliation between the houses are dissipated. How can he now avoid fighting with Tybalt? His best friend lies dead, slain in his own quarrel, through his own accursed intermeddling; and the swaggering victor, still hot from the slaughter, comes back to triumph over the dead. Who with the heart and spirit of a man could under such circumstances refrain from exclaiming,

> "Away to heaven, respective lenity!
> And fire-eyed fury be my conduct now."

Vanish gentle breath, calm words, knees humbly bowed! —his weapon in an instant glitters in the blazing sun; and as with a lightning flash,—as rapidly and resistlessly,—before Benvolio can pull his sword from the scabbard, Tybalt, whom his kindred deemed a match for twenty men, is laid by the side of him who but a moment before had been the victim of his blade. What avails the practised science of the duellist, the gentleman of the very first house, of the first and second cause!—how weak is the immortal passado, or the punto reverso, the hay, or all the other learned devices of Vincent Saviola, against the whirlwind rage of a man driven to desperation by all that can rouse fury or stimulate hatred! He sees the blood of his friend red upon the ground; the accents of gross and unprovoked outrage ring in his ears; the perverse and obstinate insolence of a bravo confident in his skill, and depending upon it to insure him impunity, has marred his hopes; and the butcher of the silk button has no chance against the demon which he has evoked. "A la stoccata" carries it not away in this encounter: but Romeo exults not in his death. He stands amazed, and is with difficulty hurried off, exclaiming against the constant fate which perpetually throws him in the way of misfortune. Well, indeed, may Friar Lawrence address him by the title of thou "fearful man!"—as a man whose career through life is calculated to inspire terror. Well may he say to him that

> "Affliction is enamour'd of thy parts,
> And thou art wedded to calamity."

And slight is the attention which Romeo pays to the eloquent arguments by which it is proved that he had every reason to consider himself happy. When the friar assures him that

> "A pack of blessings lights upon thy back,
> Happiness courts thee in her best array,"

the nurse may think it a discourse of learning and good counsel, fit to detain an enraptured auditor all the night. Romeo feels it in his case to be an idle declamation, unworthy of an answer.

The events which occur during his enforced absence, the haste of Paris to be wedded, the zeal of old Capulet in promoting the wishes of his expected son-in-law, the desperate expedient of the sleeping-draught,* the ac-

---

* Is there not some mistake in the length of time that this sleeping-draught is to occupy, if we consider the text as it now stands to be correct? Friar Lawrence says to Juliet, when he is recommending the expedient,

> "Take thou this phial, being then in bed,
> And this distilled liquor drink thou off:
> When presently through all thy veins shall run
> A cold and drowsy humour, which shall seize
> Each vital spirit, &c.
> And in this borrow'd likeness of shrunk death
> Thou shalt remain *full two and forty hours*,
> And then awake as from a pleasant sleep."

Juliet retires to bed on Tuesday night, at a somewhat early hour. Her mother says after she departs, "'Tis now near night." Say it is eleven o'clock: forty-two hours from that hour bring us to five

cident which prevented the delivery of the friar's letter, the officious haste of Balthazar to communicate

o'clock in the evening of Thursday; and yet we find the time of her awakening fixed in profound darkness, and not long before the dawn. We should allow at least ten hours more, and read,

"Thou shalt remain full *two and fifty* hours,"—

which would fix her awakening at three o'clock in the morning, a time which has been marked in a former scene as the approach of day.

"*Cap.* Come, stir, stir, stir! The second cock has crow'd,—
The curfew bell hath rung,—'tis three o'clock."

Immediately after he says, "Good faith, 'tis day." This observation may appear superfluously minute; but those who take the pains of reading the play critically will find that it is dated throughout with a most exact attention to hours. We can time almost every event. *Ex. gr.* Juliet dismisses the nurse on her errand to Romeo when the clock struck nine, and complains that she has not returned at twelve. At twelve she does return, and Juliet immediately proceeds to Friar Lawrence's cell, where she is married without delay. Romeo parts with his bride at once, and meets his friends while "the day is hot." Juliet at the same hour addresses her prayer to the fiery-footed steeds of Phœbus, too slowly for her feelings progressing towards the west. The same exactness is observed in every part of the play.

I may remark, as another instance of Romeo's ill luck, the change of the original wedding day. When pressed by Paris, old Capulet says that "Wednesday is too soon,—on Thursday let it be;" but afterwards, when he imagines that his daughter is inclined to consult his wishes, he fixes it for Wednesday, even though his wife observes that Thursday is time enough. Had this day not been lost, the letter of Friar Lawrence might still have been forwarded to Mantua to explain what had occurred.

the tidings of Juliet's burial, are all matters out of his control. But the mode of his death is chosen by himself; and in that he is as unlucky as in everything else. Utterly loathing life, the manner of his leaving it must be instantaneous. He stipulates that the poison by which he is to die shall not be slow of effect. He calls for

> " such soon-speeding gear
> As will disperse itself through all the veins,
> That the life-weary taker may fall dead."

He leaves himself no chance of escape. Instant death is in his hand; and thanking the true apothecary for the quickness of his drugs, he scarcely leaves himself a moment with a kiss to die. If he had been less in a hurry,—if he had not felt it impossible to delay posting off to Verona for a single night,—if his riding had been less rapid, or his medicine less sudden in its effect, he might have lived. The friar was at hand to release Juliet from her tomb the very instant after the fatal phial had been emptied. That instant was enough: the unlucky man had effected his purpose just when there was still a chance that things might be amended. Those who wrote the scene between Romeo and Juliet which is intended to be pathetic, after her awakening and before his death, quite mistake the character of the hero of the play. I do not blame them for their poetry, which is as good as that of second-rate writers of tragedy in general; and think them, on the whole, deserving of our commendation for giving us an additional proof how unable clever men upon town are to follow the conceptions of genius. Shakspeare, if he thought it consistent with the character which he had with so much deliberation framed, could have written a parting scene at least as good as that with which his tragedy has been supplied; but he saw the inconsistency, though his unasked assistants did not. They tell us they did it to consult popular taste. I do not believe them. I am sure that popular taste would approve of a recurrence to the old play in all its parts; but a harlotry play-actor might think it hard upon him to be deprived of a "point," pointless as that point may be.

Haste is made a remarkable characteristic of Romeo, —because it is at once the parent and the child of uniform misfortune. As from the acorn springs the oak, and from the oak the acorn, so does the temperament that inclines to haste predispose to misadventure, and a continuance of misadventure confirms the habit of haste. A man whom his rashness has made continually unlucky, is strengthened in the determination to persevere in his rapid movements by the very feeling that the "run" is against him, and that it is of no use to think. In the case of Romeo, he leaves it all to the steerage of Heaven, *i. e.* to the heady current of his own passions; and he succeeds accordingly. All through the play care is taken to show his impatience. The very first word he speaks indicates that he is anxious for the quick passage of time.

> "*Ben.* Good morrow, cousin.
> *Rom.* Is the day so young?
> *Ben.* But new struck nine.
> *Rom.* Ay me, sad hours seem long."

The same impatience marks his speech in the moment of death:

> "O true apothecary,
> Thy drugs are quick!"

From his first words to his last the feeling is the same. The lady of his love, even in the full swell of her awakened affections, cannot avoid remarking that his contract is

> "Too rash, too unadvised, too sudden,
> Too like the lightning, which does cease to be
> Ere one can say, It lightens."

When he urges his marriage on the friar,

> "*Rom.* O let us home: I stand on sudden haste.
> *Friar.* Wisely and slow. They stumble that run fast.

The metaphors put into his mouth are remarkable for their allusions to abrupt and violent haste. He wishes that he may die

> "As violently as hasty powder fired
> Doth hurry from the fatal cannon's womb."

When he thinks that Juliet mentions his name in anger, it is

> "as if that name,
> Shot from the deadly level of a gun,
> Did murder her."

When Lawrence remonstrates with him on his violence, he compares the use to which he puts his wit to

> "Powder in a skilless soldier's flask;"

and tells him that

> "Violent delights have violent ends,
> And in their triumph die; like fire and powder,
> Which, as they kiss, consume."

Lightning, flame, shot, explosion, are the favourite parallels to the conduct and career of Romeo. Swift are his loves; as swift to enter his thought, the mischief which ends them for ever. Rapid have been all the pulsations of his life; as rapid the determination which decides that they shall beat no more.

A gentleman he was in heart and soul. All his

habitual companions love him : Benvolio and Mercutio, who represent the young gentlemen of his house, are ready to peril their lives, and to strain all their energies, serious or gay, in his service. His father is filled with an anxiety on his account so delicate, that he will not venture to interfere with his son's private sorrows, while he desires to discover their source, and if possible to relieve them. The heart of his mother bursts in his calamity; the head of the rival house bestows upon him the warmest panegyrics; the tutor of his youth sacrifices everything to gratify his wishes; his servant, though no man is a hero to his *valet de chambre*, dares not remonstrate with him on his intentions, even when they are avowed to be savage-wild,

> "More fierce and more inexorable far,
> Than empty tigers or the roaring sea,"—

but with an eager solicitude he breaks his commands by remaining as close as he can venture, to watch over his safety. Kind is he to all. He wins the heart of the romantic Juliet by his tender gallantry: the worldly-minded nurse praises him for being as gentle as a lamb. When it is necessary or natural that the Prince or Lady Montague should speak harshly of him, it is done in his absence. No words of anger or reproach are addressed to his ears save by Tybalt; and from him they are in some sort a compliment, as signifying that the self-chosen prize-fighter of the opposing party deems Romeo the worthiest antagonist of his blade. We find that he fights two blood-stained duels, but both are forced upon him; the first under circumstances impossible of avoidance, the last after the humblest supplications to be excused.

> "O begone!
> By Heaven, I love thee better than myself,
> For I came hither armed against myself.
> Stay not; begone!—live, and hereafter say
> A madman's mercy bade thee run away."

With all the qualities and emotions which can inspire affection and esteem,—with all the advantages that birth, heaven, and earth could at once confer,—with the most honourable feelings and the kindliest intentions,—he is eminently an unlucky man. The record of his actions in the play before us does not extend to the period of a week; but we feel that there is no dramatic straining to shorten their course. Everything occurs naturally and probably. It was his concluding week; but it tells us all his life. Fortune was against him; and would have been against him, no matter that might have been his pursuit. He was born to win battles, but to lose campaigns. If we desired to moralize with the harsh-minded satirist, who never can be suspected of romance, we should join with him in extracting as a moral from the play

> "Nullum habes numen, si sit prudentia; sed te
> Nos facimus, Fortuna, deam, cœloque locamus;"

and attribute the mishaps of Romeo, not to want of fortune, but of prudence. Philosophy and poetry differ not in essentials, and the stern censure of Juvenal is just. But still, when looking on the timeless tomb of Romeo, and contemplating the short and sad career through which he ran, we cannot help recollecting his mourning words over his dying friend, and suggest as an inscription over the monument of the luckless gentleman,

"I THOUGHT ALL FOR THE BEST."

MIDSUMMER NIGHT'S DREAM.
BOTTOM, THE WEAVER.

———◆———

"Some men are born with a silver spoon in their mouths, and others with a wooden ladle."—*Ancient Proverb.*

"Then did the sun on dunghill shine."—*Ancient Pistol.*

It has often been remarked that it is impossible to play the enchanted scenes of Bottom with any effect. In reading the poem we idealize the ass-head; we can conceive that it represents in some grotesque sort the various passions and emotions of its wearer; that it assumes a character of dull jocosity, or duller sapience, in his conversations with Titania and the fairies; and when calling for the assistance of Messrs. Peas-blossom and Mustard-seed to scratch his head, or of the Queen to procure him a peck of provender or a bottle of hay, it expresses some puzzled wonder of the new sensations its wearer must experience in tinglings never felt before, and cravings for food until then unsuited to his appetite. But on the stage this is impossible. As the manager cannot procure for his fairies representatives of such tiny dimensions as to be in danger of being overflown by the bursting of the honey-bag of an humble-bee, so it is impossible that the art of the property-man can furnish Bottom with an ass-head capable of expressing the mixed feelings of humanity and asinity which actuate the metamorphosed weaver. It is but a pasteboard head, and that is all. The jest is over the first moment after his appearance; and, having laughed at it once, we cannot laugh at it any more. As in the case of a man who, at a masquerade, has chosen a character depending for its attraction merely on costume,—we may admire a Don Quixote, if properly bedecked in Mambrino's helmet and the other habiliments of the Knight of La Mancha, at a first glance, but we think him scarcely worthy of a second.

So it is with the Bottom of the stage; the Bottom of the poem is a different person. Shakspeare in many parts of his plays drops hints, "vocal to the intelligent," that he feels the difficulty of bringing his ideas adequately before the minds of theatrical spectators. In the opening address of the Chorus of *Henry V.* he asks pardon for having dared

> "On this unworthy scaffold to bring forth
> So great an object. Can this cockpit hold
> The vasty fields of France? or, may we cram
> Within this wooden O, the very casques
> That did affright the air at Agincourt?"

and requests his audience to piece out the imperfections of the theatre with their thoughts. This is an apology for the ordinary and physical defects of any stage,—especially an ill-furnished one; and it requires no great straining of our imaginary forces to submit to them. Even Ducrow himself, with appliances and means to boot a hundredfold more magnificent and copious than any that were at the command of Shakspeare, does not deceive us into the belief that his fifty horses, trained and managed with surpassing skill, and mounted by agile and practised riders, dressed in splendid and carefully-considered costumes, are actually fighting the battle of Waterloo, but we willingly lend ourselves to the delusion. In like manner, we may be sure that in the days of Queen Elizabeth the audience of the Globe complied with the advice of Chorus, and,

" Minding true things by what their mockeries be,"

were contented that

" Four or five most vile and ragged foils
Right ill-disposed, in brawl ridiculous,"

should serve to represent to their imagination the name of Agincourt.

We consent to this just as we do to Greeks and Romans speaking English on the stage of London, or

French on that of Paris; or to men of any country speaking in verse at all; or to all the other demands made upon our belief in playing. We can dispense with the assistance of such downright matter-of-fact interpreters as those who volunteer their services to assure us that the lion in Pyramus and Thisbe is not a lion in good earnest, but merely Snug the joiner. But there are difficulties of a more subtle and metaphysical kind to be got over, and to these, too, Shakspeare not unfrequently alludes. In the play before us,—*Midsummer Night's Dream,*—for example, when Hippolita speaks scornfully of the tragedy in which Bottom holds so conspicuous a part, Theseus answers, that the best of this kind (scenic performances) are but shadows, and the worst no worse if imagination amend them. She answers that it must be *your* imagination then, not *theirs*. He retorts with a joke on the vanity of actors, and the conversation is immediately changed. The meaning of the Duke is, that however we may laugh at the silliness of Bottom and his companions in their ridiculous play, the author labours under no more than the common calamity of dramatists. They are all but dealers in shadowy representations of life; and if the worst among them can set the mind of the spectator at work, he is equal to the best. The answer to Theseus is, that none but the best, or, at all events, those who approach to excellence, can call with success upon imagination to invest their shadows with substance. Such playwrights as Quince the carpenter,—and they abound in every literature and every theatre,—draw our attention so much to the absurdity of the performance actually going on before us, that we have no inclination to trouble ourselves with considering what substance in the background their shadows should have represented. Shakspeare intended the remark as a compliment or a consolation to less successful wooers of the comic or the tragic Muse, and touches briefly on the matter; but it was also intended as an excuse for the want of effect upon the stage of some of the finer touches of such dramatists as himself, and an appeal to all true judges of poetry to bring it before the tribunal of their own imagination; making but a matter of secondary inquiry how it appears in a theatre, as delivered by those who, whatever others may think of them, would, if taken at their own estimation, " pass for excellent men." His own magnificent creation of fairy land in the Athenian wood must have been in his mind, and he asks an indulgent play of fancy not more for Oberon and Titania, the glittering rulers of the elements, who meet

"—— on hill, in dale, forest, or mead,
 By paved fountain, or by rushy brook,
 Or on the beached margent of the sea,
 To dance their ringlets to the whistling wind,"

than for the shrewd and knavish Robin Goodfellow, the lord of practical jokes, or the dull and conceited Bottom, "the shallowest thickskin of the barren sort," rapt so wondrously from his loom and shuttle, his threads and thrums, to be the favoured lover of the Queen of Faëry, fresh from the spiced Indian air, and lulled with dances and delight amid the fragrance of the sweetest flowers, filling with their luscious perfume a moonlighted forest.

One part of Bottom's character is easily understood, and is often well acted. Amid his own companions he is the cock of the walk. His genius is admitted without hesitation. When he is lost in the wood, Quince gives up the play as marred. There is no man in Athens able to take the first part in tragedy but himself. Flute declares that he has the best wit of any handicraftman in the city. This does not satisfy the still warmer admirer,* who insists on the goodliness of his person,

---

* Act iv. sc. 2. Athens.—Quince's House.—Enter Quince, Flute, Snout, and Starveling.

" *Qui.* Have you sent to Bottom's house yet, &c.?

and the fineness of his voice. When it seems hopeless that he should appear, the cause of the stage is given up as utterly lost. When he returns, it is hailed as the "courageous day," and the "happy hour," which is to restore the legitimate drama. It is no wonder that this perpetual flattery fills him with a most inordinate opinion of his own powers. There is not a part in the play

> *Flu.* He hath simply the best wit of any man in Athens.
> *Qui.* Yea, and the best person too; and he is a very paramour for a sweet voice.
> *Flu.* You must say paragon; a paramour is, God bless us! a thing of naught."

I propose that the second admirer's speech be given to Snout, who else has not anything to say, and is introduced on the stage to no purpose. The few words he says elsewhere in the play are all ridiculous; and the mistake of "paramour" for "paragon" is more appropriate to him than to Quince, who corrects the *cacology* of Bottom himself. [Act. iii. sc. 1.

> "*Pyr.* Thisby, the flower of odious savours sweet.
> *Qui.* Odours—odours."]

And, besides, Quince, the playwright, manager, and ballad-monger,

> ["I'll get Peter Quince to write a ballad of this dream," says Bottom,]

is of too much importance in the company to be rebuked by so inferior a personage as Flute. In the original draft of their play Snout was to perform Pyramus's father, and Quince, Thisbe's father, but those parts are omitted; Snout is the representative of Wall, and Quince has no part assigned him. Perhaps this was intentional, as another proof of bungling.

which he cannot perform. As a lover he promises to make the audience weep; but his talent is still more shining in the Herculean vein of a tyrant. The manliness of his countenance, he admits, incapacitates him from acting the part of a heroine; but, give him a mask, and he is sure to captivate by the soft melody of his voice. But, lest it should be thought this melodious softness was alone his characteristic, he claims the part of the lion, which he is to discharge with so terrific a roar as to call forth the marked approbation of the warlike Duke; and yet, when the danger is suggested of frightening the ladies, who all, Amazons as they were, must be daunted by sounds so fear-inspiring, he professes himself gifted with a power of compass capable of imitating, even in the character of a roaring lion, the gentleness of the sucking dove, or the sweetness of the nightingale. He is equally fit for all parts, and in all parts calculated to outshine the rest. This is allowed; but, as it is impossible that he can perform them all, he is restricted to the principal. It is with the softest compliments that he is induced to abandon the parts of Thisbe and the lion for that of Pyramus. Quince assures him that he can play none other, because " Pyramus is a sweet-faced man; a proper man as one shall see in a summer's day; a most lovely, gentlemanlike man; *therefore* YOU must undertake it." What man of woman born could resist flattery so unsparingly administered? the well-puffed performer consents, and though he knows nothing of the play, and is unable to tell whether the part for which he is cast is that of a lover or a tyrant, undertakes to discharge it with a calm and heroic indifference as to the colour of the beard he is to wear, being confident, under any circumstances, of success, whether that most important part of the costume be straw-coloured or orange-tawny, French crown or purple in grain. With equal confidence he gets through his performance. The wit of the courtiers, or the presence of the Duke, have no effect upon his nerves. He alone speaks to the audience in his own character, not for a moment sinking the personal consequence of Bottom in the assumed port of Pyramus. He sets Theseus right on a point of the play with cool importance; and replies to the jest of Demetrius (which he does not understand) with the self-command of ignorant indifference. We may be sure that he was abundantly contented with his appearance, and retired to drink in, with ear well deserving of the promotion it had attained under the patronage of Robin Goodfellow, the applause of his companions. It is true that Oberon designates him as a " hateful fool;" that Puck stigmatizes him as the greatest blockhead of the set; that the audience of wits and courtiers before whom he has performed vote him to be an ass: but what matter is that? He mixes not with them; he hears not their sarcasms; he could not understand their criticisms; and, in the congenial company of the crew of patches and base mechanicals who admire him, lives happy in the fame of being *the* Nicholas Bottom, who, by consent, to him universal and world-encompassing, is voted to be *the* Pyramus,—*the* prop of the stage,—*the* sole support of the drama.

Self-conceit, as great and undisguised as that of poor Bottom, is to be found in all classes and in all circles, and is especially pardonable in what it is considered genteel or learned to call " the histrionic profession." The triumphs of the player are evanescent. In no other department of intellect, real or simulated, does the applause bestowed upon the living artist bear so melancholy a disproportion to the repute awaiting him after the generation passes which has witnessed his exertions. According to the poet himself, the poor player

"Struts and frets his hour upon the stage,
And then is heard no more."

Shakspeare's own rank as a performer was not high, and his reflections on the business of an actor are in general splenetic and discontented. He might have said,—though indeed it would not have fitted with the mood of mind of the despairing tyrant into whose mouth the reflection is put,—that the well-graced actor, who leaves the scene not merely after strutting and fretting, but after exhibiting power and genius to the utmost degree at which his art can aim, amid the thundering applause,—or, what is a deeper tribute, the breathless silence of excited and agitated thousands, —is destined ere long to an oblivion as undisturbed as that of his humbler fellow-artist, whose prattle is without contradiction voted to be tedious. Kemble is fading fast from our view. The gossip connected with everything about Johnson keeps Garrick before us, but the interest concerning him daily becomes less and less. Of Betterton, Booth, Quin, we remember little more than the names. The Lowins and Burbages of the days of Shakspeare are known only to the dramatic antiquary, or the poring commentator, anxious to preserve every scrap of information that may bear upon the elucidation of a text, or aid towards the history of the author. With the sense of this transitory fame before them, it is only natural that players should grasp at as much as comes within their reach while they have power of doing so. It would be a curious speculation to inquire which personally has the greater enjoyment,—the author, neglected in life, and working for immortal renown, or the actor living among huzzas, and consigned to forgetfulness the moment that his hour is past. I suppose, on the usual principle of compensation, each finds in himself springs of happiness and self-comfort. The dim distance, in its shadowy and limitless grandeur, fills with solemn musings the soul of the one; the gorgeous gilding of the sunny scenery in the foreground kindles with rapturous joy the heart of the other. Shenstone lays it down as a principle, that, if it were left to our choice whether all persons should speak ill of us to our faces, and with applause behind our backs, or, *vice versâ*, that the applause should be lavished upon ourselves, and the ill-speaking kept for our absence, we should choose the latter ; because, if we never heard the evil report, we should know nothing about our bad reputation, while, on the contrary, the good opinion others entertained of us would be of no avail if nothing reached our ears but words of anger or reproach. Since, after all, it is from within, and not from without, the sources of joy or sorrow bubble up, it does not matter so very much as the sensitive Lord of Leasowes imagines what the opinions of others concerning us may be,—at least as compared with those which, right or wrong, we form of ourselves. The question is of no great practical importance; and yet it would be somewhat curious to speculate in the manner of Hamlet, if we could do so, on the feelings of Kean and Wordsworth in the zenith of the popularity of the former, when he was worshipped as a demi-god by the unquestionable, or, at least, the scarce-questioned dispensers of daily renown; while the other by the recognised oracles of critical sagacity was set down as a jackass more obtuse than that belaboured by his own Peter Bell.

Pardon, therefore, the wearers of the sock and buskin for being obnoxious to such criticism as that lavished by Quince upon Bottom. We have no traces left us of what constituted the ordinary puffery of the Elizabethan days; but, as human nature is the same in all ages, we must suppose the trade to have been in its own way as vigorously carried on then as now. And, without hinting at anything personal, do we not week after week find attached to every performer making (whether with justice or not is no part of the consideration) pretensions to the omnifarious abilities of Bottom, some Peter Quince, who sticks to that Bottom with the tenacity of a leech, and is ready to swear that *he*, the Bottom, is the only man in Athens; that his appearance spreads an universal joy; his occultation involves the world in dramatical eclipse; that his performance of the lover can only be surpassed by his performance of the tyrant; and that it must puzzle an impartial public to decide whether nature and art, genius and study, designed him for a heroine couchant, or a rampant lion. To this it is little wonder that the object of applause lets down his ears too often donkey-like, and permits himself to be scratched by a Master Cobweb, spun though he be by a bottle-bellied spider, or a Master Peas-blossom, who can only claim Mistress Squash for his mother and Master Peascod for his father. In Peter Quince, Shakspeare shadowed forth, by anticipation, Sheridan's Puff. Quince is a fool, and Puff a rogue; and yet I think the criticism of the elder reviewer just as valuable. It is in the end as useful to the object of applause to be told, in plain terms, that he alone can act Pyramus because he is a sweet-faced man, a proper man, a most lovely, gentlemanlike man, as to have the same flummery administered under the guise of mock philosophy, with gabbling intonations about breadth, profoundness, depth, length, thickness, and so forth; which, being interpreted, signify, in many cases, "I know nothing about acting or writing, but I do know that you can give me a box or a dinner, and therefore let me play to your Bottom, Quince the carpenter, in an ass's head, intended as a representation of Aristotle the Stagirite."

Alas! I am wandering far away from the forest. I can only plead that my guide has led me into my own congenial land of newspaper from his native soil of poetry. But he never long remains out of his own domain, and the jokes and jests upon the unlucky company who undertook to perform

> "A tedious brief scene of young Pyramus
> And his love Thisbe, very tragical mirth,"

are but intrusive matter amid the romantic loves, all chivalrous and a little classical, of Theseus and Hippolita, and the jealousies unearthly, and yet so earthly, of Fairy Land. The romance of early Greece was sometimes strangely confused by the romance of the middle ages. It would take a long essay on the mixture of legends derived from all ages and countries to account for the production of such a personage as the "Duke ycleped Theseus" and his following; and the fairy mythology of the most authentic superstitions would be ransacked in vain to discover exact authorities for the

Shakspearian Oberon and Titania. But, no matter whence derived, the author knew well that in his hands the chivalrous and classical, the airy and the imaginative, were safe. It was necessary for his drama to introduce among his fairy party a creature of earth's mould, and he has so done it as in the midst of his mirth to convey a picturesque satire on the fortune which governs the world, and upon those passions which elsewhere he had with agitating pathos to depict. As Romeo, the gentleman, is *the* unlucky man of Shakspeare so here does he exhibit Bottom, the blockhead, as *the* lucky man, as him on whom Fortune showers her favours beyond measure.

This is the part of the character which cannot be performed. It is here that the greatest talent of the actor must fail in answering the demand made by the author upon our imagination. The utmost lavish of poetry, not only of high conception, but of the most elaborate working in the musical construction of the verse, and a somewhat recondite searching after all the topics favourable to the display of poetic eloquence in the ornamental style, is employed in the description of the fairy scenes and those who dwell therein. Language more brilliantly bejewelled with whatever tropes and figures rhetoricians catalogue in their books is not to be found than what is scattered forth with copious hand in *Midsummer Night's Dream.* The compliment to Queen Elizabeth,

> "In maiden meditation fancy-free,"

was of necessity sugared with all the sweets that the *bon-bon* box of the poet could supply; but it is not more ornamented than the passages all around. The pastoral images of Corin

> "Playing on pipes of corn, and versing love
> To amorous Phillida;"

the homely consequences resulting from the fairy quarrel,

> "The ox hath therefore stretch'd his yoke in vain,
> The ploughman lost his sweat, and the green corn
> Hath rotted ere his youth attain'd a beard;
> The fold stands empty in the drowned field,
> And crows are fatted with the murrain flock;"

and so on, are ostentatiously contrasted with misfortunes more metaphorically related:

> "We see
> The seasons alter; hoary-headed frosts
> Fall on the fresh lap of the crimson rose;
> And on old Hyems' chin and icy crown
> An odorous chaplet of sweet summer buds
> Is, as in mockery, set."

The mermaid chaunting on the back of her dolphin; the fair vestal throned in the west; the bank blowing with wild thyme, and decked with oxlip and nodding violet; the roundelay of the fairies singing their queen to sleep; and a hundred images beside of aërial grace and mythic beauty, are showered upon us; and in the midst of these splendours is tumbled in Bottom the weaver, blockhead by original formation, and rendered doubly ridiculous by his partial change into a literal jackass. He, the most unfitted for the scene of all conceivable personages, makes his appearance, not as one to be expelled with loathing and derision, but to be instantly accepted as the chosen lover of the Queen of the Fairies. The gallant train of Theseus traverse the forest, but they are not the objects of such fortune. The lady, under the oppression of the glamour cast upon her eyes by the juice of love-in-idleness, reserves her raptures for an absurd clown. Such are the tricks of Fortune.

Oberon, himself, angry as he is with the caprices of his queen, does not anticipate any such object for her charmed affections. He is determined that she is to be captivated by " some vile thing," but he thinks only of

> " Ounce, or cat or bear,
> Pard, or boar with bristled hair,"

animals suggesting ideas of spite or terror; but he does not dream that, under the superintendence of Puck, spirit of mischief, she is to be enamoured of the head of an ass surmounting the body of a weaver. It is so nevertheless; and the love of the lady is as desperate as the deformity of her choice. He is an angel that wakes her from her flowery bed; a gentle mortal, whose enchanting note wins her ear, while his beauteous shape enthralls her eye; one who is as wise as he is beautiful; one for whom all the magic treasures of the fairy kingdom are to be with surpassing profusion dispensed. For him she gathers whatever wealth and delicacies the Land of Faëry can boast. Her most airy spirits are ordered to be kind and courteous to this *gentleman*,—for into that impossible character has the blindness of her love transmuted the clumsy and conceited clown. Apricocks and dewberries, purple grapes, green figs, and mulberries, are to feed his coarse palate; the thighs of bees, kindled at the eyes of fiery glow-worms, are to light him to his flower-decked bed; wings plucked from painted butterflies are to fan the moonbeams from him as he sleeps; and in the very desperation of her intoxicating passion she feels that there is nothing which should not be yielded to the strange idol of her soul. She mourns over the restraints which separate her from the object of her burning affection, and thinks that the moon and the flowers participate in her sorrow.

> " The moon, methinks, looks with a watery eye,
> And when she weeps, weeps every little flower,
> *Lamenting some enforced chastity."*

Abstracting the poetry, we see the same thing every day in the plain prose of the world. Many is the Titania driven by some unintelligible magic so to waste her love. Some juice, potent as that of Puck,—the true Cupid of such errant passions,—often converts in the eyes of woman the grossest defects into resistless charms. The lady of youth and beauty will pass by the attractions best calculated to captivate the opposite sex, to fling herself at the feet of age or ugliness. Another, decked with graces, accomplishments, and the gifts of genius, and full of all the sensibilities of refinement, will squander her affections on some good-for-nothing *roué*, whose degraded habits and pursuits banish him far away from the polished scenes which she adorns. The lady of sixteen quarters will languish for him who has no arms but those which nature has bestowed; from the midst of the gilded *salon* a soft sigh may be directed towards the thin-clad tenant of a garret; and the heiress of millions may wish them sunken in the sea if they form a barrier between her and the penniless lad toiling for his livelihood,

"Lord of his presence, and no land beside."

Fielding has told us all this in his own way, in a distich, (put, I believe, into the mouth of Lord Grizzle; but, as I have not the illustrious tragedy in which it appears, before me, I am not certain, and must therefore leave it to my readers to verify this important point.) Love

"Lords into cellars bears,
And bids the brawny porter walk up-stairs."

Tom Thumb and *Midsummer Night's Dream* preach the one doctrine. It would be amusing to trace the courses of thought by which the heterogeneous minds of Fielding and Shakspeare came to the same conclusion.

Ill-mated loves are generally but of short duration on the side of the nobler party, and she awakes to lament her folly. The fate of those who suffer like Titania is the hardest. The man who is deprived of external graces of appearance may have the power of captivating by those of the mind: wit, polish, fame, may compensate for the want of youth or personal attractions. In poverty or lowly birth may be found all that may worthily inspire devoted affection—

> "The rank is but the guinea's stamp,
> The man's the gowd for a' that."

In the very dunghill of dissipation and disgrace will be raked up occasionally a lurking pearl or two of honourable feeling, or kind emotion, or irregular talent, which may be dwelt upon by the fond eye, wilfully averting its gaze from the miserable mass in which they are buried. But woe unto the unhappy lady who, like Titania, is obliged to confess, when the enchantment has passed by, that she was " enamoured of an *ass!*" She must indeed " loathe his visage," and the memory of all connected with him is destined ever to be attended by a strong sensation of disgust.

But the ass himself of whom she was enamoured has not been the less a favourite of Fortune, less happy and self-complacent, because of her late repentance. He proceeds onward as luckily as ever. Bottom, during the time that he attracts the attentions of Titania, never for a moment thinks there is anything extraordinary in the matter. He takes the love of the Queen of the Fairies as a thing of course, orders about her tiny attendants as if they were so many apprentices at his loom, and dwells in Fairy Land unobservant of its wonders, as quietly as if he were still in his workshop. Great is the courage and self-possession of an ass-head.

Theseus would have bent in reverent awe before Titania. Bottom treats her as carelessly as if she were the wench of the next-door tapster. Even Christopher Sly,* when

> * In comparing the characters of Sly and Bottom, we must be struck with the remarkable profusion of picturesque and classical allusions with which both these buffoons are surrounded. I have quoted some of the passages from *Midsummer Night's Dream* above. The Induction to the *Taming of the Shrew* is equally rich. There, too, we have the sylvan scenery and the cheerful sport of the huntsman, and there we also have references to Apollo and Semiramis; to Cytherea all in sedges hid; to Io as she was a maid; to Daphne roaming through a thorny wood. The coincidence is not casual. Shakspeare desired to elevate the scenes in which such grovelling characters played the principal part by all the artificial graces of poetry, and to prevent them from degenerating into mere farce. As I am on the subject, I cannot refrain from observing that the remarks of Bishop Hurd on the character of the Lord in the Induction to the *Taming of the Shrew* are marked by a ridiculous impertinence, and an ignorance of criticism truly astonishing. They are made to swell, however, the strange farrago of notes gathered by the variorum editors. The next editor may safely spare them.
>
> I have not troubled my readers with verbal criticism in this paper, but I shall here venture on one conjectural emendation. Hermia, chiding Demetrius, says, Act iii. sc. 2,
>
>> "If thou hast slain Lysander in his sleep,
>> Being o'er shoes in blood, wade in *the* deep,
>> And kill me too."
>
> Should we not read " *knee* deep ?" As you are already over your shoes, wade on until the bloody tide reaches your knees. In Shakspeare's time *knee* was generally spelt *kne;* and between *the* and *kne* there is not much difference in writing.

he finds himself transmuted into a lord, shows some signs of astonishment. He does not accommodate himself to surrounding circumstances. The first order he gives is for a pot of small ale; and after all the elegant luxuries of his new situation have been placed ostentatiously before him—after he has smelt sweet savours, and felt soft things—after he begins to think he is

> "A lord, indeed,
> And not a tinker nor Christopher[o] Sly;"

even then nature—or habit, which stands in the place of nature,—recurs invincible, and once more he calls for a pot of the smallest ale. (I may again cite Fielding in illustration of Shakspeare; for do we not read, in the Covent Garden tragedy, of the consolation that

> "Cold small beer is to the waking drunkard;"

and do we not hear the voice of Christopher Sly praying, for God's sake, in the midst of his lordly honours, for a draught of that unlordly but long-accustomed beverage?) In the *Arabian Night's Entertainments* a similar trick is played by the Caliph Haroun Alraschid upon Abou Hassan, and he submits, with much reluctance, to believe himself the Commander of the Faithful. But having in vain sought how to explain the enigma, he yields to the belief, and then performs all the parts assigned to him, whether of business or pleasure, of counsel or gallantry, with the easy self-possession of a practised gentleman. Bottom has none of the scruples of the tinker of Burton-heath, or the *bon vivant* of Bagdad. He sits down amid the fairies as one of themselves without any astonishment; but so far from assuming, like Abou Hassan, the manners of the court where he has been so strangely intruded, he brings the language and bearing of the booth into the glittering circle of Queen Titania. He would have behaved in the same manner on the throne of the caliph, or in the bedizened chamber of the lord; and the ass-head would have victoriously carried him through.

Shakspeare has not taken the trouble of working out the conclusion of the adventure of Sly; and the manner in which it is finished in the old play where he found him, is trifling and common-place. The Arabian novelist repeats the jest upon his hero, and concludes by placing him as a favourite in the court of the amused caliph. This is the natural ending of such an adventure; but, as Bottom's was supernatural, it was to conclude differently. He is therefore dismissed to his ordinary course of life, unaffected by what has passed. He admits at first that it is wonderful, but soon thinks it is nothing more than a fit subject for a ballad in honour of his own name. He falls at once to his old habit of dictating, boasting, and swaggering, and makes no reference to what has happened to him in the forest. It was no more than an ordinary passage in his daily life. Fortune knew where to bestow her favours.

Adieu then, Bottom the weaver! and long may you go onward prospering in your course! But the prayer is needless, for you carry about you the infallible talisman of the ass-head. You will be always sure of finding a Queen of the Fairies to heap her favours upon you, while to brighter eyes and nobler natures she remains invisible or averse. Be you ever the chosen representative of the romantic and the tender before dukes and princesses; and if the judicious laugh at your efforts, despise them in return, setting down their criticism to envy. This you have a right to do. Have they, with all their wisdom and wit, captivated the heart of a Titania as you have done? Not they—nor will they ever. Prosper therefore, with undoubting heart despising the rabble of the wise. Go on your path rejoicing; assert loudly your claim to fill every character in life; and may you be quite sure that as long as the noble race of the Bottoms continues to exist, the chances of extraordinary good luck will fall to their lot, while in the ordinary course of life they will never be unattended by the plausive criticism of a Peter Quince.

HIS LADIES.—LADY MACBETH.

> "Then gently scan your brother man,
> More gently sister woman."   BURNS.

> "Je donne mon avis, non comme bon, mais comme mien."
> MONTAIGNE.

THE ladies of Shakspeare have of course riveted the attention, and drawn to them the sympathies, of all who have read or seen his plays. The book-trained critic, weighing words and sentences in his closet; the romantic poet, weaving his verses by grove or stream; the polished occupant of the private box; the unwashed brawler of the gallery; the sedate visitant of the pit, are touched each in his several way by the conjugal devotion and melancholy fate of Desdemona, the high-souled principle of Isabella, the enthusiastic love and tragic end of Juliet, the maternal agonies of Constance, the stern energies of Margaret of Anjou, the lofty resignation of Katharine, the wit and romance of Rosalind, frolic of tongue, but deeply feeling at heart; the accomplished coquetries of Cleopatra, redeemed and almost sanctified by her obedient rushing to welcome death at the call ringing in her ears from the grave of her self-slain husband; the untiring affection of Imogen, Ophelia's stricken heart and maddened brain, or the filial constancy of Cordelia. Less deeply marked, but all in their kind beautiful, are the innocence of Miranda, the sweetness of Anne Page, the meek bearing—beneath the obtrusion of undesired honours—of Anne Boleyn, the playful fondness of Jessica;—but I should run through all the catalogue of Shakspeare's plays were I to continue the enumeration. The task is unnecessary, for they dwell in the hearts of all, of every age, and sex, and condition. They nestle in the bosoms of the wise and the simple, the sedentary and the active, the moody and the merry, the learned and the illiterate, the wit of the club, the rustic of the farm, the soldier in camp, the scholar in college; and it affords a remarkable criterion of their general effect, that, even in those foreign countries which, either from imperfect knowledge, defective taste, or national prejudice, set little value on the plays of Shakspeare,—while Hamlet, Richard, Macbeth, King John, Lear, and Falstaff, are unknown or rejected, the names of Desdemona and Juliet are as familiar as household words.

No writer ever created so many female characters, or placed them in situations of such extreme diversity; and in none do we find so lofty an appreciation of female excellence. The stories from which the great dramatists of Athens drew their plots were, in most of their striking incidents, derogatory to woman. The tale of Troy divine, the war of Thebes, the heroic legends, were their favourite, almost their exclusive sources; and the crimes, passions, and misfortunes of Clytemnestra and Medea, Phædra and Jocasta, could only darken the scene. An adulterous spouse aiding in the murder of her long-absent lord, the King of men, returning crowned with conquest; a daughter participating in the ruthless avenging by death inflicted on a mother by a son; an unpitying sorceress killing her children to satiate rage against her husband; a faithless wife endeavouring to force her shameless love on her step-son, and by false accusation consigning him for his refusal to destruction beneath his father's curse; a melancholy queen linked in incestuous nuptials to her own offspring;—these ladies are the heroines of the most renowned of the Greek tragedies! and the consequences of their guilt or misfortune compose the fable of many more. In some of the Greek plays, as the Eumenides, we have no female characters except the unearthly habitants of heaven or hell; in the most wondrous of them all, Prometheus Fettered, appears only the mythic Io; in the Persians, only the ghost of Atossa, who scarcely appertains to womankind: in some, as Philoctetes, women form no part of the *dramatis personæ;* in others, as the Seven against Thebes, they are of no importance to the action of the piece ; or, as in the Suppliants, serve but as the Chorus; and, in many more, are of less than secondary importance. Euripides often makes them the objects of those ungallant reflections which consign the misogynic dramatist to such summary punishment from the irritated sex in the comedies of Aristophanes; and in the whole number, in the thirty-three plays extant, there are but two women who can affect our nobler or softer emotions. The tender and unremitting care of Antigone for her blind, forlorn, and aged father, her unbending determination to sacrifice her lover and her life sooner than fail in paying funeral honours to her fallen brother; and, in Alcestis, her resolute urging that her own life should be taken to preserve that of a beloved husband,— invest them with a pathetic and heroic beauty. But, in the one, we are haunted by the horrid recollections of incest and fratricide; and in the other we are somewhat indignant that we should be forced to sympathize with an affection squandered upon so heartless a fellow as Admetus, who suffers his wife to perish in his stead with the most undisturbed conviction of the superior value of his own existence, pouring forth all the while the most melodious lamentations over her death, but never for a moment thinking of coming forward to prevent it. They are beautiful creations, nevertheless.

The Greek dramatists were in a great measure bound to a particular class of subjects; but, in general, the manner in which an author treats the female character, affords one of the main criteria by which the various gradations of genius may be estimated. By the highest genius woman is always spoken of with a deep feeling of the most reverential delicacy. Helen is the cause of the war immortalized by the Iliad; but no allusion to her lapse is made throughout the poem save by herself, deploring in bitter accents what she has done. She wishes that she had died an evil death before she followed Paris; she acknowledges herself to be unworthy of the kindred of those whom she describes as deserving of honour; her conscience suggests that her far-famed brothers, "whom one mother bore," are in the field when the warring chieftains meet in truce, but dare not show themselves among their peers through shame of the disgrace she has entailed upon them; and, at the last, she lays bare her internal feeling that insult is the lot she deserves by the warm gratitude with which she acknowledges, in her bitter lament over the corse of Hector, that he had the generosity never to address her with upbraiding. The wrath of Achilles is roused for the injury inflicted upon him by carrying off Briseis, dear to his heart, " spear-captured as she was." She is restored by the penitent Agamemnon, with solemn vows that she returns pure and uninsulted. Of Andromache I think it unnecessary to speak. In the Odyssey, it is true, we have Circe and Calypso; but they are goddesses couching with a mortal, and excite no human passion. We meet them in the region of "*speciosa miracula,*" where Cyclops, and Sirius, and Lotus-eaters dwell; where the King of the winds holds his court, and whence is the passage to Erebus. In that glorious mixture of adventure and allegory,—the Voyage of Ulysses,—we may take those island beauties to be the wives and sweethearts whom sailors meet in every port; or, following the stream of moralists and commentators, look upon the fable to be no more than

" Truth severe in fairy fiction dressed."

In other parts of the poem we might wish for more warm-heartedness in Penelope; but under her circumstances caution is excusable, and she must be admitted to be a pattern of constancy and devotion. The Helen of the Odyssey is a fine continuation of the Helen of the Iliad. Still full of kindly feminine impulses, still sorrowing when she thinks of the misfortunes she has occasioned, her griefs have lost the intense poignancy with which they afflicted her while leading a life degrading her in her own eyes, and exposing her to affronts of which she could not complain. Restored to the husband of her early affections, consoled by his pardon, and dwelling once more amid the scenes of her youth, —absence from which, and absence so occasioned, she had never ceased to regret in wasting floods of tears,— the Helen of the Odyssey comes before us no longer uttering the accents of ceaseless self-reproach, but soothed, if not pacified, in soul. We have the *lull* after the tempest,—the calm following the whirlwind.

Virgil is a great poet indeed, though few will now agree with Scaliger that he is equal, far less superior, to Homer. Dido is the blot upon the Æneid. The loves of the Carthaginian queen might have made, and in the hands of Virgil would have made, a charming poem, treated separately,—a poem far superior in execution to the Hero and Leander of Musæus, but a work of the same order. As it stands, the episode, if it can be so called, utterly ruins the epic character of the hero. St. Evremond has said that Æneas had all the qualities of a monk; it is plain that he had not the feelings of a gentleman; and we cannot wonder that his first wife wandered from his side, and that he met with so violent an opposition when he sought another. Virgil, after his conduct to Dido, had not the courage to introduce him to Lavinia in person, and leaves him undefended to the angry tongue of her mother. The poet was justly punished for his fourth book; for, in all those which follow, he has not ventured to introduce any female characters but incendiaries, sibyls, shrews, and furies.

When Dante took Virgil as his guide in the infernal regions, he did not follow his master in dwelling on the pleasures or the gentler sorrows of illicit love. His ghostly women appear stern, or subdued of port. The lady who is best known to the English reader, Francesca di Rimini, forms no exception. Nothing can be more grave and solemn than the tale of her hapless passion, as told in the Inferno. It is pervaded throughout by such sorrow and remorse as we might expect to find in a region whence hope is excluded. Accordingly how far different is its impression from that left on the mind by the same story when told merely as a love-tale by Mr. Leigh Hunt. I do not say this in disparagement of that picturesque and graphic poem, the *Story of Rimini*, which has been exposed to the most unjustifiable criticism; but to mark the manner in which men of talent and men of genius handle the same subject. The ladies of Tasso, though not vigorously sketched, and in general imitated from the Latin poets,—I speak of his Jerusalem,—are conceived in a spirit of romantic chivalry; and, even when the witching Armida leads Rinaldo astray, the poet diverts our attention from the blandishments of the enchantress to dazzle us by the wonders of magic groves and gardens. Poor Tasso, besides, wishes to persuade us—perhaps in some moody hours he had persuaded himself—that he intended the whole poem for an allegory, in which Armida was to play some edifying part,—I forget what. In the poets of romance we do not look for the severer style of the epic; but the forest-ranging heroines of Ariosto and Spenser, "roaming the woodland, frank and free," have an air of self-confiding independence and maiden freshness, worthy of the leafy scenes through which they move, that renders it impossible to approach them with other thoughts than those of chivalrous deference. If Spenser, in his canto of Jealousy, makes the lady of the victim of that weak passion treat her husband as he had anticipated, why, she errs with no man of mortal mould, but chooses as her mates the jolly satyrs wonning in the wood; and Spenser has his allegory too. Ariosto took no trouble to make explanations, being satisfied, I suppose, with the character given of his poetry by Cardinal Hippolyto; and even he has the grace to beg the ladies, to whose service he had from the beginning dedicated his lays, to avert their eyes when he is about to sing the strange adventures of Giocondo.*

---

* *Orlando Furioso*, canto xxii. st. 1, 2, 3.

I.

"Donne, e voi che le donne avete in pregio,
    Per Dio, non date a questa istoria orecchia,
A questa che 'l ostier dire in dispregio,
    E in vostra infamia e biasmo s'apparecchia;
Benche ne macchia vi puo dar ne fregio
    Lingua si vile; e sia l'usanza vecchia,
Che 'l volgare ignorante ognun riprenda,
E parle piu de quel meno intenda.

II.

"Lasciate questo canto, che senz' esso
    Puo star l'istoria, e non sara men chiara;
Mettendolo Turpino, anch' io l' ò messo,
    Non per malevolenzia, ne per gara;
Ch' io v' ami oltre mia lingua che l' a expresso,
    Che mai non fu di celebrarvi avara,

The theme of Milton in *Paradise Lost*, hardly admits of the development of ordinary human feelings; but his sole Eve has grace in all her steps, and all her actions too. In *Paradise Regained* his subject was

> N' ò falto mille prove, e v' o dimostro
> Ch' io son ne potrei esser se non vostro.
>
> III.
> "Passi chi vuol tre carte, o quattro, senza
>   Leggerne verso, e chi pur legge vuole
> Gli dia quella medesima credenza,
>   Che si vuol dare a finzion, e a fole," &c.

which thus may be rollingly Englished,

> Ladies, and you to whom ladies are dear,
> For God's sake don't lend to this story an ear.
> Care not for fables of slander or blame
> Which this scandalous chronicler flings on your name.
> Spots that can stain you with slight or with wrong
> Cannot be cast by so worthless a tongue.
> Well is it known, as an usage of old,
> That the ignorant vulgar will ever be bold,
> Satire and censure still scattering, and
> Talking the most where they least understand.
> Passed over unread let this canto remain,
> Without it the story will be just as plain.
> As Turpin has put it, so *I* put it too;
> But not from ill-feeling, dear ladies, to you.
> My love to your sex has been shown in my lays;
> To you I have never been niggard of praise;
> And many a proof I have given which secures
> That I am, and can never be other than yours.

badly chosen; and he feared, from religious motives, to introduce the Virgin. In *Comus* his Lady is a model of icy chastity, worthy of the classic verse in which she is embalmed; but Dalilah in *Samson Agonistes* is the more dramatic conception. Ornate and gay, she makes urgent court to her angry husband, with no better fate than to be by him inexorably repelled. She presses upon him all the topics that could lead to reconciliation, but the sense of his wrongs is too acute to allow of pardon; and at last she bursts away with the consoling reflection that, though spurned by him, and made the object of reproach in Israelitish songs,

>   Skip three or four pages, and read not a word;
>   Or, if you *will* read it, pray deem it absurd,
>   As a story in credit not better or worse
>   Than the foolish old tales you were told by the nurse.

I do not mean to defend my doggrel; but I think Ariosto has not yet had an adequate translator in English, or indeed in any language; nor, in my opinion, will he easily find one. The poem is too long, and requires the aid of the music of the original language to carry the reader through. I do not know what metre in English could contend against the prolixity; but I *do* know that Ariosto sadly wants—as what classic in the vernacular languages does not?—a better critic of his text than he has yet found in Italian.

In the above passage it is somewhat amusing to find Ariosto assuring his readers that they might pass this particular canto, because without it "*puo star l'istoria;*" as if there were a canto in the whole poem of which the same might not be said.

she shall be hymned and honoured in those of her own country as a deliverer. Milton was unhappy in his wives and daughters; and his domestic manners appear to have been harsh and unamiable. In his prose works, his *Tetrachordon* for example, he does not display any kindly feeling for the sex; but when he clothed himself in his singing robes, and soared above the cares of every-day life, to expatiate in the purer regions of poetry, the soul of the poet softened and sublimed; like his own Adam, his sterner nature relented; and, though he could not make Samson pardon Dalilah, he will not let her depart unhonoured. In *Paradise Lost*, he had spoken of her disparagingly,—

> "So rose the Danite strong,
> Herculean Samson, from the harlot lap
> Of Philistæan Dalilah;"

but when she comes before him, as it were, in bodily presence, he leaves all the words of reproach to her irritated lord, and suggests to her, topics of self-justification, dismissing her from the stage, not as a faithless wife, but as a heroic woman, who had sacrificed her affections to her country, and who retires after humiliating herself in vain to reap the reward of her patriotic conduct among her people and her kindred.

If we turn from the epic and tragic to the other departments of literature in which genius can be exercised, we shall find the feeling much the same. Those who write from observation of what is going on in the world, —the novelist, the comic writer, the satirist,—must take the world as it is, and lay it before us in its mixture of good and evil. There is no need, however, that the latter should be forcibly thrust upon us. The task of the satirists appears to me the lowest in which talent can be employed. The most famous among them, Juvenal, tells us truly that the *rigidi censura cachinni* —the part chosen by Democritus—is easy to any one. We must rise above it, as he has done in some of his satires,—as in that sublime poem in which the passage occurs, the tenth, or the thirteenth and fourteenth,— and forget the wit or the censor to assume the loftier bearing of the moralist. I should have wondered that the same mind which produced these noble effusions could have perpetrated the enormities of the sixth satire and some others, if I did not reflect that Rome, originally an asylum for robbers, was nothing more than a standing camp, with the virtues and vices, the manners and the feelings of a camp, to the day of its downfall. Rape and violence procured its first women, and it would seem as if the original act had influenced their feelings to the sex throughout. It is certain that theirs is the only literature in the world in which no female character is delineated worthy of the slightest recollection—a striking circumstance, and well deserving critical investigation; but it would now lead us too far from our subject, from which indeed I have delayed too long already. We must get back to Shakspeare, staying only to remark that if Boccacio and his imitator, Chaucer, have intermingled licentious tales in their miscellaneous collection, they have done so, only in compliance with the supposed necessity of delineating every species of life, and that they hasten to show that they could be of finer spirit when emancipated from the thraldom of custom; that Cervantes chequers the comic of *Don Quixote* with visions of graceful and romantic beauty; and that such will be found to be the case more or less in every composition that takes firm hold of the human mind. I except, of course, works of morals, science, and philosophy: and under those heads must come the unromantic and unpoetic books of wit, and even buffoonery, if they be doomed to last. Rabelais will live for ever to speak vocally to the intelligent; but mere licentiousness must perish. Indulgence in woman-scorning ribaldry inflicts due punishment upon talent itself, if it be prostituted to such miserable work. The melancholy ability which has been so successful in *La*

Pucelle affords a sufficient reason why its author failed when he attempted a *Henriade*.

Supereminent over all the great geniuses of the world and with no others have I compared him—is Shakspeare in his women. Homer was not called upon to introduce them in such number or variety, nor could they enter so intimately into the action of his poems. Still less was there opportunity for their delineation in Milton. But Shakspeare's is the unique merit that, being a dramatist wielding equally the highest tragic and the lowest comic, and therefore compelled to bring females prominently forward in every variety of circumstance, he has carefully avoided themes and situations which might either inspire horror or disgust, or excite licentious feeling. We have in him no Phædra, Clytemnestra or Medea; no story like those of Jocasta, or Monimia, or the Mysterious Mother. He would have recoiled from what is hinted at in *Manfred*. Even the Myrrha of *Sardanapalus* could not have found a place among his heroines. In none of his plots, comic or tragic, does female frailty form an ingredient. The only play in which ladies have been betrayed is *Measure for Measure;* and there he takes care that their misfortune shall be amended, by marrying Mariana to Angelo, and ordering Claudio to restore honour to

Julietta, whom he had wronged. Nowhere else does a similar example occur, and there it is set in strong contrast with the high-toned purity of Isabella. In the instances of slandered women, it seems to delight him to place them triumphant over their slanderers; as Hero in *Much Ado about Nothing*, Hermione in the *Winter's Tale*, Imogen in *Cymbeline*. All his heroes woo with the most honourable views; there is no intrigue in any of his plays, no falsehood to the married bed. Those who offer illicit proposals are exposed to ruin and disgrace. Angelo falls from his lofty station. Prince John is driven from his brother's court. Falstaff, the wit and courtier, becomes a butt, when his evil star leads him to make lawless courtship to the Wives of Windsor. The innocent and natural love of Miranda in the *Tempest* affords a striking contrast to the coarse and disgusting passion of Dorinda: a character thrust into the play as an improvement by no less a man than Dryden. Here again we may remark how great is the distance which separates genius of the first order even from that which comes nearest to it. The two most detestable women ever drawn by Shakspeare—Regan and Goneril—are both in love with Edmund; but we have no notice of their passion until the moment of their death, and then we find that, wicked as were the thoughts which rankled in their bosoms, no infringement of the laws of chastity was contemplated; marriage was their intention: " I was contracted to them both," says Edmund; " all three now marry in an instant." With his dying breath he bears testimony that in the midst of their crimes they were actuated by the dominant feeling of woman:

> " Yet Edmund was beloved ;
> The one the other poisoned for his sake,
> And after slew herself."

Emilia is accused by Iago in soliloquy as being suspected of faithlessness to his bed, but he obviously does not believe the charge:—

> " I hate the Moor;
> And it is thought abroad that 'twixt my sheets
> He has done my office; *I know not if 't be true,*
> But I, for mere suspicion in that kind,
> Will do as if for surety."

He uses it merely as an additional excuse for hating the Moor; a palliation to his conscience in the career which he is about to pursue. Queen Gertrude's marriage with her brother-in-law is made the subject of severe animadversion; but it does not appear that she had dishonoured herself in the life of her first husband, or was in any manner participant in the crime of Claudius. Hamlet, in the vehemence of his anger, never insinuates such a charge; and the Ghost, rising to moderate his violence, acquits her by his very appearance at such a time, of any heinous degree of guilt. As for the gross theory of Tieck respecting Ophelia, it is almost a national insult. He maintains that she had yielded to Hamlet's passion, and that its natural consequences had driven her to suicide. Such a theory is in direct opposition to the retiring and obedient purity of her character, the tenour of her conversations and soliloquies, the general management of the play, and what I have endeavoured to show is the undeviating current of Shakspeare's ideas. If the German critic propounded this heresy to insult English readers through one of their greatest favourites in revenge for the ungallant reason which the Archbishop of Canterbury,* in *Henry V.*, assigns as the origin of the Salique law, he might be pardoned; but, as it is plainly dictated by a spirit of critical wicked-

---

* *Henry V.* act i. sc. 2. Archbishop Chicheley's argument is

"The land Salique lies in Germany,
Between the floods of Sala and of Elbe,
Where Charles the Great, having subdued the Saxons,
There left behind and settled certain French,
Who, holding in disdain the German women
For some dishonest manners of their life,
Established there this law, to wit, no female
Should be inheritrix in Salique land."

ness and blasphemy, I should consign him, in spite of learning, acuteness, and Shakspearian knowledge, without compassion, to the avenging hands of Lysistrata.*

Such, in the plays where he had to create the characters, was the course of Shakspeare. In the historical plays, where he had to write by the book, it is not at all different. Scandal is carefully avoided. Many spots lie on the fame of Queen Elinor, but no reference is made to them by the hostile tongue which describes the mother-queen as a second Até, stirring her son, King John, to blood and strife. Jane Shore, of whom ʻRowe, a commentator on Shakspeare too, made a heroine, is not introduced on the stage in *Richard III.* Poor Joan of Arc is used brutally, it must be owned; but it is not till she is driven to the stake that she confesses to an infirmity which not even her barbarous judges can seriously believe. We must observe, besides, that the first part of *Henry VI.* can scarcely be considered a play of Shakspeare, for he did little more than revise the old play of that name. To the charge of the older dramatist, too, must be set the strange exhibition of Margaret of Anjou mourning over the head of the Duke of Suffolk

* Aristoph. Lysistr.

in the second part. When Shakspeare has that vigorous woman to himself, as in *Richard III.*, she shows no traces of such weakness: she is the heroic asserter of her husband's rights, the unsubdued but not-to-be-comforted mourner over her foully slaughtered son. He makes the scenes of the civil wars sad enough; the father kills the son, the son the father, under the eyes of the pitying king; but there is no hint of outrage on women. He contrives to interest us equally in Katharine of Aragon and Anne Boleyn. Everything that poetry can do, is done, to make us forget the faults of Cleopatra, and to incline us to think that a world was well lost for that *petit nez retroussé*. We should in vain search the writings of the Romans themselves for such Roman ladies as those of *Coriolanus* and *Julius Cæsar*. In his camps and armies we have much military tumult and railing, but nowhere the introduction of licentious scenes. If Alcibiades be attended by his Phrynia and Timandra, and Falstaff have his poll clawed like a parrot by Doll Tearsheet, the Athenian ladies are introduced as a vehicle for the fierce misanthropy of Timon, and the fair one of Eastcheap acts as a satire upon the impotent desires of the withered elder, the dead elm, whom she clasps in her venal embraces. They are drawn in their true colours:

no attempt is made to bedeck them with sentimental graces—to hold them up to sympathetic admiration with the maudlin novelist, or to exhibit them as " interesting young females" with the police reporter. They lift not their brazen fronts in courts and palaces; in obscure corners they ply their obscene trade. We know that it is their vocation, and dismiss them from our minds. There is no corruption to be feared from the example of the inmates of Mr. Overdone's establishment or Mrs. Quickly's tavern. Shakspeare exhibits only one fallen lady in all his plays—and she is Cressida. But *Troilus and Cressida* deserves a separate paper, if for no other reason, yet because it is a play in which Shakspeare has handled the same characters as Homer. It is worth while to consider in what points these greatest of poets agree, and in what they differ.

Such, then, is the female character as drawn in Shakspeare. It is pure, honourable, spotless,—ever ready to perform a kind action,—never shrinking from a heroic one. Gentle and submissive where duty or affection bids,—firm and undaunted in resisting the approaches of sin, or shame, or disgrace. Constant in love through every trial;—faithful and fond in all the great relations of life, as wife, as daughter, as sister, as mother, as friend,—witty or refined, tender or romantic, lofty or gay,—her failings shrouded, her good and lovely qualities brought into the brightest light, she appears in the pages of the mighty dramatist as if she were the cherished daughter of a fond father, the idolized mistress of an adoring lover, the very goddess of a kneeling worshipper. I have catalogued most of the female names which adorn the plays. One is absent from the list. She is absent; the dark lady of that stupendous work which, since the Eumenides, bursting upon the stage with appalling howl in quest of the fugitive Orestes, electrified with terror the Athenian audience, has met no equal. I intend to maintain that Lady Macbeth, too, is human in heart and impulse,— that she is not meant to be an embodiment of the Furies.

Macbeth is the gloomiest of the plays. Well may its hero say that he has supped full of horrors. It opens with the incantations of spiteful witches, and concludes with a series of savage combats, stimulated by quenchless hate on one side, and by the desperation inspired by the consciousness of unpardonable crime on the other. In every act we have blood in torrents. The first man who appears on the stage is the *bleeding* captain. The first word uttered by earthly lips is,

"What *bloody* man is that?" The tale which the captain relates is full of fearful gashes, reeking wounds, and *bloody* execution. The murder of Duncan in the second act stains the hands of Macbeth so deeply as to render them fit to incarnadine the multitudinous seas, and make the ·green—one red. His lady imbrues herself in the crimson stream, and gilds the faces of the sleeping grooms with gore. She thus affords a pretence to the thane for slaughtering them in an access of simulated fury.

> "Their hands and faces were all badged with *blood*,
> So were their daggers, which unwiped we found
> Upon their pillows."

Macbeth carefully impresses the sanguinary scene upon his hearers:

> "Here lay Duncan,
> His silver skin laced with his golden *blood*,
> And his gashed stabs looked like a breach in nature
> For ruin's wasteful entrance; there the murderers,
> Steeped in the colours of their trade, their daggers
> Unmannerly breeched in *gore*."

Direful thoughts immediately follow, and the sky itself participates in the horror. The old man who can well remember threescore and ten, during which time he had witnessed dreadful hours and strange things, considers all as mere trifles, compared with the sore night of Duncan's murder.

> "The'heavens,
> Thou seest, as troubled with man's act,
> Threaten his *bloody* stage ; by the clock 'tis day,
> And yet dark night strangles the travelling lamp."

The horses of Duncan forget their careful training, and their natural instincts, to break their stalls and eat each other. Gloom, ruin, murder, horrible doubts, unnatural suspicions, portents of dread in earth and heaven, surround us on all sides. In the third act, desperate assassins, incensed by the blows and buffets of the world, weary with disasters, tugged with fortune, willing to wreak their hatred on all mankind, and persuaded that Banquo has been their enemy, set upon and slay him, without remorse and without a word. The prayer of their master to Night, that she would, with

> "*Bloody* and invisible hand,
> Cancel and tear to pieces that great bond"

which kept him in perpetual terror, is in part accomplished; and he who was his enemy in, as he says,

> "Such *bloody* distance,
> That every minute of his being thrusts
> Against my life,"

lies breathless in the dust. The murderers bring the witness of their deed to the very banquet-chamber of the expecting king. They come with *blood* upon the face. The hardened stabber does not communicate the tidings of his exploit in set phrase. He minces not the matter,—his language is not culled from any trim and weeded vocabulary; and the king compliments him in return, in language equally vernacular and unrefined.

> "*Mur.* My lord, his throat is cut; that I did for him.
> *Mac.* Thou art the best o' the cut-throats."

Cheered by this flattering tribute to his merits, the accomplished artist goes on, in all the pride of his profession, to show that he had left no rubs or botches in his work. Macbeth, after a burst of indignation at the escape of Fleance, recurs to the comfortable assurance of Banquo's death, and asks, in the full certainty of an answer in the affirmative,

> " But Banquo's safe?
> *Mur.* Ay, my good lord : safe in a ditch he bides,
>   With twenty trenched gashes on his head;
>   The least a death to nature.
> *Mac.* Thanks for that."

Presently the gory locks of Banquo's spectre attest

the truth of what the murderer has told, and the banquet breaks up by the flight, rather than the retirement, of the astonished guests; leaving Macbeth dismally, but fiercely, pondering over thoughts steeped in slaughter. The very language of the scene is redolent of blood. The word itself occurs in almost every speech. At the conclusion of the act, come the outspeaking of suspicions hitherto only muttered, and the determination of the Scottish nobles to make an effort which may give to their tables meat, sleep to their eyes, and free their feasts and banquets from those bloody knives, the fatal hue of which haunted them in their very hours of retirement, relaxation, or festival.

The sanguine stain dyes the fourth act as deeply. A head severed from the body, and a bloody child, are the first apparitions that rise before the king at the bidding of the weird sisters. The blood-boltered Banquo is the last to linger upon the stage, and sear the eyes of the amazed tyrant. The sword of the assassin is soon at work in the castle of Macduff; and his wife and children fly from the deadly blow, shrieking " murder "—in vain. And the fifth act,— from its appalling commencement, when the sleeping lady plies her hopeless task of nightly washing the blood-stained hand, through the continual clangour of trumpets calling, as clamorous harbingers, to blood and death, to its conclusion, when Macduff, with dripping sword, brings in the freshly hewn-off head of the "dead butcher," to lay it at the feet of the victorious Malcolm, — exhibits a sequence of scenes in which deeds and thoughts of horror and violence are perpetually, and almost physically, forced upon the attention of the spectator. In short, the play is one clot of blood from beginning to end. It was objected to Alfieri, (by Grimm, I believe,) that he wrote his tragedies not in tears, but blood. Shakspeare could write in tears when he pleased. In Macbeth he chose to dip his pen in a darker current.

Nowhere in the course of the play does he seek to beguile us of our tears. We feel no more interest in the gracious Duncan, in Banquo, in Lady Macduff, than we do in the slaughtered grooms. We feel that they have been brutally murdered; and, if similar occurrences were to take place in Wapping or Rotherhithe, London would be in commotion. All the police from A to Z would be set on the alert, the newspapers crammed with paragraphs, and a hot search instigated after the murderer. If taken, he would be duly tried, wondered at, gazed after, convicted, hanged and forgotten. We should think no more of his victim than we now think of Hannah Browne. The other characters of the play, with the exception of the two principal, are nonentities. We care nothing for Malcolm or Donalbain, or Lenox or Rosse, or the rest of the Scottish nobles. Pathetic, indeed, are the words which burst from Macduff when he hears the astounding tidings that all his pretty chickens and their dam have been carried off at one fell swoop; but he soon shakes the woman out of his eyes, and dreams only of revenge. His companions are slightly affected by the bloody deed, and grief is in a moment converted into rage. It is but a short passage of sorrow, and the only one of the kind. What is equally remarkable is, that we have but one slight piece of comic in the play,—the few sentences given to the porter;* and

---

* The speech of this porter is in blank verse.

  Here is a knocking indeed! If a man
  Were porter of hell-gate, he should have old
  Turning the key. Knock—knock—knock! Who is there,
  In the name of Beelzebub? Here is a farmer
  That hanged himself [up] on the expectation
  Of plenty: come in time. Have napkins enough
  About you. Here you'll sweat for it. Knock—knock!
  Who's there, in the other devil's name? [I'] faith
  Here's an equivocator, that could swear
  In both the scales 'gainst either scale; [one] who

their humour turns upon a gloomy subject for jest,—the occupation of the keeper of the gates of hell. With these two exceptions,—the brief pathos of Macduff, and the equally brief comedy of the porter,—all the rest is blood. Tears and laughter have no place in this cavern of death.

Of such a gory poem, Macbeth is the centre, the moving spirit. From the beginning, before treason has entered his mind, he appears as a man delighting in blood. The captain announcing his deeds against Macdonwald, introduces him bedabbled in slaughter.

> Committed treason enough for God's sake, yet
> Cannot equivocate to heaven. Oh! come in,
> Equivocator. Knock—knock—knock! Who's there?
> 'Faith, here's an English tailor come hither
> For stealing out of a French hose. Come in, tailor.
> Here you may roast your goose.
>   Knock—knock—
>   Never in quiet.
> Who are you? but this place is too cold for hell.
> I'll devil-porter it no longer. I had thought
> T' have let in some of all professions,
> That go the primrose-path to th' everlasting darkness.

The alterations I propose are very slight. *Upon* for *on, i' faith* for *'faith*, and the introduction of the word *one* in a place where it is required. The succeeding dialogue is also in blank verse. So is the sleeping scene of Lady Macbeth; and that so palpably, that I wonder it could ever pass for prose.

> "For brave Macbeth,—well he deserves that name,—
> Disdaining fortune, with his brandished steel,
> Which smoked with bloody execution,
> Like valour's minion carved out his passage
> Until he faced the slave:
> And ne'er shook hands, nor bade farewell to him,
> Till he unseamed him from the nave to the chops,*
> And fixed his head upon our battlements."

After this desperate backstroke, as Warburton justly calls it,* Macbeth engages in another combat equally sanguinary. He and Banquo

> "Doubly redoubled strokes upon the foe;
> Except they meant to bathe in reeking wounds,
> Or memorize another Golgotha,
> I cannot tell."

Hot from such scenes, he is met by the witches. They promise him the kingdom of Scotland. The glittering prize instantly affects his imagination; he is so wrapt in thought at the very moment of its announcement that he cannot speak. He soon informs us what is the hue of the visions passing through his mind. The witches

---

* Warburton proposes that we should read " from the *nape* to the chops," as a more probable wound. But this could hardly be called *unseaming*; and the wound is intentionally horrid to suit the character of the play. So, for the same reason, when Duncan is murdered, we are made to remark that the old man had much blood in him.

had told him he was to be king: they had not said a word about the means. He instantly supplies them:

> "Why do I yield to that suggestion
> Whose horrid image doth unfix my hair,
> And make my seated heart knock at my ribs
> Against the use of nature."

The dreaded word itself soon comes:

> "My thought, whose MURDER yet is but fantastical,
> Shakes so my single state of man, that function
> Is smothered in surmise."

To a mind so disposed, temptation is unnecessary. The thing was done. Duncan was marked out for murder before the letter was written to Lady Macbeth, and she only followed the thought of her husband.

Love for him is in fact her guiding passion. She sees that he covets the throne,—that his happiness is wrapt up in the hope of being a king,—and her part is accordingly taken without hesitation. With the blindness of affection, she persuades herself that he is full of the milk of human kindness, and that he would reject false and unholy ways of attaining the object of his desire. She deems it, therefore, her duty to spirit him to the task. Fate and metaphysical aid, she argues, have destined him for the golden round of Scotland.

Shall she not lend her assistance? She does not ask the question twice. She will. Her sex, her woman's breasts, her very nature, oppose the task she has prescribed to herself; but she prays to the ministers of murder, to the spirits that tend on mortal thoughts, to make thick her blood, and stop up the access and passage of remorse; and she succeeds in mustering the desperate courage which bears her through. Her instigation was not in reality wanted. Not merely the murder of Duncan, but of Malcolm, was already resolved on by Macbeth.

> " The Prince of Cumberland! That is a step
> On which I must fall down, or else o'erleap,
> For in my way it lies. Stars! hide your fires,
> Let not light see my black and dark desires!"

As the time for the performance of the deed approaches, he is harassed by doubts; but he scarcely shows any traces of compunction or remorse. He pauses before the crime,—not from any hesitation at its enormity, but for fear of its results,—for fear of the poisoned chalice being returned to his own lips,—for fear of the trumpet-tongued indignation which must attend the discovery of the murder of so popular a prince as Duncan,—one who has borne his faculties so meekly, and loaded Macbeth himself with honours. He is not haunted by any feeling for the sin, any compassion for his victim;—the dread of losing the golden opinions he has so lately won, the consequences of failure, alone torment him. His wife has not to suggest murder, for that has been already resolved upon; but to represent the weakness of drawing back, after a resolution has once been formed. She well knows that the momentary qualm will pass off,—that Duncan is to be slain, perhaps when time and place will not so well adhere. Now, she argues,—now it can be done with safety. Macbeth is determined to wade through slaughter to a throne. If he passes this moment he loses the eagerly desired prize, and lives for ever after a coward in his own esteem; or he may make the attempt at a moment when detection is so near at hand, that the stroke which sends Duncan to his fate will be but the prelude of the destruction of my husband. She therefore rouses him to do at once that from which she knows nothing but fear of detection deters him; and, feeling that there are no conscientious scruples to overcome, applies herself to show that the present is the most favourable instant. It is for him she thinks—for him she is unsexed—for his ambition she works—for his safety she provides.

Up to the very murder, Macbeth displays no pity—no feeling for anybody but himself. Fear of detection still haunts him, and no other fear.

> " Thou sure and steadfast earth,
> Hear not my steps which way they walk, for fear
> The very stones prate of my whereabout."

As Lady Macbeth says, it is the frustrated attempt, not the crime, that can confound him. When it has been accomplished, he is for a while visited by brain-sick fancies; and to her, who sees the necessity of prompt action, is left the care of providing the measures best calculated to avert the dreaded detection. She makes light of facing the dead, and assures her husband that

> " A little water clears us of this deed.
> How easy it is then ! "

Does she indeed feel this ? Are these the real emotions of her mind ? Does she think that a little water will wash out what has been done, and that it is as easy to make all trace of it vanish from the heart as from the hand ? She shall answer us from her sleep, in the loneliness of midnight, in the secrecy of her chamber. Bold was her bearing, reckless and defying her tongue, when her husband was to be served or saved; but the sigh bursting from her heavily-charged breast, and her deep agony when she feels that, so far from its being easy to get rid of the witness of murder, no washing can obliterate the damned spot, no perfume sweeten the hand once redolent of blood, prove that the recklessness and defiance were only assumed. We find at last what she had sacrificed, how dreadful was the struggle she had to subdue. Her nerve, her courage, mental and physical, was unbroken during the night of murder; but horror was already seated in her heart. Even then a touch of what was going on in her bosom breaks forth. When urging Macbeth to act, she speaks as if she held the strongest ties of human nature in contempt.

> "I have given suck, and know
> How tender 'tis to love the babe that milks me:
> I would, when it was smiling in my face,
> Have plucked my nipple from his boneless gums,
> And dashed the brains out, had I but so sworn
> As you have done to this."

Is she indeed so unnatural—so destitute of maternal, of womanly feeling? No. In the next scene we find her deterred from actual participation in killing Duncan, because he resembled her father in his sleep. This is not the lady to pluck the nipple from the boneless gums of her infant, and dash out its brains. Her language is exaggerated in mere bravado, to taunt Macbeth's infirmity of purpose by a comparison with her own boasted firmness; but if the case had arisen, she who had recoiled from injuring one whose life stood in the way of her husband's hopes from a fancied resemblance to her father, would have seen in the smile of her child a talisman of resistless protection.

The murder done, and her husband on the throne, she is no longer implicated in guilt. She is unhappy in her elevation, and writhes under a troubled spirit in the midst of assumed gaiety. She reflects with a settled melancholy that

> " Nought's had, all's spent,
> When our desire is got without content,
> 'Tis safer to be that which we destroy,
> Than by destruction dwell in doubtful joy."

This to herself. To cheer her lord, she speaks a different language in the very next line.

> " How now, my lord! why do you keep alone,
> Of sorriest fancies your companions making;
> Using those thoughts which should indeed have died
> With those they think on?"

Her own thoughts, we have just seen, were full as sorry as those of her husband; but she can wear a mask. Twice only does she appear after her accession to the throne; once masked, once unmasked. Once seated at high festival, entertaining the nobles of her realm, full of grace and courtesy, performing her stately hospitalities with cheerful countenance, and devising with rare presence of mind excuses for the distracted conduct of her husband. Once again, when all guard is removed, groaning in despair.

The few words she says to Macbeth after the guests have departed, almost driven out by herself, mark that her mind is completely subdued. She remonstrates with him at first for having broken up the feast; but she cannot continue the tone of reproof, when she finds that his thoughts are bent on gloomier objects. Blood is for ever on his tongue. She had ventured to tell him that the visions which startle him, were but the painting of his brain, and that he was unmanned in folly. He takes no heed of what she says, and continues to speculate, at first in distraction, then in dread, and lastly in savage cruelty, upon blood. The apparition of Banquo almost deprives him of his senses. He marvels that such things could be, and complains that a cruel exception to the ordinary laws of nature is permitted in his case. Blood, he says,

" —— has been shed ere now in the olden time,
Ere human statute purged the gentle weal,"—

and in more civilized times also; but, when death came, no further consequences followed. Now not even twenty mortal murders [he remembered the number of deadly gashes reported by the assassin] will keep the victim in his grave. As long as Banquo's ghost remains before him, he speaks in the same distracted strain. When the object of his special wonder, by its vanishing, gives him time to reflect, fear of detection, as usual, is his first feeling.

"It will have blood, they say; blood will have blood!"

The most improbable witnesses have detected murder. Stones, trees, magotpies, choughs, have disclosed the secretest man of blood. Then come cruel resolves, to rid himself of his fears. Mercy or remorse is to be henceforward unknown; the firstlings of his heart are to be the firstlings of his hand,—the bloody thought is to be followed instantly by the bloody deed. The tiger is now fully aroused in his soul.

"I am in blood
Stept in so far, that, should I wade no more,
Returning were as tedious as go o'er."

He sees an enemy in every castle; everywhere he plants his spies; from every hand he dreads an attempt upon his life. Nearly two centuries after the play was written, the world beheld one of its fairest portions delivered to a rule as bloody as that of the Scottish tyrant; and so true to nature are the conceptions of Shakspeare, that the speeches of mixed terror and cruelty, which he has given to Macbeth, might have been uttered by Robespierre. The atrocities of the Jacobin, after he had stept so far in blood, were dictated by fear. "Robespierre," says a quondam satellite,* "devenait plus sombre; son air renfrogné repoussait tout le monde; il ne parlait que d'assassinat, encore d'assassinat, toujours d'assassinat. Il avait peur que son ombre ne l'assassinât."

Lady Macbeth sees this grisly resolution, and ceases to remonstrate or interfere. Her soul is bowed down before his, and he communicates with her no longer. He tells her to be ignorant of what he plans, until she can applaud him for what he has done. When he abruptly asks her,

> "How say'st thou,—that Macduff denies his person
> At our great bidding?"

she, well knowing that she has not said anything about it, and that the question is suggested by his own fear and suspicion, timidly inquires,

> "Have you sent to him, *sir?*"

---

* *Causes secretes de la Révolution de 9 au 10 Thermidor;* by Vilate, ex-juré révolutionnaire de Paris.

The last word is an emphatic proof that she is wholly subjugated. Too well is she aware of the cause, and the consequence, of Macbeth's *sending* after Macduff; but she ventures not to hint. She is no longer the stern-tongued lady urging on the work of death, and taunting her husband for his hesitation. She now addresses him in the humbled tone of an inferior; we now see fright and astonishment seated on her face. He tells her that she marvels at his words, and she would fain persuade herself that they are but the feverish effusions of an over-wrought mind. Sadly she says,

"You lack the season of all nature,—sleep."

Those are the last words we hear from her waking lips; and with a hope that repose may banish those murky thoughts from her husband's mind, she takes, hand in hand with him, her tearful departure from the stage; and seeks her remorse-haunted chamber, there to indulge in useless reveries of deep-rooted sorrow, and to perish by her own hand amid the crashing ruin of her fortunes, and the fall of that throne which she had so fatally contributed to win.

He now consigns himself wholly to the guidance of the weird sisters; and she takes no part in the horrors which desolate Scotland, and rouse against him the insurrection of the enraged thanes. But she clings to him faithfully in his downfall. All others except the agents of his crimes, and his personal dependents, have abandoned him; but she, with mind diseased, and a heart weighed down by the perilous stuff of recollections that defy the operation of oblivious antidote, follows him to the doomed castle of Dunsinane. It is evident that he returns her affection, by his anxious solicitude about her health, and his melancholy recital of her mental sufferings. He shows it still more clearly by his despairing words when the tidings of her death are announced. Seyton delays to communicate it; but at last the truth must come,—that the queen is dead. It is the over-flowing drop in his cup of misfortune.

"She should have died hereafter;—
There would have been a time for such a word."

I might have borne it at some other time; but now—now—now that I am deserted by all—penned in my last fortress—feeling that the safeguards in which I trusted are fallacious,—now it is indeed the climax of my calamity, that she, who helped me to rise to what she thought was prosperity and honour,—who clung to me through a career that inspired all else with horror and hate,—and who, in sickness of body, and agony of mind, follows me in the very desperation of my fate, should at such an hour be taken from me,—I am now undone indeed. He then, for the first time, reflects on the brief and uncertain tenure of life. He has long dabbled in death, but it never before touched him so closely. He is now aweary of the sun—now finds the deep curses which follow him sufficiently loud to pierce his ear,—now discovers that he has already lived long enough,—and plunges into the combat, determined, if he has lived the life of a tyrant, to die the death of a soldier, with harness on his back. Surrender or suicide does not enter his mind; with his habitual love of bloodshed, he feels a savage pleasure in dealing gashes all around; and at last, when he finds the charms on which he depended, of no avail, flings himself, after a slight hesitation, into headlong conflict with the man by whose sword he knows he is destined to fall, with all the reckless fury of despair. What has he now to care for? The last tie that bound him to human kind was broken by the death of his wife, and it was time that his tale of sound and fury should come to its appropriate close.

Thus fell he whom Malcolm in the last speech of the play calls " the dead butcher." By the same tongue Lady Macbeth is stigmatized as the fiend-like queen.

Except her share in the murder of Duncan,—which is, however, quite sufficient to justify the epithet in the mouth of his son,—she does nothing in the play to deserve the title; and for her crime she has been sufficiently punished by a life of disaster and remorse. She is not the tempter of Macbeth. It does not require much philosophy to pronounce that there were no such beings as the weird sisters; or that the voice that told the Thane of Glamis that he was to be King of Scotland, was that of his own ambition. In his own bosom was brewed the hell-broth, potent to call up visions counselling tyranny and blood; and its ingredients were his own evil passions and criminal hopes. Macbeth himself only believes as much of the predictions of the witches as he desires. The same prophets, who foretold his elevation to the throne, foretold also that the progeny of Banquo would reign; and yet, after the completion of the prophecy so far as he is himself concerned, he endeavours to mar the other part by the murder of Fleance. The weird sisters are to him, no more than the Evil Spirit which, in Faust, tortures Margaret at her prayers. They are but the personified suggestions of his mind. She, the wife of his bosom, knows the direction of his thoughts; and, bound to him in love, exerts every energy, and sacrifices every feeling, to minister to his hopes and aspirations. This is her sin, and no more. He retains, in all his guilt and crime, a fond feeling for his wife. Even when meditating slaughter, and dreaming of blood, he addresses soft words of conjugal endearment; he calls her " dearest chuck," while devising assassinations, with the fore-knowledge of which he is unwilling to sully her mind. Selfish in ambition, selfish in fear, his character presents no point of attraction but this one merit. Shakspeare gives us no hint as to her personal charms, except when he makes her describe her hand as " little." We may be sure that there were few " more thoroughbred or fairer fingers," in the land of Scotland than those of its queen, whose bearing in public towards Duncan, Banquo, and the nobles, is marked by elegance and majesty; and, in private, by affectionate anxiety for her sanguinary lord. He duly appreciated her feelings, but it is pity that such a woman should have been united to such a man. If she had been less strong of purpose, less worthy of confidence, he would not have disclosed to her his ambitious designs, less resolute and prompt of thought and action, she would not have been called on to share his guilt; less sensitive or more hardened she would not have suffered it to prey for ever like a vulture upon her heart.

She affords, as I consider it, only another instance of what women will be brought to, by a love which listens to no considerations, which disregards all else beside, when the interests, the wishes, the happiness, the honour, or even the passions, caprices, and failings of the beloved object are concerned; and if the world, in a compassionate mood, will gently scan the softer errors of sister-woman, may we not claim a kindly construing for the motives which plunged into the Aceldama of this blood-washed tragedy the sorely urged and broken-hearted Lady Macbeth?

TIMON OF ATHENS.

THE story of Timon the Misanthrope was popular not only in his native land of Greece, but in the English literature of the Middle Ages. Classical readers, who are of course acquainted with the lively dialogue of Lucian, were once apt to look upon the philosopher of Samosata as affording the original of the play of Shakspeare; but I doubt if Lucian, though familiar to the learned, was popularly known even at the end of the sixteenth century in England. Shakspeare was indebted for the hint, and the principal incidents of his drama, to Plutarch, translated from the French of Amyot by Sir Thomas North, and to *Painter's Palace of Pleasure*. Dr. Farmer, in his very shallow and pretending *Essay on the Learning of Shakspeare*, announces this important fact among others equally important, with much flourish; and those who feel inclined for such inquiries, will find sufficient to satisfy their curiosity in the voluminous notes gathered by the industry of Malone, Steevens, and Boswell.

To use the phrase of Dr. Farmer, which immediately succeeds his notice of Timon, " were this a proper place for such a disquisition," I should have something to say, not merely on the learning of Shakspeare,—a point on which I differ exceedingly with the Master of Emanuel,—but on the utility of learning to a dramatist. I should be prepared to contend, that though the greater the store of knowledge, no matter whence derived,—from books, from observation, from reflection,—possessed by a writer on any subject, and the larger the field whence an author of works of imagination can cull or compare, so much more copious will be his sources of thought, illustration, ornament, and allusions; yet that the dramatist, and indeed the poet in general, (the exceptions are few, and easily accounted for,) should not travel far out of the ordinary and beaten path for the main staple and material of his poem. Without immediately referring to the question of classical learning, many reasons exist for thinking that Richard the Third was not so deformed either in mind or body as he is represented in the two plays in which he appears in Shakspeare, or in the single one into which they are both clumsily rolled for the stage; but popular opinion, and the ordinary chronicles of the times, so represented him. Northern antiquaries are generally of opinion that Macbeth was the true king, and that the blood-stained mantle of cruelty and oppression ought to be shifted to the shoulders of the " gracious Duncan," who was in reality the usurper. In like manner we can conceive that if the authorities of Saxo-Grammaticus or Geoffry of Monmouth could be hunted up, a different colouring might be given to the tales of Hamlet or Lear. But what is all this to the purpose? It is no part of the duty of the dramatist to invade the province of the antiquary or the critic; and yet, for confining himself to his proper department, he incurs the censure of Farmer, and other persons of the same calibre of intellect. If Shakspeare had had all the concentrated knowledge of all the antiquarian societies of Denmark, Scotland, Norway, or Wales, he would have completely forgotten, what it was utterly impossible *he* should forget,—the first principles of dramatic art, if he depicted Macbeth, Lear, or Hamlet in any other manner than that which he has chosen. He would not have taken the trouble, even if editions of Saxo-Grammaticus or Hector Boethius were as plenty as blackberries, to turn over a single page of their folios. He found all that his art wanted in the historians or romance-writers of the day,—in Hall or Holinshed, 'or the *Tragical History of Hamblet*, and that, too, translated, not from the Latin of the Danish annalist, but from the French of the story-teller Belleforest. Common sense would dictate this course; but if the learned languages be wanted to support it, I may quote Horace, who, being eminently the poet of common sense, speaks for all times and countries.

"Rectius Iliacum carmen deducis in actus.
Quàm si proferres ignota indictaque primus."

Take the tale or the legend as it is popularly believed for the foundation of your drama, and leave to others the obscure glory of hunting after new lights, or unheard-of adventures.

In his classical plots the same principle holds. In his *Antony and Cleopatra, Julius Cæsar, Coriolanus,* and *Timon of Athens*, "it is notorious," to use the words of Dr. Farmer, "that much of his *matter-of-fact* knowledge is deduced from Plutarch; but in what language he read him, hath yet been the question." A more idle question could not have been asked. He might, for anything we know to the contrary, have *read* him in Greek; but for dramatic purposes he *used* him in English. Sir Thomas North's translation of Plutarch was a remarkably popular book; and Shakspeare, writing not for verbal critics, anxiously collating the version with the original, and on the look-out to catch slips of the pen or mistakes of the press,* but

---

* Such as *Lydia* for *Libya*, in *Antony and Cleopatra*. Act iii. Sc. 6.
"―――― made her
Of Lower Syria, Cyprus, *Lydia*,
Absolute queen."

Upton, correcting it from the text of Plutarch, substituted *Libya;* and Dr. Johnson and other commentators adopted the correction. Farmer had the great merit of discovering that the word is *Lydia* in North, whom Shakspeare followed. It was a great shame indeed that he had not noticed the error, and collated the English with the Greek! In the same spirit of sagacious criticism it is remarked, that Cæsar is made to leave to the Roman people his gardens, &c. "on *this* side Tiber," whereas it should be "on *that* side Tiber,"—the original being πέραν τοῦ ποταμοῦ. North translates it, however, "on *this* side," and Shakspeare again follows him without turning to the Greek. Farmer, with an old rhetorical

for the ordinary frequenters of the theatre, consulted the volume of the English knight, not that of the Bœotian biographer. If he had been as learned as Isaac Casaubon, he would have acted precisely in the same manner. The minute and unceasing study of

artifice, says, " I could furnish you with many more instances, but these are as good as a thousand." He had given *three*—and I extremely doubt if he could have given three more. He bids us "turn to the translation from the French of Amyot, by Thomas North, in folio, 1579, and you will at once see the *origin* of the mistake." It is hard to say in what sense Farmer uses the word " origin;" but the mistakes originate in Amyot, who translates the former passage "Royne d'Egypte, de Cypre, de *Lydie*," and the latter " et qu'il laissoit au peuple des jardins et vergers *deça* la rivière du Tybre." I agree with Farmer, however, in thinking that, if he could adduce the thousand instances of which he speaks, his argument would be nothing the better. It would only prove that Shakspeare, for the purposes of his plays, consulted North in English, and not Plutarch in Greek; a fact which may be readily conceded, and, as I have said in the text, completely justified on the true principles of the drama.

I do not agree with Upton and others in their proposed alteration of these two passages, which, however they may differ from the text of Plutarch, I would suffer to remain as they appear in the folio, because I am sure that Shakspeare so wrote them. Of the third, referred to by Dr. Farmer, I am not so clear. In *Antony and Cleopatra*, Act iv. Sc. 1. Augustus, in reply to Antony's challenge, says:

> "Let the old ruffian know
> I have many other ways to die—meantime,
> Laugh at his challenge."

classical literature since the days of Shakspeare has banished blunders from our editions and translations, and not even the most carelessly educated would deem

"What a reply is this!" says Upton: "it is acknowledging he should fall under the unequal combat. But if we read,

> Let the old ruffian know
> *He* hath many other ways to die: meantime,
> *I* laugh at his challenge.

we have the poignancy and the very repartee of Cæsar in Plutarch." To this reading, which has been generally adopted, Dr. Farmer objects that, though it is certainly so in the Greek and the modern translation, "Shakspeare was misled by the ambiguity of the old one." Antonius sent again to challenge Cæsar to fight him, to which Cæsar answered, "That *he* had many other ways to die." The doctor ought to have told us that the ambiguity here proceeded from Amyot; " Cesar luy fit reponse, qu'*il* avoit beaucoup d'autres moyens de mourir que celuy-là;" but it is not an ambiguity of a very puzzling kind. It appears to me that Shakspeare would have followed his text literally as usual, and borrowed the word "*he*." I am, therefore, in favour of Upton's reading; especially as it mends the metre, which in the present text is somewhat out of joint.

> " Cæsar to Antony. Let the old ruffian know
> I have many other ways to die—meantime,
> Laugh at his challenge.
>   *Mæc.*   Cæsar must think," &c.

The proposed reading would make it much smoother.

> " Cæsar to Antony. Let the old ruffian
> Know he hath many other ways to die:
> Meantime, I laugh at 's challenge.
>   *Mæc.*   Cæsar must think," &c.

o

it pedantic or misplaced in a dramatist to write with a constant reference to the original, no matter in what language, from which he drew his story; but, on the other hand, we should deem him a very dull critic indeed who would insist upon it that in a play avowedly written after Hooke, or Gibbon, or Mitford, its author should verify every quotation, and take care that their authorities were given with all the perfections of the last " editio aliis longè locupletior."

Ben Jonson took another course, and his success was as indifferent as that of Shakspeare was overwhelming. His *Sejanus* and *Catiline* are treasures of learning. Gifford truly says of the latter, that " the number of writers whom Jonson has consulted, and the industry and care with which he has extracted from them every circumstance conducive to the elucidation of his plot, can only be conceived by those who have occasion to search after his authorities. He has availed himself of almost every scattered hint from the age of Sallust to that of Elizabeth for the correct formation of his characters, and placed them before our eyes as they appear in the writings of those who lived and acted with them." The consequence is, that *Catiline* is absolutely unbearable on the stage, and fails to please in the closet, because the knowledge with which it abounds is conveyed in an inappropriate form. If Jonson had bestowed the same pains, and expended the same learning, upon a history of the Catilinarian conspiracy, he might have produced a historical treatise to be applauded, instead of a tragedy to be at most but tolerated. His learning oppressed him. He was too full of knowledge to borrow his plots, not to say from North, but from Plutarch himself. The inaccuracies of the old story-teller would have constantly shocked his scholar-like mind; and, instead of drawing characters or inventing situations, he would have been in perpetual quest of authorities to corroborate or contradict his principal text. Had there been any such thing as a Plutarchian life of Catiline, or " a Tragical History of the bloody conspiracy of Rome, showing how they swore upon a bowl of blood to burn the town, and murder the senators; with the particulars of the execution of some of the conspirators, and the killing of the rest in a bloody battle near unto the Italian mountains called the Alpes," the subject might have attracted the attention of Shakspeare, who would have assuredly looked no farther. The gossiping biographer or the prating ballad-monger would suffice for his purpose; and all other authors, from the age of Sallust to that of Elizabeth, might rest unconsulted in peace. We should, however, have had characters which, if they were not as correctly formed, "and placed before our eyes as they appear in the *writings* of those who lived and acted with them," would have been placed before us as they appeared in the eyes of men themselves who saw them live and act. He would not have dressed up the dry-bones of history, skeleton-fashion; but clothed them with flesh, and sent upon the stage, not critical abstractions, but actual men. It is usual to talk of the art of Jonson as something opposed to the genius of Shakspeare. With deference to those who employ this language, it is not over-wise. In everything material the possession of genius includes the possession of art; and in their common pursuit it would be easy to prove that Jonson was as much inferior in dramatic art, as it is admitted he was in dramatic genius, to his illustrious contemporary. I am much mistaken if I could not support my opinion by the authority of no less a person than Aristotle himself, of whom Jonson thought so highly as to write a commentary on his Poetics. I do not say this out of any disparagement of that great writer, whose name, on many accounts, stands eminently high for erudition and genius in our own, as it would in any other literature, and whose memory was shamefully used by some of the Shakspearian commentators of the last century; but I refer to him because the acknowledged failure of his learned dramas affords, in my mind, a full justification of the course pursued by Shakspeare, and ought to put an end to the idle gabble as to the learning of him whom Dr. Farmer so complacently calls "the old bard." But the full discussion of this question, with the numberless incidental disquisitions to which it must give rise, would occupy too large a space to be ventured upon in these fleeting essays; and might make the readers of *Bentley's Miscellany* set me down, if its editor were rash enough to inflict such toil upon them, as a bore of the first magnitude for intruding my dry criticisms upon his pleasant and festive pages. I am rather afraid that they are something inclined to think me so already, and am unwilling farther to jeopardy my reputation on that score. I must confine myself to Timon.

Lucian introduces Timon after his fall from riches, besieging Jupiter with a storm of epithets, and railing at the dotage into which the god has fallen, and his imbecility in permitting so much evil in the world. He reminds him of the former times, in which his lightning and thunder were in constant occupation; when his ægis was perpetually shaken, his bolts darted like clouds of arrows, his hail rattled down as through a sieve; and how once on a great occasion he drowned the world in an universal deluge, leaving but a spark of life behind in a cock-boat stranded upon Lycorea for the propagation of greater wickedness. After some general reflections, he comes to his own particular case, and upbraids the god for allowing him to be treated with so much ingratitude, especially as he had so often sacrificed at the jovial festivals with so much liberality. His clamours succeed in arresting the attention of Jupiter, who had been scared away for some time from looking into Athens by the noisy disputes of the philosophers; and, recognizing his claims on divine attention, he despatches Mercury to find Plutus, and bring him to Timon in the desert. The messenger of the gods willingly undertakes the commission; and a pleasant dialogue between him and Plutus, on the difficulty of keeping or retaining wealth, the difference its possession and its want makes in the human character, and other similar topics, ensues. Plutus is soon introduced to Timon, drives away Poverty, and defends himself against the accusations of the misanthrope, by referring to his own reckless extravagance, and want of discrimination in the choice of associates. Recommending Timon to dig vigorously, he departs. The digging is abundantly successful. It turns up gold in countless quantities, and presently arrive troops of flatterers, allured by the mere smell of the metal. Some who had treated him with remarkable ingratitude are among the number, and Timon resolves on vengeance. As one by one they approach,—some under pretence that their visits were paid for the sake of doing him service, others promising him public honours and dignities,—he assaults them with his spade, and sends them home battered and broken-headed. At last the visitors become too numerous for this close combat, and determined, like the old man in the story, to try what virtue is in stones, he commences a battery upon them, which soon compels them to retreat, but "not," as Timon says in the concluding sentence of the dialogue, "bloodless or unwounded."

Such is a hasty sketch of what is generally looked upon to be one of the most finished compositions of Lucian. The style throughout is gay and airy, (though somewhat hampered by its mythology, for Plutus is made to bear the incompatible characters of the God of Gold, and of gold itself, which every now and then comes in awkwardly,) and the characters are pleasantly sketched. But Lucian nowhere reaches the height of the comic; and over tragic or pathetic, or satire, in its loftier range, he has scarcely any power. The objects of his ridicule are comprised within a small compass. His readers may well exclaim with Lord Byron, "Oh!

thou eternal Homer!" for he can scarcely write two pages without some jeering reference to the Iliad or Odyssey, the spirit of which divine poems he did not in the slightest degree comprehend. The wranglings of the sophists among whom he lived, and to which he attached a wonderful importance, form another topic of which he is never tired. Sketches of Athenian manners and society abound, often graphic, but perpetually filled with complaints of the insolence and upstart pride of the rich. He is always on the watch to remind them of the transitory nature of their possessions; and to condemn them to insult and disgrace at the hands of the poorer classes, whom they had treated with *hauteur* during life, when they descend to another world. He repeats in several places the comparison of life to a theatrical procession, in which magnificent parts are assigned to some, who pass before the eyes of the spectators clothed in costly garments, and bedecked with glittering jewels; but, the moment the show is over, are reduced to their original nothingness, no longer kings and heroes, but poor players whose hour has been strutted out. It gives him wonderful pleasure to call Crœsus, and Midas, and the other generous princes of old times on the Asiatic coast, whose names are everlastingly hacked to pieces in the common-place satires, or squibs, or homilies of the Greeks, wretches and offscourings; and to exhibit Cyrus, Darius, or Xerxes, occupied in degrading tasks in the infernal regions. These topics, with perpetual sneers at the then tumbling mythology of Paganism, almost exclusively occupy the pages of Lucian.

His vein of satire was small, and its direction not elevated. It is easy to see that petty feelings of personal spite or envy are at the bottom of all he writes. He was jealous of the attention paid to wealth, and anxious to show the world its mistake in not bestowing exclusive homage on those far superior persons who could write witty dialogue, sparkling *persiflage*, or smart reviews. In the sketch which is called his Life, he lets us into the secret. His father was anxious to make him a sculptor, and apprenticed him to an uncle, who had obtained some reputation as an artist. His uncle treated him harshly, and he took a dislike to the business. He then tells us of his dream, in which the Goddesses of Art and Eloquence contended for him; and, after hearing the pleadings of both, he decided for the latter. The argument which weighed most with him, was, the power conferred by a successful career on a public orator of assuming the port and insolence of the great. I doubt not that Lucian in his prosperous circumstances—it is said that he died Procurator. *i.e.*

Lord Lieutenant, of Egypt—was fully as arrogant, and as sensible of all the privileges of his position, as the most swelling and presumptuous of those whom he belabours in his Dialogues. Swift said that he wrote for no other reason than that he might be treated as if he were a lord; Lucian's ambition for literary renown was stimulated by the hope that he might treat others in what he conceived to be lordly fashion. In other respects the game he pursues is, in general, small. Living in the pestilential atmosphere of a literary town, he thought the squabbling and quibbling of the pædagogues by whom he was surrounded things of vital moment. It was, in his eyes, matter well worthy of all the satirical powers he possessed, to quiz the slovenly dress, or the quack pretensions, of a set of poor devils whose very names must have been unknown beyond the narrow precincts in which they bustled. Greece, in his days, could not boast of any productions of genius; the commentating and criticising age had come; and the classics of bygone times were the subject of everlasting chatter among sects of reviewers anxious to show off their own wit and cleverness. The country had for ages ceased to take any interest in politics; and nothing remained to console national vanity but perpetual declamations on Marathon and Salamis, and vapourings about their skirmishing and buccaneering wars against the Persians. Philip, and his "god-like son," were, for many reasons which I need not stop to recapitulate, no favourites with the scribbling tribes of fallen Greece, and in general they make their appearance only for some such silly purpose as

"To point a moral, and adorn a tale."

Of the events which occurred in the four or five centuries which elapsed from the death of Alexander to the days of Lucian, no notice is taken. We have scarcely a hint, except in one or two essays of dubious authenticity, of the existence and progress of Christianity, which was with relentless hand knocking to pieces those gods who were so often made the butts of Lucian's ineffective jesting. If there remained to us nothing but his writings, we should be ignorant almost of the existence of the great Roman empire under which he lived. His vision is confined to the gossip of Athens; what he sees there, he depicts with a pleasant and faithful hand; his world is that of sophists and reviewers, and on their concerns he is shrewd, witty, and instructive. Nothing in its style can be better, for example, than the Cobbler and the Cock; but the manners there depicted, and the foibles satirized, are trifling. The Art of writing

History is a perfect model of a review; but then it is no more than a review. The Auction of Slaves is a capital squib; but nothing more than a squib. He has often been compared to Rabelais, who has sometimes borrowed largely from him; (Epistemon's account of what he saw in the other world, for example, is taken not only in conception, but in many of its details, from the Necyomantia of Lucian;) but those who know how to read the Gargantua and Pantagruel in the manner recommended by Rabelais himself in his address to the " *beuveurs trez illustres*," and the others to whom he dedicates his writings, will appreciate the deep difference between a light and sparkling wit, amusing himself with offhand pleasantries on literary folly or provincial absurdity, and the long-pondering old man filled with omnigenous knowledge, rioting in bitter-souled buffoonery over all that can affect the interests or agitate the passions of mankind. Compare Lucian's True History, with the Voyage of Panurge in quest of the Holy Bottle. The Greek has the merit of the original idea, which has since suggested all other imaginary voyages, and supplied no few materials to Gulliver himself, and a pleasant history it must indeed be allowed to be; but what is it after all, but a quiz or parody (often an unfair one) on Herodotus and Homer? In the other, literature and its concerns hold but a trifling place; but as the vessel steered by Xenomanes, glides onward through allegoric lands, and prodigious adventures, to its final destination, it leaves untouched no coast where matter is to be found for reflections on law, religion, medicine, science, politics, philosophy, in all their ramifications, poured forth from a bosom filled with unbounded erudition, and a heart perfectly fearless of those to whom it could trace superstition, imposture, quackery, or corruption.

I have dwelt perhaps too long—certainly longer than I had intended—on Lucian; but I wish to point out the inutility of looking to him, even if he had been at Shakspeare's elbow, as supplying in any degree elements for the character of the dramatic Timon of Athens. *He* is the more energetic misanthrope. *He* indeed *hates* mankind. The Greek is not in earnest. In the depth of his indignation he turns away to jest upon some trifle of manners. He can recollect the ill-breeding and gluttony of the philosopher who licks up the rich sauce off the plate with his fingers; and he can stop to bandy jests with the hungry parasite, or the venal orator. His opening address to Jupiter, commences with a frolic recapitulation of the epithets addressed to the Olympian ruler by the poets; and the misanthrope is so far forgotten in the litterateur, that he pauses before entering on his own calamities and wrongs, to laugh at the brain-stricken poets who are obliged to stop the gap of a yawning rhythm, or to prop up a halting metre, by an epithet. This misanthropy did not very seriously affect the patient; nor are the evils of which he complains, amounting as they do to little more than his being cut by his old acquaintances now that he is poor, so dreadful or extraordinary as to make him

> "———— bid the thunder-bearer shoot,
> Or tell tales of them to high-judging Jove."

The wrath of the Timon of Shakspeare is conceived in a different spirit. No jesting escapes his lips while he hurls his hatred on Athens. His withering malediction touches all the points on which we are most sensitive; many, from the mere consideration of which we instinctively turn away. He prays for the incontinence of matrons, the disobedience of children, the degradation of nobles before slaves and fools, the foul desecration of virgins beneath the eyes of their parents, the bursting of all social bonds, the preternatural cruelty of boyhood to age:

> "Son of sixteen,
> Pluck the lined crutch from thy old limping sire,
> And beat his brains out!"

The utter uprooting of all the civilized institutions, all the charitable feelings, all the honourable or holy thoughts that link mankind together:

> "Piety and fear,
> Religion to the gods, peace, justice, truth,
> Domestic awe, night-rest, and neighbourhood,
> Instruction, manners, mysteries and trades,
> Degrees, observances, customs and laws,
> Decline to your confounding contraries,
> And yet confusion live."

This is no mock hatred; it is the harrowing language of a man thoroughly aroused to indignation, and desperate against his kind. Compare it with the parallel passage of Lucian, and we shall see, without recurring to any such foolish inquiry as to what was the precise quantity of the "less Greek" allowed to Shakspeare by Ben Jonson, that to no other source than that which supplied the maledictions of Lear, or Constance, or Margaret, need we look for the bursting imprecations of Timon.

He is introduced, at the commencement of the play, surrounded with all the pomp and circumstance of profuse wealth. The poet, the painter, the jeweller, await his appearance with the tributes of the pen, the pencil, and the mine. The noblest men of his city bow before him, cap in hand; the humble look up to him as their surest stay in distress, and none depart disappointed. All conditions and all minds, the poet says in the florid style,

> "As well of glib and slippery creatures* as
> Of grave and austere quality, tender down
> Their service to Lord Timon. His large fortune,
> Upon his good and gracious nature hanging,
> Subdues and properties to his love and tendance
> All sorts of hearts; yea, from the glass-faced flatterer,
> To Apemantus, that few things loves better
> Than to abhor himself."

His first appearance on the stage is to release a prisoner by paying the debt; to give the dowry required to make two lovers happy in their union; to bestow lavish recompense, and, what is fully as dear to the ear of painter or poet, commendations equally lavish on the productions offered to his patronage; to receive with abounding hospitality Alcibiades and his train; to preside at a magnificent banquet, heaping his guests with gifts, and entertaining them with all the splendour that taste and prodigal expense can command. His own heart, proud and gratified, swells with a strong desire to do still more:

* Should not this be "creature," *i.e.* creation?

> "Methinks I could deal kingdoms to my friends,
> And ne'er be weary."

He is happy in being the instrument of contributing to the happiness of others. It is his delight—his pleasure —his hobby. Not to be generous, is not to be himself. His profuse and liberal habit blinds him to all suspicions that the rest of the world is not of the same temper. The time comes when he is to be cruelly undeceived, and when his sincerity in these professions of universal love and benevolence is to be severely tested. His wealth, which he thought inexhaustible, has taken to itself wings and fled. But even this does not make any very deep impression upon him. He listens with characteristic impatience to the tale of his ruin told by the disconsolate Flavius. He answers in brief and hasty sentences, and soon bids him " sermon no further." He has his own resources left, his own plans to fall back upon. He remembers his wish when in the height of imagined prosperity ; he had often desired to be poorer, in order that he might come nearer his friends. He had been affected even to tears when, with overflowing heart, he thought of the precious comfort of having so many persons knit together so closely, that, like brothers, they commanded each other's fortunes. He reflects with a

P

justifiable pride, that his generosity was not directed to unworthy purposes, or called forth by unworthy feelings:

> "No villanous bounty yet hath past my heart;
> Unwisely, not ignobly have I given."

He will not listen to the suggestions of his steward that he can find any difficulty in borrowing. Even when he learns that the senators, on whom he had public claims, and from whom he expected a large sum of money for the mere asking, have turned a deaf ear to applications made in his name, he is not discouraged. He utters a slight expression of spleen, "You gods reward them!" and at once bidding Flavius look cheerly, proceeds to account for their ingratitude as an exception to the general rule, arising from the lack of kindly warmth in cold-blooded age. Elsewhere he is secure of success:

> "———— Ne'er speak or think
> That Timon's fortunes 'mong his friends can sink."

All these hopes are dashed to the ground in a moment. His attempts at borrowing are worse than unsuccessful; they make his difficulties notorious, and, instead of assisting his wants, cause his house to be besieged with clamorous creditors. Shakspeare has not written the scene in which the ungrateful refusals of his friends are communicated to him; but he shows us the effect of the communication on Timon's mind. It strikes him with instant sickness. " Take it on my soul," says his servant Servilius,

> " My lord leans wondrously to discontent.
> His comfortable temper has forsook him ;
> He is much out of health, and keeps his chamber."

This is the cold fit of the ague by which he is smitten. The hot fit of fever is soon at hand. He bursts in controlless rage through the files of opposing duns ; plans a whimsical, but a decisive revenge ; and having executed it, parts from the crowd of

> " Smiling, smooth, detested parasites,
> Courteous destroyers, affable wolves, meek bears,
> The fools of fortune, trencher-friends, time-flies,
> Cap-and-knee slaves, vapours, and minute-jacks,"

whose prodigious ingratitude had driven him almost mad, with a stern resolution never more to expose himself to similar causes of grief and indignation, by herding again with mankind.

It is useless to say that such a determination was unjust. He who affects to be a misanthrope, is a pitiful and troublesome coxcomb ; real misanthropy is madness, and in the concluding acts of the play,

Timon is actually insane. He had no friends. His money and his dinners attracted dependents and guests in abundance; but he ought to have known that they went *for* the money and the dinner, and nothing else. The entertainer and the entertained were on a level. If they had the pleasure of receiving, he had the glory of giving, and neither party had a right to complain. The course of life he led, was calculated expressly to drive from him all who were possessed of qualities capable of inspiring respect and friendship. No honourable or high-minded man would frequent the house of Timon, to be exposed to the suspicion of going there with sordid or selfish views. He gathered around him throngs of people whom he corrupted into sycophancy, and he is unreasonable enough to complain of the very meanness which was chiefly of his own creation or encouragement. He set no value on what he flung away with lavish hand, and in reality cared as little for those to whom he flung it. While dispensing his boundless hospitalities, or scattering his magnificent gifts, he had in him, though undeveloped, and even by himself unsuspected, the seeds of misanthropy as deeply set as when he was howling against

"All feasts, societies, and throngs of men,"

in the desert. He consulted merely his own whim in giving. He thought that no profusion could exhaust his wealth; and he therefore was profuse, as he imagined, in security. If we held the purse of Fortunatus, or could chain

> " Volatile Hermes, and call up unbound,
> In various forms, old Proteus from the sea,
> Drawn through a limbeck to his native form,"

and achieve the discovery of the philosopher's stone, where would be our merit in dispensing gold all around? We give nothing when we give that which costs us nothing. We do not see that Timon makes any sacrifice, or puts himself to any inconvenience; and we must esteem but lightly that liberality which looks forward to recompense or return. In his prosperity he cherished chance companions without consideration; and with equal want of consideration, he curses all mankind in his adversity. The difference between his feelings in the two cases amounts to no more than this, that Timon, rich, quietly showed his contempt of the ill-chosen circle of parasites with which he had surrounded himself, by a careless bounty showered without distinction on the base as on the worthy; and Timon, poor, clamorously exhibited his hatred of all mankind, hastily judging them by the wretched sample with which he had associated; in a strain of general imprecation as reckless and undiscriminating.

A servile or sensual mind would have adopted the plan of Gnatho in the Eunuchus, who, after he had wasted in " riotous living " whatever property he possessed,—after *patria abligurierat bona,*—seized on such a gull as Thraso, and have endeavoured to live upon others, as others had lived upon him. A good-natured or thoughtless fellow would have tried to mend his luck, called for fresh cards, and begun again. He, no doubt, would be at first especially annoyed by the loss of his money, and still more by the reflection that he had been choused and ill-treated by those whom he took to be his friends, and who, at all events, were the partners of his gayer hours. But the fit would soon pass, the bile would be got rid of, and (if of English tongue) after a few of those national prayers which have obtained us a celebrated *sobriquet* among all the other people of the earth, liberally distributed to all and sundry, he would regain his temper, and philosophically sing

> Why should we quarrel for riches,
>   Or other such glittering toys?
> A light heart and a thin pair of breeches
>   Will go through the world, my brave boys!

He would struggle on, and puzzle it out in one way or another; and, if Fortune smiled once more, be as ready as ever to commence the old game, forgetting and forgiving everything and everybody, and as open as before to be imposed upon by those who gave themselves the trouble to do so.

But Timon could not adopt either of these courses. Too high-bred, too haughty of thought, he could never have descended to be a trencher-slave: too selfishly awake to his own importance, he could never have pardoned those who had hurt his pride, or mortified his vanity.

Such contrasts as these, Shakspeare had no notion of opposing to him. But he has chosen the appropriate contrast in Apemantus, the snarling philosopher,* who is modelled after the cynics, particularly after Diogenes. In Timon's prosperity, he haunts his entertainments for the purpose of indulging his impertinent humour of carping at the company he meets there. Like Diogenes himself, he is no more than an ill-mannered hound, who

* He is thus introduced at Timon's banquet. "Then comes, dropping after all, Apemantus discontentedly, *like himself.*" There has been some deep criticism on these words; but, as they do not convey any very brilliant meaning, I incline to think the direction was, "Then comes, dropping after all, Apemantus discontentedly, *by* himself."

deserves perpetual kickings, and is tolerated only for his wit. It is a character easy to assume and to support, requiring nothing more than a sufficient stock of cool impudence and effrontery. Vanity is at the bottom. A desire to brazen out the inconveniences of low breeding and awkward manners, and a love of notoriety, no matter how obtained, are enough to make a cynic. The well-known repartees of Plato and Aristippus set the character of Diogenes in its true light: we may be certain that Alexander, in their celebrated dialogue, looked upon him merely as a buffoon, tumbling about for his diversion in a peculiar fashion; but he was undoubtedly possessed of much wit and humour. The jesting of Apemantus, is as plain-spoken and ill-natured, if not as good, as that of the famed tenant of the tub; and Timon keeps him at his table as an original—a sort of lion, who is as much a part of the diversion of the evening, as the masque of the Amazons, or the lofty strain of the hautboys. There are some touches of nature in the fellow, however; for he sees with regret the approaching downfall of his liberal host, and warns him against the consequences of the course he is pursuing, with a grumbling kindness.

His cynicism is not misanthropy; it is of the same stamp as that of the hero of a celebrated play, which its celebrated author intended as an exhibition of the feelings and propensities of a man-hater, and gave it accordingly the name of *Le Misantrope.* It would be absurd to offer eulogies to Molière, but it is undeniable that he has made a mistake in the title of his play. Alceste is a testy and fretful man; nothing more. There is none of the insane rage, and consequently none of the poetry, of the misanthrope about him. It is hard to say what puts him out of humour; and, indeed, he can hardly tell the reason, except that

"Moi, je veux me fâcher, et ne veux point entendre."

When he comes to matters more specific, we find him repeating the complaints, almost the phrases, of Apemantus:

"Non : je ne puis souffrir cette lâche méthode
Qu'affectent la plupart de vos gens à-la-mode ;
Et je ne hay rien tant que les contorsions
De tous ces grands faiseurs de protestations :"

or again,

"Mes yeux sont trop blessés ; et la cour et la ville
Ne m'offrant rien qu'objets à m'échauffer la bile,
J'entre en une humeur noire, en un chagrin profond,
Quand je vois vivre entre eux les hommes comme ils font.
Je ne trouve par-tout que lâche flaterie,
Qu'injustice, intérêt, trahison, fourberie ;

> Je ne puis plus tenir, j'enrage, et mon dessein
> Est de rompre en visière à tout le genre humain."

It was hardly worth while to come to so desperate a determination for so small a cause. His friend Philinte may well say

> "Je ne vois pas, moi, que le cas soit pendable."

Even Apemantus is of higher strain on the same subject of insincere politeness:

> "Aches contract and starve your supple joints!
> That there should be small love 'mongst these sweet knaves,
> And all this courtesy! The strain of man 's bred out
> Into baboon and monkey.
>   Who lives that 's not
> Depraved, and depraves? who dies, that bears
> Not one spurn to their graves of their friends' gift?
> I should fear, those that dance before me now
> Would one day stamp upon me. It has been done;
> Men shut their doors against a setting sun.
>   What a coil 's here!
> Serving of becks, and jutting out of bums!
> I doubt whether their legs be worth the sums
> That are given for them. Friendship 's full of dregs;
> Methinks, false hearts should never have sound legs.
> Thus honest fools lay out their wealth on courtesies."

In this strain Apemantus is consistent throughout. Alceste is not. Oronte reads to him a silly sonnet, and le Misantrope is as careful of the usages of society in conveying his censure, as any of the flatterers he condemns. His disapproval is conveyed indirectly; instead of saying at once that the verses are sad trash, he veils his criticism under the pretence of its having been addressed to another:

> "Mais, un jour, à quelqu'un dont je tairai le nom,
> Je disois," &c.

The treatment which the poet experiences from Apemantus is of a more decisive character. Alceste, besides, so far from having determined to break " en visière à tout le genre humain," is in love, and in love with a flirt of the first magnitude. He is desperately jealous of his rivals; and instead of supporting his misanthropical character is ready to defy them *à l'outrance* for laughing at him. A duellist, not a misanthrope, would have said,

> "Par le sangbleu! messieurs, je ne croyois pas être
> Si plaisant que je suis."

He experiences all the usual vicissitudes of love,— jealousy, anger, quarrels, reconciliations, and so forth. If we did not find it in the *Misantrope*, we should be inclined to ascribe the following tender *morçeau*—and there are more beside—to as love-smitten a swain as ever talked " softely to his ladye love."

Alceste says to Celimone;

"Ah! que vous sçavez bien ici contre moi-même,
Perfide! vous servir de ma foiblesse extrême,
Et ménager pour vous l'excès prodigieux
De ce fatal amour, né de vos traitres yeux!"

We find nothing like this, in the misanthrope drawn by a more vigorous hand. Molière himself seems to have a sharp misgiving as to the consistency of his character, for he makes Philinte say with astonishment

"De l'humeur dont le Ciel a voulu le former,
Je ne sçai pas comment il s'avise d'aimer."

He may indeed be well amazed; but it is also not a little to be wondered that the same consideration did not induce the author to choose a different title for his comedy.

The snarler living in society, and the furious man who has fled from it, meet in the wood. The scene which ensues is the master-piece of the play. The contrast between the hardened practitioner in railing at mankind, the long-trained compound of impudent humorist and sturdy beggar, who never had felt an honourable or generous emotion, and whose career had been devoted to procure under the cover of philosophy and independence, an inglorious living in lazy idleness, by amusing those whose taste lay that way with scurril ribaldry; and the man who, born in lofty rank, had enjoyed all the luxuries and the splendours of life, who had the mouths, the tongues, the eyes, and hearts of men paying homage to him, who had never bent for favour, save when he thought that he did honour to those of whom he asked it; and now deprived of all that had been his glory and happiness, the gods of his idolatry shattered at one blow, his brilliant sky suddenly overcast, and the rich and bright-coloured rainbow reduced to its original mist and vapour;—the contrast between these,—one content with his lot, and even vain of the position into which he has thrust himself; the other, torn by all the passions of anger and mortification,—is finely conceived and admirably executed. Apemantus tells Timon that his present character springs only from change of fortune; that he is a fool to expose himself to the rigour of woods which have outlived the eagle, while his flatterers wear silk, drink wine, lie soft, and have forgotten his existence; that his sour cold habit has been put on enforcedly; that he would again be a courtier, if he were not a beggar; and, as a moral of his discourse, recommends him to imitate the practices of those who ruined him,—to hinge his knee, crouch, flatter, and betray in turn:

"'Tis most just
That thou turn rascal; hadst thou wealth again,
Rascals should have it."

Timon scarcely replies to the railing of the cynic, and utterly disdains to notice the scoundrel advice with which he concludes: but he retorts on his unwelcome visitor, that his character also was framed by his circumstances; that he was born a beggar, and bred a dog; that his nature commenced in sufferance, and that time made him hard in it; and that, if he had not been from the earliest moment of his life the most degraded of mankind, he would be a knave and flatterer. In these mutual censures there is a mixture of truth and injustice. That Timon's misanthropy was forced upon him by the downfall of his fortunes, and the faithlessness of his friends, is true; but Apemantus does not do him justice when he says, that he would return to his old mode of life, if he were to regain his former wealth. The iron has entered too deeply into his soul. Nor has the cynic properly appreciated the character of Timon, when he recommends him to turn rascal. Here he speaks from himself, and is laid defencelessly open to the powerful retort of the fallen gentleman. "Hadst thou," says Timon,

> "Like us, from our first swath, proceeded
> The sweet degrees that this brief world affords
> To such as may the passive drugs of it
> Freely command, thou wouldst have plunged thyself
> In general riot; melted down thy youth
> In different beds of lust, and never learned
> The icy precepts of respect; but followed
> The sugared game before thee."

The same selfish mood of temper that rendered the beggar Apemantus insolent, and desirous of vexing whomsoever he met, "always a villain's office, or a fool's," would have made the high-born Apemantus pursue such a course as is here described by Timon; and, if he had broken down in his career, there can scarcely be a doubt that he would have followed the servile advice he tenders. The beggared prodigal would have become a sycophant. But Timon, too, is unjust towards Apemantus when he says,

> "All villains that do stand by thee are pure;"

for the cynic had no other villany than impudence and idleness. The fact is, that neither can defend his own conduct, and each is driven to take the ground of impugning that of his accuser. Such a conversation can have but the one end. It must conclude, as it does here in a torrent of mutual abuse; and they depart with increased scorn and contempt of each other.

With the fourth act, the Shakspearian Timon may be said to begin and end. The first act, exhibiting his prodigal extravagance; the second his tottering estate; and the third, his mortification and revenge, are taken from Plutarch; or, if we must speak by the card, from North. There is nothing remarkable in the characters of a prodigal host, a confiding friend, or an irritated benefactor soured by unlooked-for ingratitude. The fourth act is Shakspeare's own. Alarm had made way for rage; rage now bursts into madness uncontrolled. In the other sketches of Timon, he is shown as a splenetic wit; and those who visit him in the hour of his returning wealth are no more than ordinary parasites, plying their well-understood vocation. In the fifth act Shakspeare dramatizes some of the old traditionary stories of the man-hater, and the force and energy which he had imparted to the character are immediately weakened. The invitation of all Athenians "in the sequence of degree" to hang themselves, is a touch of mere comedy;* and even his answers to the senators,

---

* Shakspeare, in introducing this story of the tree, did not take the trouble of recollecting that it is a town story, and not suited for the desert.

> "I have a tree, which grows here in my close
> That mine own use invites me to cut down,
> And I must fell it."

though savage enough, are far removed from the intensity of frenzied hatred exhibited in the fourth act. There he is indeed the *misanthropos* who hates mankind. The poetry of the misanthropic feeling is there fully developed. In Apemantus, his hatred of mankind is a tolerated impertinence, which obtains admission to lordly tables, and affords an opportunity of railing and carping without being exposed to their proper consequences. In Alceste, there is in reality no misanthropy at all; Philinte may well call it a folly:

> " C'est une folie, à nulle autre seconde,
> De vouloir se mêler de corriger le monde."

In Timon it is absolute madness. He goes not about displaying his wit or his ill-nature at the expense of those whom he meets. He flies from all society, and confounds the universal race of man in one common curse. As for correcting the world, he dreams not of such folly. It suits him better to pray for its universal ruin and damnation.

This is the only light in which misanthropy can be

He hardly had a close of his own, or indeed a tree of his own, in the desert, where he dwelt in a cave; besides, he had no necessity for felling any particular tree, or, if he had, there remained enough for the purposes he recommended.

considered for the purposes of poetry. If we do not look upon it as madness, it becomes contemptible. Timon, born to great estate, wastes it in riotous living; and, when his money is gone, he finds it not quite so easy to borrow as it had been with him to lend. The case is far from being uncommon; and it is borne in different ways, according to the different temperaments of men. It drives Timon out of his senses. Gold, and the pomps and vanities which it procures, had been to him everything. Nature had not supplied him with domestic attachments; he is without wife or children, kindred or relations, and he has made no friend. All that he regarded, vanished with his wealth. His soul, like that of the licentiate, Perez Garcia, lay in his purse; when the purse was lost, he lost his senses too. In his prosperity we do not find any traces of affection, honourable or otherwise, for women. In his curses, disrespect for the female sex is remarkably conspicuous. The matron is a counterfeit, her smiling babe is spurious; the virgin is a traitor, there is no chastity which is not to be sacrificed for Gold, that

> " Ever young, fresh, loved, and delicate wooer,
>   Whose blush doth thaw the consecrated snow
>   That lies on Dian's cheek; "

and those who do make the sacrifice are instantly converted into the plagues and torments of mankind. "There's more gold," he says to Phryne and Timandra, after a speech of frenzied raving;

"Do you damn others, and let this damn you,—
And ditches grace you all!"

These philosophical ladies assure him that they will do anything for gold, and thank him for his compliments:

"More counsel with more money, bounteous Timon!"

He readily believes them to be no worse than the rest of their sex; and, as gold had been his all-in-all, feels no scruple in thinking that its operation ought to be resistless in subverting the honour of women, as well as the faith of men. Nothing, I repeat, except insanity, could raise such a character from contempt; but invest him with madness, and poetry will always be able to rivet our attention, and excite our sympathies for the moody passions of the man hated of the gods, wandering alone over the limitless plain of life without end or object, devouring his own heart, and shunning the paths of men.

No women appear in this play except Phryne and Timandra, and they but in one short scene, when they do not speak, between them, fifty words. This, of itself, is sufficient to keep the play off the stage, for few actresses will be desirous of appearing in such characters. They are precisely the description of women suited to confirm Timon in his hatred of the human race, and his conviction of the power of money over all. It is unnecessary to say that ladies of a different class of soul are to be found in Shakspeare, but their place is not here. Isabels and Imogens, Juliets and Desdemonas, would have scorned the riot and sycophancy of his prosperous hours, and would have scared away by their unpurchaseable purity the degrading visions of his misanthropical fancies in the wood. The mistresses of Alcibiades [the real Alcibiades, I should imagine, was much " better accommodated" than he appears to be in this play] are Timon's patterns of womankind; as the parasite train, who infested his house, are his patterns of mankind. Yet even he might have seen that his estimate was unjust. The churlish Apemantus, who ate roots while others revelled at his overloaded board, seeks him in the forest to offer something better than roots to mend his feast. His steward, Flavius, approaches him in his calamity with a tender of his duteous service. Alcibiades, the most honoured of his guests, and who never had received any favours at his hands, offers him assistance unasked. These touches of kindness might have abated his censure, and made him waver in his opinion that he should find in the woods

"The unkindest beast more kinder than mankind."

But no. The feeling which was at the root of his madness is as conspicuous in his reception of these offers, as in all other parts of his conduct. He patronizes to the end. He is touched by the devotion of Flavius, because he recognises Timon in the light of a master; he declines the gold of Alcibiades, because he wishes to show that *he* has more gold, and can still lavish it; but Apemantus he spurns. He will not accept assistance from a beggar, and a beggar upon whom it would be no matter of pride to waste his bounty, even if the perverse snarler would receive it.

Insanity, arising from pride, is the key of the whole character; pride indulged, manifesting itself indirectly in insane prodigality,—pride mortified, directly in insane hatred. Apemantus was wrong when he told him that he was long a madman, and then a fool. He should have reversed it. Timon was first a fool, and then a madman. Alcibiades sees at a glance that

"his wits
Are drowned and lost in his calamities;"

and for such a catastrophe nothing can be a more unerring preparation than the stubborn will of pride. "Assuredly," says the Laureate, " in most cases, madness is more frequently a disease of the will than of the intellect. When Diabolus appeared before the town of Mansoul, and made his oration to the citizens at Eargate, Lord Will-be-will was one of the first that was for consenting to his words, and letting him into the town." Well may Dr. Southey conclude his speculations on this subject by saying, "In the humorist's course of life, there is a sort of defiance of the world and the world's law; indeed, any man who departs widely from its usages, avows this; and it is, as it ought to be, an uneasy and uncomfortable feeling wherever it is not sustained by a high state of excitement, and that state, if it be lasting, becomes madness."* The Laureate in this sentence has written an unconscious commentary on the Timon of Shakspeare. The soul-stung Athenian, when he

> " made his everlasting mansion
> Upon the beached verge of the salt flood,''

called himself a misanthrope:—he was a madman!

W. M.

---

* *The Doctor,* &c. vol. iii. pp. 272 and 281. I believe no secret is violated in attributing this work to Dr. Southey.

₊ The text of *Timon of Athens* is about the most corrupt of the plays. I suggest a few alterations.

Act iii. Scene 1. Lucullus, wishing to bribe Flavius, says, " Here's three *solidores* for thee." Steevens declares this coin to be from the mint of the poet. It is *saludores, i. e. saluts-d'or,*—a piece coined in France by our Henry V. See Holinshed, Ruding, Ducange, &c. It is mentioned by Rabelais more than once.

Act iv. Scene 3. " *Raise* me this beggar, and denude the lord,
    The senator shall bear contempt hereditary,
    The beggar native honour."

Read—" *Robe* me this beggar," *i. e.* array the beggar in the robes of the senator, and reduce the senator to the nakedness of the beggar, and contempt and honour will be awarded according to their appearance.

Act iv. Scene 3. Timon, addressing gold, says,
    " O thou sweet *king-killer*, and dear divorce
    'Twixt natural son and sire!"

Read " *kin-killer,*" *i.e.* destroyer of all kindred affection. King-killing was no crime in Athens, where, as Shakspeare knew, there was no king ; and all Timon's apostrophes to the wicked power of gold relate not to the artificial laws of society, but to the violation of natural ties, as between son and sire, husband and wife.

Same scene.
    " Thou bright defiler
    Of Hymen's purest bed ! thou valiant Mars!
    Thou ever young, *fresh, loved,* and delicate wooer," &c.

Perhaps, *fresh-lived.*

POLONIUS.

This is a character which few actors like to perform. Custom exacts that it must be represented as a comic part, and yet it wants the stimulants which cheer a comedian. There are no situations or reflections to call forth peals of laughter, or even fill the audience with ordinary merriment. He is played as a buffoon; but the text does not afford the adjuncts of buffoonery; and, in order to supply their place, antic gesture and grimace are resorted to by the puzzled performer. It is indeed no wonder that he should be puzzled, for he is endeavouring to do what the author never intended. It would not be more impossible—if we be allowed to fancy degrees of impossibility—to perform the pantomimic Pantaloon seriously in the manner of King Lear, than to make the impression which Shakspeare desired that Polonius should make, if he be exhibited in the style of the dotard of Spanish or Italian comedy, or the Sganarelle whom Molière has borrowed from them. There is some resemblance in Lord Ogleby; but we cannot persuade ourselves to think that George Colman, elder or younger, could have written any part in *Hamlet*. I doubt not that both thought their own comedies far superior.

Polonius is a ceremonious courtier; and no more ridicule attaches to him than what attaches to lords of the bedchamber, or chamberlains, or other such furniture of a court in general. It is deemed necessary that kings should be hedged not only by the divinity of their regal honours, but by the more corporal entrenchments of officers of state. In fact it must be so; and in every history of the world we find these functionaries, differing only in name. We know not the internal arrangements of the palaces of the kings that reigned in the land of Edom before there reigned any king over the children of Israel;[*] but we may be sure that Bela the son of Beor, and Hadad the son of Bedad, who smote Midian in the field of Moab, and Saul of Rehoboth by the river, and Hadar, whose city was Pau, and whose wife was Matred, the daughter of Mezahab, and the other princes of the house of Esau, who appear for a brief moment in the earliest record of human affairs in the book of the world's generation, but to die and make way for others to reign in their stead, had courtiers around them, to whom were allotted duties in fashion different, in spirit

[*] Gen. xxxvi. 31—39.

the same as those which were performed by the courtly officials of the Byzantium emperors, the togaed comites of the Cæsars, the ruffled and periwigged *gens de la cour* of the Grand Monarque, or the gold sticks and silver sticks of Queen Victoria;—and performed, no doubt, for the same reason—for that con-si-de-ra-ti-on, which, whether in the shape of flocks and herds, or land and beeves, or the more easily managed commodity of shekels and sovereigns, when the secret of "a circulating medium" was discovered, has ever been the stimulants of the general herd attracted to a court. It would be indeed travelling far from the purpose of these papers to talk morals or politics on such a subject; but there can be no harm in saying that, in times of difficulty or danger, when "uneasy is the head that wears a crown," it is not to them its wearer must look for zeal or assistance. The dog loves the master—the cat loves the house. The nobler animal who couches not in the drawing-room, and is not caressed and pampered with soothing and officious hand, but who guards the dwelling, and follows to the field, may, if treated with kindness, be depended upon to the last. He will die at the feet of a master returning in the twentieth year—will couch upon his grave—will seize his murderer by the throat.

The mere domestic creature, following her instinct, will cling to the house through every change of dynasty, ready to welcome with gratulatory purr whatever hand may rub down her glossy coat, and supply her with customary food, even if that hand should be reeking with the blood of the fallen owner of the mansion in which she had been reared. But the cat is not to be blamed. She acts as nature meant her to act; and what nature is to a cat, habit is to a courtier. Nothing can be more improbable than that the Queen should bother herself—I talk Hibernically— with reading these papers;—nothing is more certain than that, if she does, she will not believe a word of what I am saying. Yet if she lives to the age of the great lady in whose days the creator of Polonius flourished,—and may she so live, equally glorious in her character of Queen, and far happier in her character of woman!—she may be inclined to think that I am right, and that the profession of etiquette, well calculated as it may be to dignify the ceremonial of state, is not to be confounded with the loyalty which inspires

"The manly hearts to guard a throne."

But it is perfectly natural that the professors of the

science should set a high value upon it. The chamberlain who gave up the monarchy as lost when he saw M. Roland enter the presence of the king with ribbons in his shoes* was perfectly sincere. It was no part of his business to inquire farther than what he saw before him; he had not to ask into the remoter causes which gave M. Roland the courage or the presumption to violate the laws of court decorum, which the staff-bearer had throughout his life considered to be as steadfast as the laws that regulated the motions of the earth, if indeed he ever condescended to think on such uncourtly trifles. It is easy to laugh at this chamberlain; but he was substantially right. The kingdom of the doomed Louis did not depend upon stockings or buckles; but it depended upon the belief that the person of the king was inviolate, and the breach of decorum was but the first step leading to the scaffold. The clown, who troubles not himself with astronomical, meteorological, or chemical studies, knows well that harvest is to follow seed-time, and prognosticates with unerring certainty that the grain which he is scattering in the ground is to ripen into a golden ear; so our court functionary, who had never dreamt of political speculations, never consulted any

* "Roland the Just with ribbons in his shoes."—*Anti-Jacobin.*

philosophical observers—looked not beyond the circle of the Tuilleries, and would not have understood a single word of Mr. Carlyle's eloquent theories—saw in this one grain of disrespect the coming crop of destruction. I know nothing of his after history—perhaps he emigrated with others of his order; but if he did not originally commit that false step,—and I hope for the honour of so shrewd an observer that he did not—[for what had *he* to do with chivalry?]—I have little doubt that he found his fitting place among the gold-laced suite of the Emperor,—welcomed with well-trained bows the return of Louis the Eighteenth,—served Charles the Tenth with appropriate ceremony,—and is, I trust, now in his old age discussing the glories of the powdered and rapiered circle of Louis Quinze, beneath the approving smile of Louis Philippe.

Of this race was Polonius. Let not the abstracted sage or the smug sneerer imagine that it was a race of fools. In such courts as those which Shakspeare contemplated they were far from it indeed. They had been bred in camps and colleges—[Polonius had been at the university, where in the dramatic entertainments, usual in the seats of learning in Shakspeare's time, he was selected to perform no less a part than that of Julius Cæsar]—had acquired the polish of courts, if, indeed, we should not rather say they created it—mingled habitually among the great and the witty, the graceful and the wise;—but, from perpetually confining themselves to one class of society, and that the most artificial of all classes, and deeming all other interests depending upon that of their masters, as they saw all other persons bowing in subservience before them, it is no wonder that their world was bounded by the precincts of a palace, and their wisdom or ability exerted, as everybody's ability or wisdom is exerted, to shine or thrive by the arts which contributed to make way in the world wherein their lot was cast. Their sphere of courtly duty made them appear to be frivolous;—it does not follow that they were so in life elsewhere.

This distinction is admirably kept up in Polonius. In the presence he is all ceremony and etiquette. He will not open the business of Hamlet's addresses to his daughter, while the ambassadors from Norway are waiting an audience.

> "Give first admittance to the ambassadours,
> Thy news shall be the fruit of that great feast."

Who could be better qualified to introduce them with due honours? The king appoints him to the duty at once:—

"Thyself do grace to them, and bring them in."

He performs his courtly mission, and waits its conclusion before he commences to speak on what concerns his daughter.

"This business is well ended;"

and now for a speech.

"My liege, and madam, to expostulate
What majesty should be, what duty is,
Why day is day, night night, and time is time,
Were nothing but to waste night, day, and time."

This is the exordium. We now proceed to the propositio.

"Therefore, since brevity is the soul of wit,
And tediousness the limbs and outward flourishes,
I will be brief. Your noble son is mad."

The narratio should follow; but a parenthetical remark cannot be resisted.

"Mad call I it."

You must take it on my assertion—

"For to define true madness,
What is 't but to be nothing else but mad?
But let that go."

The queen agrees with the orator that it might as well be let go,—for she desires "more matter," with less art. Her chamberlain, of course, like all rhetoricians, disclaims the employment of rhetorical artifice,—

> "Madam, I swear, I use no art at all,"

and proceeds to the narratio, which is again stopped for a moment by a trick of the art which he denies that he is using.

> "That he is mad, 'tis true; 'tis true, 'tis pity;
> And pity 'tis, 'tis true: a foolish figure;
> But farewell it, for I will use no art.
> Mad let us grant him then: and now remains
> That we find out the cause of this effect;
> Or, rather say, the cause of this defect;
> For this effect, defective, comes of cause."

[The argument is strictly logical. It being granted that he is mad, we must find the cause of what logicians call effect—which in common parlance, as applied to the madness of Hamlet, would be called a defect,—we must find it, I say; because whatever an effect may be, defective or not, it must arise from a cause.]

> "Thus it remains, and the remainder thus perpend.*
> I have a daughter," &c.

In due course of reasoning he exhibits his proofs— Hamlet's verses and letter, and Ophelia's confessions.

---

* This line is unnatural. The metre would be right, and the technical arrangement of the style more in character if we read,
> Thus it remains: remainder thus perpend.

In equally strict order follows the argument, consisting of an elaborately arranged enumeration of the circumstances attendant on Hamlet's madness:

> "And he, repulsed, (a short tale to make)
> Fell into a sadness; thence into a fast;
> Thence to a watch; [and] thence into a weakness;
> Thence to a lightness; and, by this declension,
> Into the madness wherein now he raves,
> And all we mourn for."

At this period of the speech, if it were delivered in the House of Commons, there would be loud cries of "Hear, hear," and the right honourable gentleman would be obliged to pause for several minutes. If he were a rising member, all his friends would come up to congratulate him on his success, and the impression he had obviously made; if an established speaker, the friends of his party would exclaim, "How admirable!" —"Polonius surpasses himself to-night,"—"Did you ever hear anything so fine, so close, so logical," &c., &c. The opposite side would be obliged to look candid, and say that it certainly was clever.

All that remains is the peroratio. Cheered by the success of his arguments, he proceeds triumphantly in gratulation of his own sagacity.

> "Hath there been such a time (I 'd fain know that)
> That I have positively said, 'Tis so,
> When it proved otherwise?"

[The king says, "Not that I know"—which is equivalent to "cheers from the ministerial benches."]

> "Take this from this, if this be otherwise."

[This is a sample of *gestus*. He points to his head and shoulder.]

> "If circumstances lead me, I will find
> Where truth is hid, though it were hid indeed
> Within the centre."

The speech is over, complete in all its parts. There is scarcely an oratorical figure which is omitted, and it might serve as an unequalled model for many a crack speech "elsewhere." Who is there that has not heard promises of brevity made preludes to tediousness, and disclaimers of art vehicles of rhetorical flourish? What figure more used than amplification such as that, —prefaced, as usual in such cases, by a declaration that the tale will be short,—in which Polonius employs half a dozen lines to detail the degrees of the madness of Hamlet?—and what practice more common than passionate appeals to the past conduct of the speaker as guarantees for the wisdom and uprightness of the course which on the present occasion he is about to pursue? The speech of Polonius translated into Ciceronian Latin would be worthy of Cicero himself;—expanded into three columns of a newspaper report, would be the topic of conversation the day after its delivery in all the clubs, and the welcome theme of applause or confutation by the leading-article-manufacturers of both sides of the question.

Here Polonius was in his character of courtier and privy councillor. He had the ear of the King, and he held it fast. His Majesty and his royal consort duly appreciated the merits of the old orator; but as usual in courts, he does not win the same favour in the eyes of Hamlet. The ministers of the existing prince are seldom favourites with his heir-apparent—his immediate Camarilla never. Youth also generally thinks itself wiser than age; and we wonder not to find in the next scene that Hamlet treats Polonius as a driveller. The old gentleman bears courteously with the incivilities of one whom he considers to be either a mere madman or a prankish jester, and, recurring to the days of his youth, excuses the prince for indulging in feelings which lead to derangement of ideas. Even the recollections, however, of the days when, like his contemporary the gravedigger, " he did love, did love," cannot overcome him to the degree of confessing that he was actually mad. He suffered much extremity; but, after all, he was only " very near madness."*

When the players are introduced, it is only be-

* Is not this dialogue in blank verse? The speech of Polonius certainly is,
> " Still harping on
> My daughter! Yet he knew me not at first.
> He said, I was a fishmonger. He is
> Far gone, far gone; and truly, in my youth
> I suffered extremity for love:
> Very near this. I 'll speak to him again."

I recommend all future editors of *Hamlet* to restore the original reading of the passage immediately preceding,—
> " For if the sun breed maggots in a dead dog,
> Being a *good*-kissing carrion. Have you a daughter?"

in spite of Warburton's magnificent comment, which, according to Johnson, sets the critic on a level with the author. "The illative particle [for]," says the bishop, "shows the speaker to be reasoning from something he had said before: what that was we learn in these words, '*To be honest, as this world goes, is to be one picked out of ten thousand.*' Having said this, the chain of ideas led him to reflect upon the argument which libertines bring against Providence from the circumstance of abounding *evil*. In the next speech, therefore, he endeavours to answer that objection, and vindicate Providence even on a supposition of the fact that almost all men were wicked. His argument in the two lines in question is to this purpose. *But why need we wonder at this abounding of evil? For, if the sun breed maggots in a dead dog, which though a god, yet shedding its heat and influence upon carrion.* Here he stops short, lest, talking too consequentially, the hearer might suspect his madness to be feigned,—and so turns

coming that he who had so long known what was the *mode* should be their principal critic,—and his criticisms are in the most approved style of *politesse.*

him off from the subject by inquiring of his daughter. But the inference which he intended to make was a very noble one, and to this purpose: If this (says he) be the case, that the effect follows the thing operated upon [*carrion*], and not the thing operating [*a god*], why need we wonder that the Supreme Cause of all things diffusing its blessings on mankind, who is as it were a dead carrion, dead in original sin,—man, instead of a proper return of duty, should breed only corruption and vices? This is the argument at length, and is as noble a one in behalf of providence as could come from the schools of divinity. But this wonderful man had an art not only of acquainting the audience with what his actors *say*, but with what they *think*. The sentiment, too, is altogether in character: for Hamlet is perpetually moralizing, and his circumstances make this reflection very natural."

Surely never before nor since was any poor illative particle, *for*, pressed to perform such hard duty. If Hamlet had *said* all that his theological commentator makes him *think*, Polonius would have set him down as mad, beyond all hope of recovery. I have often thought, while reading this note, that it was a pity Warburton had not written a commentary on the pleadings of the Lord of Baisecul and his antagonist before Pantagruel, and on the judgment delivered in the case by that renowned giant. If he discovered an essay on original sin in this illative particle *for*, he would assuredly have dug up a whole Corpus Theologicum in the law-arguments in Rabelais. The *etc.* of Lyttleton which conveyed so much meaning to the mind of Coke, is not to be compared with the *for* of Warburton. He changed the old reading, " a *good*-kissing carrion," into " a *god* kissing carrion."

When Hamlet speaks his part of the tragedy, of course Polonius compliments him for the good accent and good discretion with which he has spoken it.

The meaning of the passage is this. Hamlet suspects that Polonius knows of his love for Ophelia, and that he intends to "loose his daughter to him." He therefore calls him a fishmonger, *i.e.* a purveyor of loose fish. It would not be agreeable in pages which must fall into the hands of the young and fair to follow up the allusion. Polonius interprets the word literally, and is instantly assured that the chances are ten thousand to one if he is as honest as the mere tradesman who sells actual fish. The prince, in his affectation of craziness, proceeds to hint that the consequences of exposing a young lady to the temptations of persons in high rank or of warm blood may be dangerous, and couples the *outré* assertion that the sun can breed maggots with a reference to Polonius's daughter. *Let her not walk in the sun.* Let her not put herself in the peculiar danger to which I allude, and to which her father's performing the part of fishmonger may lead. The sun is a good-kissing carrion—[*carogne*—it is a word which elsewhere occurs in Shakspeare. Quickly, in the *Merry Wives of Windsor*, is called a carrion, &c.]—a baggage fond of kissing. In *Henry IV*. Prince Hal compares the sun to a fair hot wench in flame-coloured taffeta; and if the sun can breed maggots in a dead dog, who knows what may happen elsewhere?

There is a troublesome word in *King Lear*, of which I have never seen a satisfactory interpretation. In the storm of abusive epithets which Kent pours upon the steward, he calls him "a barber-monger." The guesses at the meaning are all insufficient. Perhaps it should read "barbe*l*-monger,"—that is, fishmonger in a peculiar sense. I throw out my conjecture to be rejected at pleasure. I must remark, however, that those who are puzzled by the meaning of a "hundred-pound knave" may find it in

When the player delivers the remainder of the speech, the critic finds it too long. Rebuked by the prince for his censure, he takes the earliest opportunity of declaring that an affected phrase, which startles Hamlet somewhat, to declare that it is good. In the end, when the player displays an emotion roused by his art, Polonius, according to the rules of *goût*, desires that an end should be put to the performance. When the play is actually performed before the king, etiquette keeps him silent until he sees that there is something in it displeasing " in a high quarter," and then the shrewd courtier stops it at once. It is his voice which directs that they should " give o'er the play." He is throughout the ceremonious but sagacious *attaché* of a palace; and the king and queen accordingly treat him with the utmost deference, and

---

Rabelais or Sir Thomas Urquhart. It is a word of reproach addressed to the heavy *pondres-pondres* Germans. It occurs in Bridlegoose's famous story of the pugnacious Gascon in the camp at Stockholm. Sir John Hawkins, in his absurd life of Dr. Johnson, imagines that it is a word invented by Urquhart, with no more meaning than the ordinary slang words of the day.

In the conclusion of the scene between Hamlet and Polonius, the former exclaims, " These tedious old fools!" Would it not be better, " Thou tedious old fool!"—for it is plain that Hamlet is thinking only of the troublesome old man who has been pestering him.

consult him in their most critical emergencies. He dies in their service, fitly practising a stratagem in perfect accordance with the *morale* of the circle in which he has always moved, and in which he has engaged to show his wisdom, devotion, and address.*
Hamlet well characterizes the class of men to which the slain courtier belonged in his farewell to the body.

> " Thou busy, rash, intruding fool, farewell;
> I took thee for thy better,—take thy fortune.
> Thou findest to be too busy is some danger."

But Polonius is no fool, though he is so called here. Hamlet is annoyed by his meddling and officiousness, and therefore applies the epithet. He marks his sense of his general respect for the old man, even when he is most pestered by his interference. In a peevish exclamation he styles him a " tedious old fool;" but when he sees that the players are inclined to follow

---

* " Behind the arras I'll convey myself,
To hear the process; I'll warrant she'll tax him home.
And, as you said, and wisely was it said,
'Tis meet that some more audience than a mother,
Since nature makes them partial, should o'erhear
The speech of vantage. Fare you well, my liege.
I'll call upon you ere you go to bed,
And tell you what I know."

his own example, he checks them by an authoritative command,

"Follow that lord, and look you mock him not."

If he calls him to Rosencrantz and Guildenstern " a great baby, not yet out of his swaddling clouts," and jeers him in their presence, it is partly to show that he is but mad north-north-west, and can know a hawk from a hand-saw when the wind is southerly, and partly to mark that he has discovered the conspiracy against him, and to display his contempt for all engaged in it.

Abstracted from his courtier-character, Polonius is a man of profound sense, and of strict and affectionate attention to his duties. A man whom his children love can never be contemptible. No one, it is said, can be a hero to his *valet de chambre*, because he sees all the petty physical wants and moral defects of his master. How much more difficult to be the object of esteem and devotion in the eyes of those who have turned their eyes upon us from childhood. Natural affection will, of course, do much; but the buffoon of the stage never could have inspired the feelings exhibited by his children, who must have been perpetually grieved and disgraced by antic buffoonery, of which they, from their connexion with the court, must have been constant witnesses. Laertes, a fine high-spirited young gentleman, and Ophelia, the Rose of May, the grace and ornament of the circle in which she moved, could not have so deeply reverenced and so bitterly deplored their father, if he had been indeed a great baby still in his swaddling clouts. The *double* of Pantaloon, whom we see tumbling about in Drury Lane or Covent Garden, would not have roused the blood of Laertes to fury, still less led him to justify assassination in avenging his fall; nor would his death have driven Ophelia to madness. Such a father might be dead and gone,

> "And at his head a grass-green turf,
> And at his heels a stone,"

according to the inflexible laws of mortality; but his son would soon wipe the natural tears he might drop, and let him lie in his grave without any complaint of

> "His obscure funeral;
> No trophy, sword, nor hatchment o'er his bones;
> No noble rite, nor formal ostentation."

Nor would his daughter, in her broken-hearted insanity, have imagined that at his death violets, the sweetest flowers of the spring, had universally withered. Let me observe, that by this remark I mean no disrespect to our actors, many of the most eminent of whom have performed the part. They yield to long-established custom, and, as the part is not of the same importance in the play as Shylock in the *Merchant of Venice*, it is not probable that any Macklin will arise to rescue him from buffoonery. Besides, as it is necessary that he should in one part of the play designedly act up to the follies of Hamlet, it would be difficult to make the distinction between the assumed and the natural character; and yet perhaps it ought to be attempted, for, as it is played at present, it is perhaps the least attractive of the prominent *dramatis personæ* of Shakspeare.

Even in the very part to which I have just alluded, where he is fooling Hamlet to the top of his bent, he cannot avoid displaying glances of his habitual shrewdness. He suspects the reality of the madness from the beginning. The insulting taunts addressed to him at second hand from Juvenal only call forth the reflection that there is method in the madness. In the end he plainly considers it as nothing more than a prank. He bids the Queen

> "Tell him his pranks have been too broad to bear with,
> And that your grace hath screened and stood between
> Much heat and him."

Neither Laertes nor Ophelia are present while he is

engaged in bandying folly against folly, and he therefore does not such before those by whom he most desires to be respected. When alone with them, his true character appears;—and what can be more sensible? His counsels to his son have never been for worldly wisdom surpassed. The ten precepts of Lord Burleigh, addressed to his son Robert, on which it is generally supposed the apophthegms of Polonius are based, are perhaps equal in shrewdness, but they want the pithiness and condensation of verse. Neither are they as philosophical, being drawn, to talk logically, *à posteriori*, while those of Shakspeare are deduced *à priori*. Take, for example, Lord Burleigh's fifth maxim on borrowing and lending money:—

"Beware of suretyship for thy best friends. He that payeth another man's debts seeketh his own decay. But if thou canst not otherwise choose, rather lend thy money thyself upon good bonds, although thou borrow it; so shalt thou secure thyself, and pleasure a friend. Neither borrow money of a neighbour or a friend, but of a stranger, where, paying for it, thou shalt hear no more of it, otherwise thou shalt eclipse thy credit, loose thy freedom, and pay as dear as to another. But in borrowing of money be precious of thy word, for he that takes care of keeping payment is lord of another man's purse."

Full of practical good sense, no doubt, as indeed is everything that " wise Burleigh spoke;" but it might occur to minds of smaller calibre than that of the Lord High Treasurer. Polonius takes higher ground.

> "Neither a borrower nor a lender be;
> For loan oft loses both itself and friend;
> And borrowing dulls the edge of husbandry."

Lord Burleigh gives us but the petty details,—in Shakspeare we find the principle.

Again, his Lordship's ninth precept is:—

" Trust not any man with thy life, credit, or estate; for it is mere folly for a man to enthrall himself to a friend, as though, occasion being offered, he should not care to become thine enemy."

It is good advice; but how much better done by Polonius!

> "This above all. To thine own self be true,
> And it must follow, as the night the day,
> Thou canst not then be false to any man."

A comparison of all the precepts of the poet and the statesman would yield a similar result. And yet nobody ever thought of exhibiting Burleigh, inferior as he is in dramatical wisdom, as an object of merriment upon the stage for many a year after he had been gathered to his fathers, until it pleased the author of the *Critic* to put him forward to make his oracular nod. There is no use in moralizing, but we cannot help reflecting that Sheridan would have done better in life if he could have followed the prudential advice of the great minister whom he mocked. It is certain that if he had avoided mimicking him at humble distance elsewhere, and never thought of playing at Parliament,—if, content with winning dramatic honours only second to those of Molière, he had eschewed throwing himself into paths where the half-nods of the less than tenth-rate Burleighs are of more weight than all the wit and genius of the *School for Scandal*, there would not have been any necessity that his death should be neglected and his funeral honoured, with a contempt and a sympathy equally characteristic of those whom his Lordship calls " the glow-worms, I mean parasites and sycophants, who will feed and fawn upon thee in the summer of prosperity, but in adverse storms they will shelter thee no more than an arbour in winter."

That the austere Lord High Treasurer might have been the mark for the covert wit of the dramatist,— covert indeed, for in his time, or in that which immediately succeeded it, there was no safety in making unseemly jests too openly about him,—is highly probable; and the enemy of Essex and Raleigh* could not be an object of admiration in the eyes of Shakspeare. Lord Burleigh, in his courtly demeanour, was as observant of etiquette as Polonius, and as ready in using indirections to find thereby directions out. The Queen was fond both of ceremony and statecraft: but I doubt much that the old gentleman in *Hamlet* is intended for anything more than a general personification of ceremonious courtiers. If Lord Chesterfield had designed to write a commentary upon Polonius, he could not have more completely succeeded than by writing his famous letters to his son. His Lordship, like every man of taste and virtue, and what Pope has comprehended in the expressive term of " all that," in his time utterly

---

* Even in these precepts his lordship cannot avoid a " gird " at those remarkable men whose accomplishments were, however, much more likely to please poets and adventurers than sober statesmen. We know how Spenser immortalizes the *Shepherd of the Ocean*, and with what pomp of verse "the general of our gracious emperess" is introduced almost by name in the chorus of *Henry V.* Shakspeare's most national play, as a fit object of comparison with the hero of Azincour himself. In Lord Burleigh they only appear as suiteth examples to point the moral of a maxim. "Yet I advise thee not to affect or neglect popularity too much. *Seek not to be Essex—shun to be Raleigh.*"

despised Shakspeare. There is nothing to blame in this. What can we talk on but of what we know? One of the grandest of the herd, Horace Walpole, wrote the *Mysterious Mother*, and therefore he had a right (had he not?) to offer an opinion on *Macbeth*, and to pronounce *Midsummer Night's Dream* a bundle of rubbish, far more ridiculous than the most absurd Italian opera. Lord Chesterfield wrote nothing, that I know of, to give him a name as an author, except his letters. Of course he wrote despatches, protocols, and other such ware, worthy, no doubt, of the Red Tapery of which he was so eminent a member.

IAGO.

I HAVE been accused by some who have taken the trouble of reading these papers, that I am fond of paradoxes, and write not to comment upon Shakspeare, but to display logical dexterity in maintaining the untenable side of every question. To maintain that Falstaff was in heart melancholy and Jaques gay, to contrast the fortunes of Romeo and Bottom, or to plead the cause of Lady Macbeth, is certainly not in accordance with the ordinary course of criticism; but I have given my reasons, sound or unsound as they may be, for my opinions, which I have said with old Montaigne, I do not pretend to be good, but to be *mine*. What appears to me to be the distinguishing feature of Shakspeare is, that his characters are real men and women, not mere abstractions. In the best of us all there are many blots, in the worst there are many traces of goodness. There is no such thing as angels or devils in the world. We have passions and feelings, hopes and fears, joys and sorrows, pretty equally distributed among us; and that which actuates the highest and the lowest, the most virtuous and the most profligate, the bravest and meanest, must, in its, original elements, be the same. People do not commit wicked actions from the mere love of wickedness; there must always be an incentive of precisely the same kind as that which stimulates to the noblest actions—ambition, love of adventure, passion, necessity. All our virtues closely border upon vices, and are not unfrequently blended. The robber may be generous—the miser, just—the cruel man, conscientious—the rake, honourable—the fop, brave. In various relations of life, the same man may play many characters as distinct from one another as day from night. I venture to say that the creatures of Boz's fancy, Fagin or Sikes, did not appear in every circle as the unmitigated scoundrels we see them in *Oliver Twist.* It is, I suppose, necessary to the exigencies of the tale, that no other part of their characters should be exhibited; but, after all, the Jew only carries the commercial, and the housebreaker the military principle, to an extent which society cannot tolerate. In element, the feeling is the same that covers the ocean with the merchant-flags of England, and sends forth the hapless boys to the trade of picking pockets—that inspires the highwayman to stop a traveller on Hounslow, and spirits the soldier to face a cannon at Waterloo. Robber, soldier, thief, merchant, are all equally men. It is necessary for a critical investigation of character, not to be content with taking things merely as they seem. We must endeavour to strip off the covering with which habit or necessity has enveloped the human mind, and to inquire after motives as well as look to actions. It would not be an unamusing task to analyze the career of two persons starting under similar circumstances, and placed in situations not in essence materially different, one ending at the debtors' door of Newgate, amid hootings and execrations, and the other borne to his final resting-place in Westminster Abbey, graced by all the pomps that heraldry can bestow.

As Shakspeare therefore draws men, and not one-sided sketches of character, it is always possible to treat his personages as if they were actually existing people; and there is always some redeeming point. The bloody Macbeth is kind and gentle to his wife; the gore-stained Richard, gallant and daring; Shylock is an affectionate father, and a good-natured master; Claudius, in *Hamlet*, is fond of his foully-won queen, and exhibits, at least, remorse for his deed in heart-rending soliloquies; Angelo is upright in public life, though yielding to sore temptation in private; Cloten is brutal and insulting, but brave; the ladies are either wholly without blemishes, or have merits to redeem them: in some plays, as *Julius Cæsar, Coriolanus, Antony and Cleopatra, Romeo and Juliet*, and several others, no decidedly vicious character is introduced at all. The personages introduced are exposed to the frailties of our nature, but escape from its grosser crimes and vices.

But Iago! Ay! there's the rub. Well may poor Othello look down to his feet, and not seeing them different from those of others, feel convinced that it is a fable which attributes a cloven hoof to the devil. His next test,

"If that thou be'st a devil, I cannot kill thee" *—

affords a proof that Iago is not actually a fiend, for he wounds him; but still he cannot think him anything less than a "demi-devil," being bled, not killed. Nor is it wonderful that the parting instruction of Lodovico to Cassio, should be to enforce the most cunning cruelty of torture on the hellish villain, or that all the party should vie with each other in heaping upon him words of contumely and execration. He richly deserved them. He had ensnared the soul and body of Othello to do the most damnable actions; he had been the cause of the cruel murder of Desdemona; he had killed his own wife, had plotted the assassination of Cassio, had betrayed and murdered Roderigo. His determination to keep silence when questioned, was at least judicious:

"Demand me nothing: what you know, you know;
From this time forth I never will speak word:"

for with his utmost ingenuity he could hardly find any-

---

* After this line he wounds Iago. Then follows:

"*Lod.* Wrench his sword from him.
Iago. I bleed, sir, but not killed."

This is strange language. Should it not be "I, [*i. e.* Ay, as usual in Shakspeare,] *bled*, sir, but not killed?"

thing to say for himself. Is there nothing, then, to be said for him by anybody else?

No more than this. He is the sole exemplar of studied personal revenge in the plays. The philosophical mind of Hamlet ponders too deeply, and sees both sides of the question too clearly, to be able to carry any plan of vengeance into execution. Romeo's revenge on Tybalt for the death of Mercutio is a sudden gust of ungovernable rage. The vengeances in the historical plays are those of war or statecraft. In Shylock, the passion is hardly personal against his intended victim. A swaggering Christian is at the mercy of a despised and insulted Jew. The hatred is national and sectarian. Had Bassanio or Gratiano, or any other of their creed, been in his power, he would have been equally relentless. He is only retorting the wrongs and insults of his tribe, in demanding full satisfaction, and imitating the hated Christians in their own practices.

> " And if you wrong us, shall we not revenge?
> If we are like you in the rest, we will
> Resemble you in that. If a Jew wrong
> A Christian, what is *his* humility?
> Revenge!
> [And] if a Christian wrong a Jew, what should
> His sufferance be by Christian example?
> Why, [sir] revenge! The villany you teach me

> I'll execute, and it shall go hard, but
> I'll better the instruction."*

It is, on the whole, a passion remarkably seldom exhibited in Shakspeare in any form. Iago, as I have said, is its only example, as directed against an individual.

Iago had been affronted in the tenderest point. He felt that he had strong claims on the office of lieutenant to Othello, who had witnessed his soldierly abilities

> "At Rhodes, at Cyprus, and on other grounds,
> Christian and heathen."

The greatest exertion was made to procure it for him, and yet he is refused. What is still worse, the grounds

---

* Printed as prose in the editions. The insertion of *and* before *if*, where it may serve as the ordinary copulative,—or as the common form, *an if*, perpetually recurring, as in Romeo, "*an if* a man did need a poison now," [on which form I may remark in passing, Horne Tooke talks ignorantly enough in his *Diversions of Purley*,]—and of a monosyllable between *why* and *revenge*, makes the whole passage metrical. I am inclined to think that *revenge* should be repeated in the concluding lines. "If a Jew wrong a Christian, what is his humility? REVENGE!" If, on the contrary, a Christian wrong a Jew, what should his sufferance be?

> "REVENGE! REVENGE! The villany you teach me
> I'll execute."

As an editor I might scruple to exhibit the text thus. I should recommend it to an actor in place of the prosaic and unmetrical—*Why, revenge*.

of the refusal are military: Othello evades the request of the bowing magnificoes

"with a bombast circumstance,
Horribly stuffed with epithets of war."

He assigns to the civilians reasons for passing over Iago, drawn from his own trade, of which they of course could not pretend to be adequate judges. And worst of all, when this practised military man is for military reasons set aside, who is appointed? Some man of greater renown and skill in arms? *That* might be borne; but it is no such thing. The choice of Othello lights upon

" Forsooth, a great arithmetician,
One Michael Cassio, a Florentine,
A fellow almost damned in a fair wife,*

---

* This is one of the most puzzling lines in Shakspeare. All the explanations are forced. Cassio had no wife, and his treatment of Bianca, who stands in place of one, is contemptuous: nor does he let her stand in the way of his duty. She tenderly reproaches him for his long absence, and he hastily sends her home, harshly saying,

" I do attend here on the general,
And think it no addition, nor my wish
To have him see me *woman'd*."

Tyrwhitt reads *damned in a fair life;* interpreting it as an allusion to the judgment denounced in the gospel, against those of whom all men speak well, which is very far-fetched indeed. If *life* were the reading, it might signify that Cassio was damned for the rough life of a soldier by the fair, *i. e.* the easy life he had hitherto led. John-

> That never set a squadron in the field,
> Nor the division of a battle knows,
> More than a spinster; unless the bookish theoric,
> Wherein the toged consuls can propose
> As masterly as he : mere prattle, without practice,
> Is all his soldiership."

It is an insult hard to be borne, as many an H. P. will be ready to testify. We will find in many professional periodical works the complaint reiterated, that son gives it up, as a passage "which, for the present, must be resigned to corruption and obscurity." A writer in one of the early volumes of *Blackwood's Magazine*, proposed somewhat ingeniously

> " A great arithmetician,
> A fellow almost damned : in a fair *wise*,
> Who never set a squadron in the field."

But this is not satisfactory. Why is Cassio a fellow almost damned? Like Dr. Johnson, " I have nothing that I can, with any approach to confidence, propose," but I think that the word " damned " is a corruption of some word which signified delicate, soft, dainty, or something of the kind, and that for " *in* " we should read " as." "A fellow almost as soft and delicate as a fair wife," as dainty as a woman. I am not fortunate to supply it, but I have somewhat thought it was

> " A fellow almost *trimmed* as a fair wife."

Such a fellow as the " neat and *trimly* dressed " courtier, "perfumed as a milliner," who excited the impatience of Hotspur. *As a fair wife*, corresponds to *more than a spinster*, in the conclusion of the sentence. I throw out my hint for the leading or misleading of future editors.

I cannot help remarking that Colonel Mitchell, in his noble life of Wallenstein, seems to have no better opinion of the " arithmeti-

"there's no remedy, 'tis the curse of service:
Preferment goes by letter and affection,
Not by old gradation, where each second
Stood heir to the first:"

and many a curse, loud and deep, is inflicted on that account upon the Horse Guards and Admiralty, who fortunately have no individual responsibilities on which the disappointed ancients can fasten. I am sure that no British soldier or sailor would carry his anger farther than a passing growl, but the example of Bellingham shows that even in our assassin-hating nation, a feeling of injustice done by a superior, will drive a man to satiate his vengeance even upon those who have not done him wrong.

cians" of Shakspeare's day than Iago. George Basta, the celebrated tactician, was contemporary with Shakspeare. Wallenstein served under him, and Colonel Mitchell makes somewhat the same complaint of the want of preferment of his hero as the disappointed ancient. "As to George Basta," he says, "if we may judge of him by his system of tactics, which was then exactly what Saldera's is now, and which, when the object of such a system is considered, must be looked upon as second only, in feebleness and insufficiency, to the one followed in our own time, he was not a likely person to appreciate talent, or to encourage and call forth genius." Nor, indeed, is the Colonel very complimentary to the army to which Iago belongs. He calls them "the worthless mercenaries of Venice, troops constantly kept in a state of mutiny and insufficiency, by the ignorant fears of their despicable government."

In the country of Iago, whether from his name we conclude it to be Spain, or from his service, Italy, none of the scruples, or rather principles, which actuate or restrain English gentlemen, existed. Least of all were they to be found in the motley armies of adventurers gathered from all quarters, the outcasts

>―" of all foreign lands,
> Unclaimed by town or tribe, to whom belongs
> Nothing, except the universal sun:"*

and Iago could not be expected to be very scrupulous as to his method of compassing his revenge. But how effect it? He is obliged to admit that Othello's standing in the state is too important to render it possible that public injury could be done to him. He is well aware that

> "the state
> * * * * *
> Cannot with safety cast him; he's embarked
> With such loud reasons to the Cyprus war,
> Which e'en now stands in act, that for their souls
> Another of his fathom they have not
> To lead their business."

In his unhoused condition no point of vantage presented itself whence harm could be wrought. Just then, when

---

* Schiller. *The Piccolomini*, Ac. iv. s. 5.

Iago's heart was filled with rage, and his head busily but vainly occupied in devising means for avenging himself on the man by whom that rage was excited, just then *Até*, the Goddess of Mischief, supplies him with all that deepest malignity could desire, by the hasty, ill-mated, and unlooked-for marriage of Othello. It was a devil-send that the most sanguine spirit could not have anticipated, and Iago clutched it accordingly with passionate eagerness. He was tempted and he fell.

When he first conceived his hatred against Othello, he had no notion that it would be pushed to such dire extremity. Revenge is generally accompanied by vanity, indeed there must be always a spice of vanity in a revengeful disposition. He who so keenly feels and deeply resents personal injury or affront, must set no small value upon himself. The proud are seldom revengeful—the great never. We accordingly find that Iago engages in his hostilities against Othello, more to show his talents than for any other purpose. He proudly lauds his own powers of dissimulation, which are to be now displayed with so much ability.

> "When my outward action doth demonstrate.
> The native act and figure of my heart
> In compliment extern, 'tis not long after

> But I will wear my heart upon my sleeve
> For daws to peck at. I am not what I am."*

He fancies himself superior to all around in art and knowledge of the world. Roderigo is a mere gull:—

> "Thus do I ever make my fool my purse;
> For I mine own gain'd knowledge should profane,
> If I should time expend with *such a snipe*,
> But for my sport and profit."

Cassio he considers to be not merely unskilled in war, but a fool:—

> "For while *this honest fool*
> Plies Desdemona to repair his fortunes," &c.

Othello is an ass in his estimation:—

> "The Moor is of a free and open nature,
> That thinks men honest that but seem to be so,
> And will as tenderly be led by the nose
> *As asses are.*"

The "*inclining*" Desdemona he utterly despises, as one who fell in love with the Moor merely for his bragging, and telling fantastical lies. His wife he calls a

---

* Can these last words be intended as a somewhat profane allusion to the title by which the Almighty reveals himself to Moses? Exod. iii. 14. I AM THAT I AM is the name of the God of truth. *I am not what I am* is therefore a fitting description of a premeditated liar.

fool; and with these opinions of his great superiority of wisdom and intellect, he commences operations to enmesh them all, as if they were so many puppets. It would be a strange thing, indeed, he reflects, if I were to permit myself to be insulted, and my rights withheld, by such a set of idiots, whom I can wind round my finger as I please.

He seated him in the seat of the scorner, a character which he who is accounted the wisest of men continually opposes to that of true wisdom. " Seest thou," says Solomon, in the Proverbs copied out by the men of Hezekiah, King of Judah, which, whether they be inspired or not, are aphorisms of profound and concentrated wisdom,—" seest thou a man wise in his own conceit? there is more hope of a fool than of him."* And the career of Iago ends with his own destruction, amid the abomination set down in another chapter of Proverbs as the lot of the scorner. The jealousy of Othello is not more gradually and skilfully raised and developed than the vengeance of Iago. At first angry enough, no doubt; but he has no defined project. He follows the Moor to take advantage of circumstances to turn them to his own use. Nothing of peculiar

* Prov. xxvi. 12. "The scorner is an abomination to men," occurs in chap. xxiv. 9.

malignity is thought upon: if he can get Cassio's place, he will be satisfied.

> "Cassio's a proper man: let me see now,
> To get his place——."

The marriage and the sight of Desdemona point out to him a ready way of accomplishing this object. The thought occurs suddenly, and he is somewhat startled at first. He asks himself with eager repetition,

> "How? how?"

and pauses to think—

> "Let me see ——."

It is soon settled.

> "After some time, to abuse Othello's ear,
> That he is too familiar with his wife."

But it still alarms him:

> "I have it—It's engendered: Hell and night
> Must bring this monstrous birth to the world's light."

The plot is not matured even when they all arrive at Cyprus.

> "'Tis here, but yet confused—
> Knavery's plain face is never seen till used."

When once fairly entered upon, however, it progresses with unchecked rapidity. He is himself hurried resistlessly forward by the current of deceit and iniquity in which he has embarked. He is as much a tool or passive instrument as those whom he is using as such.

Some critics pronounce his character unnatural, as not having sufficient motive for the crimes he commits. This is not wise. He could not help committing them. Merely to put money in his purse, he gulled Roderigo into a belief that he could assist the poor dupe in his suit to Desdemona. There is no remarkable crime in this. Nor can we blame him for being angry at being somewhat scornfully passed over; we can, at all events, enter into his feelings when he wishes to undermine one whom he considers to be unworthily preferred to him, and to obtain a place which he thinks should be his own, if patronage had been justly dispensed. It was a base thing, indeed, to malign a lady, and possess her husband with jealousy; but he could not have calculated on the harvest of death and crime which the seed of suspicion that he was sowing was destined to bring up. When he makes Cassio drunk, he only anticipates that he will put him in such action as may offend the isle. When framing the device that is to destroy the lieutenant, no thoughts of murder arise before him.

He has no regard for the feelings of Othello, but dreams not that he will kill Desdemona, whom he says he loves. As for the lady herself, his low estimation of woman would of course lead him to think but little about her peace and quiet. He excuses himself, besides, by referring to the rumour that Othello had given him cause to be jealous. It is plain that he does not pretend to lay any great stress upon this; nor can we suppose that, even if it were true, it would deeply affect him; but he thinks lightly of women in general, and has no respect whatever for his wife. Indeed, Othello does not hold Emilia in much esteem; and her own conversation with Desdemona, as she is undressing her for bed (act iv. scene 3), shows that her virtue was not impregnable. The injury, therefore, Iago was about to do Desdemona, in lessening her in the respect of her husband by accusing her of such an ordinary offence as a deviation from chastity, and one which *he* did not visit with any particular severity on his own wife, must have seemed trivial. He could not have been prepared for the dire tempest of fury which his first hint of her unfaithfulness aroused in the bosom of Othello. Up to that moment he had done nothing more than gull a blockhead, and endeavour by unworthy means to undermine a rival; trickery and slander, though not very honourable qualities, are not of such rare occurrence in the world as to call for the expression of any peculiar indignation, when we find them displayed by a clever and plotting Italian.

They have, however, led him to the plain and wide path of damnation. He cannot retract his insinuations. Even if he desired, Othello will not let him:

"Villain, be sure you prove my love a whore."

[We may observe that he still, though his suspicions are so fiercely roused, calls her his *love*. It is for the last time before her death. After her guilt is, as he thinks, proved, he has no word of affection for her. She is a convicted culprit, to be sacrificed to his sense of justice.]

"Be sure of it; give me the ocular proof:
Or, by the worth of mine eternal soul,
Thou hadst been better have been born a dog
Than answer my waked wrath,

— — —

Make me to see 't, or, at the least, so prove it,
That the probation bear no hinge, nor loop
To hang a doubt on; or woe upon thy life!"

Iago, therefore, had no choice but to go forward. He was evidently not prepared for this furious outburst; and we may acquit him of hypocrisy when he prays Othello to let her live. But Cassio must die:—

> "He hath a daily beauty in his life
> That makes me ugly."

A more urgent reason immediately suggests itself:—

> "And besides, the Moor
> May unfold me to him: there stand I in much peril.
> *No—he must die.*"

The death of Desdemona involves that of Roderigo:—

> "Live Roderigo?
> He calls me to a restitution large
> Of gold and jewels, that I bobb'd from him
> As gifts to Desdemona.
> *It must not be.*"

Here is the direct agency of necessity. He *must* remove these men. Shortly after, to silence the clamorous testimony of his wife, he *must* kill her. He is doomed to blood.

PICTURES,

GRAVE AND GAY.

THE CONFESSIONS OF AN ELDERLY GENTLEMAN;

CONTAINING HIS LAST LOVE.

THE Countess of Blessington need not be afraid that I shall interfere with her work in the unhappy tale which I am about to begin; my scene will be laid in a very different walk of life, and the lady whose charms have wounded my heart bear no resemblance whatever to the aristocratic beauties which grace the book of the Countess. My arrangement ever goes upon an opposite principle to hers; her elderly gentleman proceeds from first to last, getting through his fates and fortunes in regular rotation, as if they were so many letters of the alphabet, from A to Z: I read mine backward, in the manner of Turks, Jews, and other infidels; for worse than Turk or Jew have I been treated by the fair sex!

When I confess to being an elderly gentleman, I leave my readers to their own conjectures as to the precise figure of my age. It is sufficient to say that I have arrived at the shady side of fifty,—how much further it is unnecessary to add. I have been always what is called a man in easy circumstances. My father worked hard in industrious pursuits, and left me, his only son, a tolerably snug thing. I started in life with some five or six thousand pounds, a good business as a tobacconist, a large stock-in-trade, excellent credit and connection, not a farthing of debt, and no encumbrance in the world. In fact, I had, one way or another, about a thousand a year, with no great quantity of trouble. I liked business, and stuck to it; became respected in my trade and my ward; and have frequently filled the important office of common-councilman with considerable vigour and popularity. As I never went into rash speculations, and put by something every year, my means are now about double what they were some thirty-five years ago, when Mr. Gayless, sen. departing this life, left the firm of Gayless, Son, and Company, to my management.

It is not to be wondered at, that a man in such circumstances should occasionally allow himself relaxation from his labours. I entered heartily into all the civic festivities; and, at my snug bachelor's country-house on Fortress terrace, Kentish Town, did the thing genteelly enough every now and then. Many an excursion have I made up and down the river, to Greenwich, Richmond, Blackwall, &c.; have spent my summer at Margate, and once went to the Lakes of Westmoreland. Some of that party proposed to me to go over to see the Lakes of Killarney; but I had by that time come to years of discretion, and was not such a fool as to trust myself among the Irish. I however did go once to Paris, but, not understanding the language, I did not take much interest in the conversation of the Frenchmen; and as for talking to English people, why I can do that at home, without distressing my purse or person.

The younger portion of my fair readers may be anxious to know what is the personal appearance of him who takes the liberty of addressing them. I have always noticed that young ladies are very curious on this point; and it is difficult, if not impossible, to persuade them how irrational is their anxiety. It is in vain to quote to them the venerable maxims of antiquity, such as, " It is not handsome is, but handsome does," or, " When Poverty enters the door, Love flies out of the window," or, " All is not gold that glitters," or many more adages of equal wisdom. It is generally of no avail to dilate upon the merits of mind and intellect to persons whose thoughts run after glossy locks and sparkling eyes, and to whose imagination a well-filled ledger is of secondary importance to a well-tripped quadrille. In my own knowledge, a young lady of our ward refused to accept the hand of a thriving bill-broker in Spital-square,—a highly respectable middle-aged man, who had made a mint of money by sharp application to his business,—and chose a young barrister of the Inner Temple, whose bill, to my certain knowledge, was refused discount by the Spital-square broker at twenty-five per cent. I have been assured by officers in the army, that the case has sometimes occurred of girls in garrison towns preferring an ensign to a major of many years' service; and I have heard, on authority which I have reason to credit, of a West-end lady rejecting an actual governor of a colony, on the ground that he was a withered fellow as old and prosy as her grandfather,—as if there was anything disgraceful in that,—and shortly afterwards cocking her cap at a penniless dog, because he had romantic eyes, and wrote rubbish in albums and pocket-books. I really have no patience with such stuff. Middle-aged ladies are far less fastidious.

If I must delineate myself, however, here goes. So far from deteriorating by age, I think I have improved, like Madeira. A miniature of me, taken in my twenty-first year by an eminent artist who lived in Gutter-lane, and drew undeniable likenesses at an hour's sitting for half-a-guinea, forms a great contrast to one by Chalon, painted much more than twenty years afterward. You really would never think them to represent the same man, and yet both are extremely alike. I was in my youth a sallow-faced lad, with hollow cheeks, immense staring eyes, and long thin sandy hair, plastered to the side of my head. By the course of living which I have led in the city, the sallow complexion has been replaced by a durable red, the lean cheek is now comfortably plumped out, the eyes pursed round and contracted by substantial layers of fat, and the long hair having in general taken its departure has left the remainder considerably improved by the substitution of a floating silver for the soapy red. Then, my stature, which, like that of many celebrated men of ancient and modern times, cannot be said to be lofty, gave me somewhat an air of insignificance when I was thin-gutted and slim; but, when it is taken in conjunction with the rotundity I have attained in the progress of time, no one can say that I do not fill a respectable space in the public eye. I have also conformed to modern fashions; and when depicted by Chalon in a flowing mantle, with

"*Jour à gauche*" (whatever that may mean) written under it, I am as grand as an officer of hussars with his martial cloak about him, and quite as distinct a thing from the effigy of Mr. M'Dawbs, of Gutter-lane, as the eau de Portugal which now perfumes my person, is, from the smell of the tobacco which filled my garments with the odour of the shop when first I commenced my amorous adventures.

Such was I, and such am I; and I have now said, I think, enough to introduce me to the public. My story is briefly this:—On the 23rd of last December, just before the snow, I had occasion to go on some mercantile business to Edinburgh, and booked myself at a certain hotel, which must be nameless, for the journey—then rendered perilous by the weather. I bade adieu to my friends at a genial dinner given, on the 22nd, in the coffee-room, where I cheered their drooping spirits by perpetual bumpers of port, and all the consolation that my oratory could supply. I urged that travelling inside, even in Christmas week, in a stage-coach, was nothing nearly so dangerous as flying in a balloon; that we were not to think of Napoleon's army perishing in the snows of Russia, but rather of the bark that carried the fortunes of Cæsar; that great occasions required more than ordinary exertions;

and that the last advices concerning the house of Screw, Longcut, and Co., in the High-street, rendered it highly probable that their acceptances would not be met unless I was personally in Edinburgh within a week. These and other arguments I urged with an eloquence which, to those who were swallowing my wine, seemed resistless. Some of my own bagmen, who had for years travelled in black rappee or Irish blackguard, shag, canaster, or such commodities, treated the adventure as a matter of smoke; others, not of such veteran experience, regarded my departure as an act of rashness not far short of insanity. "To do such a thing," said my old neighbour, Joe Grabble, candlestick-maker and deputy, "at your time of life!"

I had swallowed perhaps too much port, and, feeling warmer than usual, I did not much relish this observation. "At my time of life, Joe," said I; "what of that? It is not years that make a man younger or older; it is the spirits, Joe,—the life, the sprightliness, the air. There is no such thing now, Joe, as an old man, an elderly man, to be found anywhere but on the stage. Certainly, if people poke themselves eternally upon a high stool behind a desk in a murky counting-house in the city, and wear such an odd quiz of a dress as you do, they must be accounted old."

"And yet," said Joe, "I am four years younger than you. Don't you remember how we were together at school at old Muddlehead's, at the back of Honey-lane-market, in the year seventeen hundred and eighty-fou—?"

"There is no need," said I, interrupting him, "of quoting dates. It is not considered genteel in good society. I do not admit your statement to be correct."

"I'll prove it from the parish register," said Joe Grabble.

"Don't interrupt, Joe," said I; "interrupting is not considered genteel in good society. I neither admit nor deny your assertion; but how does that affect my argument? I maintain that in every particular I am as young as I was thirty years ago."

"And quite as ready to go philandering," said Joe, with a sneer.

"Quite," replied I, "or more so. Nay, I venture to say that I could at this moment make myself as acceptable to that pretty young woman at the bar, as nine-tenths of the perfumed dandies of the West-end."

"By your purse, no doubt," said Joe, "if even that would obtain you common civility."

I was piqued at this; and, under the impulse of the moment and the wine, I performed the rash act of betting a rump and dozen for the present company, against five shillings, that she would acknowledge that I was a man of gaiety and gallantry calculated to win a lady's heart before I left London, short as was the remaining space. Joe caught at the bet, and it was booked in a moment. The party broke up about nine o'clock, and I could not help observing something like a suppressed horselaugh on their countenances. I confess that, when I was left alone, I began to repent of my precipitancy.

But faint heart never won fair lady; so, by a series of manœuvring with which long practice had rendered me perfect, I fairly, in the course of an hour, entrenched myself in the bar, and, at about ten o'clock, was to be found diligently discussing a fragrant remnant of broiled chicken and mushroom, and hobnobbing with the queen of the pay department in sundry small glasses of brandy-and-water, extracted from the grand reservoir of the tumbler placed before me. So far all was propitious; but, as Old Nick would have it, in less than ten minutes the party was joined by a mustachoed fellow, who had come fresh from fighting,—or pretending to fight—for Donna Isabella, or Don Carlos,—Heaven knows which, (I dare say he didn't,)—and was full of Bilboa, and San Sebastian, and Espartero, and Alaix pursuing Gomez, and Zumalacarregui, and General Evans, and all that style of talk, for which women have open ears. I am sure that I could have bought the fellow body and soul—at least all his property real and personal—for fifty pounds; but there he sate, crowing me down whenever I ventured to edge in a word, by some story of a siege, or a battle, or a march, ninety-nine hundred parts of his stories being nothing more or less than lies. I know I should have been sorry to have bulled or beared in Spanish on the strength of them; but the girl (her name is Sarah) swallowed them all with open mouth, scarcely deigning to cast a look upon me. With mouth equally open, he swallowed the supper and the brandy for which I was paying; shutting mine every time I attempted to say a word by asking me had I ever served abroad. I never was so provoked in my life; and, when I saw him press her hand, I could have knocked him down, only that I have no practice in that line, which is sometimes considered to be doubly hazardous.

I saw little chance of winning my wager, and was in no slight degree out of temper; but all things, smooth or rough, must have an end, and at last it was time that we should retire. My Spanish hero desired to be called at four,—I don't know why,—and Sarah said, with a most fascinating smile,

"You may depend upon 't, sir; for, if there was no one else as would call you, I 'd call you myself."

"Never," said he, kissing her hand, "did Boots appear so beautiful!"

"Devil take you!" muttered I, as I moved up stairs with a rolling motion; for the perils of the journey, the annoyance of the supper-table, the anticipation of the lost dinner and unwon lady, aided, perhaps, by what I had swallowed, tended somewhat to make my footsteps unsteady.

My mustachoed companion and I were shown into adjacent rooms, and I fell sulkily asleep. About four o'clock I was aroused by a knocking, as I at first thought, at my own room, but which I soon found to be at that of my neighbour. I immediately caught the silver sound of the voice of Sarah summoning its tenant.

"It 's just a-gone the three ke-waters, sir, and you ought to be up."

"I am up already, dear girl," responded a voice from inside, in tones as soft as the potations at my expense of the preceding night would permit; "I shall be ready to start in a jiffy."

The words were hardly spoken when I heard him emerging, luggage in hand, which he seemed to carry with little difficulty.

"Good-b'ye, dear," said he; "forgive this trouble."

"It's none in the least in life, sir," said she.

And then—god of jealousy!—he kissed her.

"For shame, sir!" said Sarah. "You mustn't. I never permit it; never!"

And he kissed her again; on which she, having, I suppose, exhausted her stock of indignation in the speech already made, offered no observation. He skipped down stairs, and I heard her say, with a sigh, "What a nice man!"

The amorous thought rose softly over my mind. "Avaunt!" said I, " thou green-eyed monster; make way for Cupid, little god of love. Is my rump and my dozen yet lost? No. As the song says,

> "When should lovers breathe their vows?
> When should ladies hear them?
> When the dew is on the boughs,
> When none else is near them."

Whether the dew was on the boughs, or not, I could not tell; but it was certain that none else was near us. With the rapidity of thought I jumped out of bed, upsetting a jug full of half-frozen water, which splashed all over, every wretch of an icicle penetrating to my very marrow, but not cooling the ardour of my love. After knocking my head in the dark against every object in the room, and cutting my shins in various places, I at last succeeded in finding my dressing-gown, knee smalls, and slippers, and, so clad, presented myself at the top of the staircase before the barmaid. She was leaning over the balustrade, looking down through the deep well after the departing stranger, whose final exit was announced by the slamming of the gate after him by the porter. I could not help thinking of Fanny Kemble in the balcony scene of *Romeo and Juliet*.

She sighed, and I stood forward.

"Oh!" she screamed. "Lor' have mercy upon us! what's this?"

"Be not afraid," said I, "Sarah; I am no ghost."

"Oh, no," said she, recovering, "I didn't suppose you were; but I thought you were a Guy Fawkes."

"No, angelic girl, I am not a Guy Fawkes; another

flame is mine!" and I caught her hand, endeavouring to apply it to my lips.

"Get along, you old ———." I am not quite certain what the angelic Sarah called me; but I think it was a masculine sheep, or a goat.

"Sarah!" said I, "let me press this fair hand to my lips."

Sarah saved me the trouble. She gave me—not a lady's "slap," which we all know is rather an encouragement than otherwise,—but a very vigorous, well-planted, scientific blow, which loosened my two fore-teeth; and then skipped up stairs, shut herself in her room, and locked the door.

I followed, stumbled up stairs, and approached in the dark towards the keyhole, whence shone the beams of her candle. I was about to explain that innocence had nothing to fear from me, when a somewhat unintelligible scuffling up the stairs was followed by a very intelligible barking. The housedog, roused by the commotion, was abroad,—an animal more horrid even than the schoolmaster,—and before I could convey a word as to the purity of my intentions, he had caught me by the calf of the leg so as to make his cursed fangs meet in my flesh, and bring the blood down into my slippers. I do not pretend to be Alexander or Julius Cæsar, and I confess that my first emotion, when the brute let me loose for a moment, and prepared, with another fierce howl, for a fresh invasion of my personal comforts, was to fly, —I had not time to reflect in what direction; but, as my enemy came from below, it was natural that my flight should be upwards. Accordingly, up stairs I stumbled as I could, and the dog after me, barking and snapping every moment, fortunately without inflicting any further wound. I soon reached the top of the staircase, and, as further flight was hopeless, I was obliged to throw myself astride across the balustrade, which was high enough to prevent him from getting at me without giving himself more inconvenience than it seems he thought the occasion called for.

Here was a situation for a respectable citizen, tobacconist, and gallant! The darkness was intense; but I knew by an occasional snappish bark whenever I ventured to stir, or to make the slightest noise, that the dog was couching underneath me, ready for a spring. The thermometer must have been several yards beneath the freezing point, and I had nothing to guard me from the cold but a night-gown and shirt. I was barelegged and barefooted, having lost my slippers in the run. The uneasy seat on which I was perched was as hard as iron, and colder than ice. I had received various bruises in the adventures of the last few minutes, but I forgot them in the smarting pain of my leg, rendered acute to the last degree by exposure to the frost. And then I knew perfectly well, that, if I did not keep my seat with the dexterity of a Ducrow, I was exposed by falling on one side to be mangled by a beast of a dog watching my descent with a malignant pleasure, and, on the other, to be dashed to pieces by tumbling down from the top to the bottom of the house. The sufferings of Mazeppa were nothing compared to mine. He was, at least, safe from all danger of falling off his unruly steed. They had the humanity to tie him on.

Here I remained, with my bedroom candle in my hand,—I don't know how long, but it seemed an eternity,—until at length the dog began to retire by degrees, backwards, like the champion's horse at the coronation of George the Fourth, keeping his eyes fixed upon me all the time. I watched him with intense interest as he slowly receded down the stairs. He stopped a long time peeping over one stair so that nothing of him was visible but his two great glaring eyes, and then they disappeared. I listened. He had gone.

I gently descended; cold and wretched as I was, I actually smiled as I gathered my dressing-gown about me, preparatory to returning to bed. Hark! He was coming back again, tearing up the stairs like a wild bull. I caught sight of his eyes. With a violent spring I caught at and climbed to the top of an old press that stood on the landing, just as the villainous animal reared himself against it, scratching and tearing to get at me, and gnashing his teeth in disappointment. Such teeth too!

"Why, what is the matter?" cried the beauteous Sarah, opening her chamber door, and putting forth a candle and a nightcap.

"Sarah, my dear!" I exclaimed, "call off the dog, lovely vision!"

"Get along with you!" said Sarah; "and don't call me a lovely vision, or I'll scream out of my window into the street. It serves you right!"

"Serves me right, Sarah!" I exclaimed, in a voice which I am quite certain was very touching. "You'll not leave me here, Sarah; look, look at this dreadful animal!"

"You're a great deal safer there than anywhere else," said Sarah; and she drew in her head again, and locked the door, leaving me and the dog gazing at each other with looks of mutual hatred.

How long I continued in this position I feel it impossible to guess; it appeared to me rather more than the duration of a whole life. I was not even soothed by the deep snoring which penetrated from the sleeping apartment of the fair cause of all my woes, and indicated that she was in the oblivious land of dreams.

I suppose I should have been compelled to await the coming of daylight, and the wakening of the household, before my release from my melancholy situation, if fortune had not so far favoured me as to excite, by way of diversion, a disturbance below stairs, which called off my guardian fiend. I never heard a more cheerful sound than that of his feet trotting down stairs; and, as soon as I ascertained that the coast was clear, I descended, and tumbled at once into bed, much annoyed both in mind and body. The genial heat of the blankets, however, soon produced its natural effect, and I forgot my sorrows in slumber. When I woke it was broad daylight,—as broad, I mean, as daylight condescends to be in December,—an uneasy sensation surprised me. Had I missed the coach? Devoting the waiters to the infernal gods, I put my hand under my pillow for my watch; but no watch was there. Sleep was completely banished from my eyes, and I jumped out of bed to make the necessary inquiries; when, to my additional horror and astonishment, I found my clothes also had vanished. I rang the bell violently, and summoned the whole *posse comitatûs* of the house, whom I accused in the loftiest tones, of misdemeanors of all descriptions. In return I was asked who and what I was, and what brought me there; and one of the waiters suggested an instant search of the room, as he had shrewd suspicions that I was the man with the carpet-bag, who went about robbing hotels. After a scene of much tumult, the appearance of Boots at last cut the knot. I was, it seems, " No. 12, wot was to ha' gone by the Edenbry coach at six o'clock that morning, but wot had changed somehow into No. 11, wot went at four."

" And why," said I, " didn't you knock at No. 12?"

" So I did," said Boots; " I knocked fit to wake the dead, and, as there warn't no answer, I didn't like to wake the living: I didn't knock no more, 'specially as Sarah——"

" What of Sarah?" I asked in haste.

" —'Specially as Sarah was going by at the time, and told me not to disturb you, for she knowd you had been uneasy in the night, and wanted a rest in the morning."

"I waited for no further explanation, but rushed to my room, and dressed myself as fast as I could, casting many a rueful glance on my dilapidated countenance, and many a reflection equally rueful on the adventures of the night.

My place was lost, and the money I paid for it; that was certain: but going to Edinburgh was indispensable. I proceeded, therefore, to book myself again; and on doing so, found Joe Grabble in the coffee-room talking to Sarah. He had returned, like Paul Pry, in quest of his umbrella, or something else he had forgotten the night before, and I arrived just in time to hear him ask if I was off. The reply was by no means flattering to my vanity.

"I do not know nothink about him," said the indignant damsel, "except that, whether he's off or on, he's a nasty old willin."

"Hey-day, Peter!" exclaimed Joe, "So you are not gone? What is this Sarah says about you?"

"May I explain," said I, approaching her with a bow, "fair Sarah?"

"I don't want your conversation at no price," was

the reply. "You're an old wretch as I wouldn't touch with a pair of tongs!"

"Hey-day!" cried Joe. "This is not precisely the character you expected. The rump and dozen ——"

But the subject is too painful to be pursued. My misfortunes were, however, not yet at an end. I started that evening by the mail. We had not got twenty miles from town when the snow-storm began. I was one of its victims. The mail stuck somewhere in Yorkshire, where we were snowed up and half starved for four days, and succeeded only after a thousand perils, the details of which may be read most pathetically related in the newspapers of the period, in reaching our destination. When there, I lost little time in repairing to our agent, —a W.S. of the name of M'Cracken,—who has a handsome flat in Nicholson-street, not far from the College. He welcomed me cordially; but there was something dolorous in his tone, nevertheless.

"Sit ye down, Master Gayless; sit ye down, and tak' a glass o' wine; it wull do ye guid after yer lang and cauld journey. I hae been looking for ye for some days."

"What about the house of Screw and Longcut?" I inquired, with much anxiety.

"I am vera sorry to say, naething guid."

"Failed?"

"Why, jest that; they cam' down three days ago. They struggled an' struggled, but it wad no do."

"What is the state of their affairs?"

"Oh! bad—bad—saxpence in the pund forby. But, why were you no here by the cotch o' whilk ye advised me. That cotch cam' in safe eneuch; and it puzzled me quite to see yer name bookit in the way-bill, an' ye no come. I did no ken what to do. I suppose some accident detained you?"

"It was indeed an accident," replied I faintly, laying down my untasted glass.

"I hope it's of nae consequence elsewhere," said Mr. M'Cracken, "because it is unco unlucky *here;* for if ye had been in E'nbro' on the Saturday, I think—indeed I am sure—that we wad hae squeezed ten or twelve shillings in the pund out o' them,—for they were in hopes o' remittances to keep up; but, when the Monday cam' they saw the game was gane, and they are now clane dished. So you see, Mr. Gayless, ye're after the fair."

"After the *fair*, indeed," said I; for men can pun even in misery.

What my man of business told me, proved to be true.

The dividend will not be sixpence in the pound, and it is more than six hundred and fifty pounds odd out of my pocket. I had the expense (including that of a lost place) of a journey to Edinburgh and back for nothing. I was snowed up on the road, and frozen up on the top of a staircase. I lost a pair of teeth, and paid the dentist for another. I was bumped and bruised, bullied by a barmaid, and hunted by a dog. I paid my rump and dozen amid the never-ending jokes of those who were eating and drinking them; and I cannot look forward to the next dog-days without having before my eyes the horrors of hydrophobia.

Such was my last love!

A NIGHT OF TERROR.

[This story is partly translated, partly imitated, from the French. The French author, I suppose, was indebted to some German original. It is no great matter, so the reader likes it. Let us therefore, without further preface, begin.]

I.

You will recollect that, three years ago, we had a dreadful winter throughout Europe. It was severe in those quarters where the climate is usually genial: in the north it was absolutely dreadful. My sister and I were on a visit to our old friend, the Princess N——, at her Lithuanian castle. The thing was arranged that Adelaide was to be married to the Princess's son, Sobieski, who was daily expected from Spain. I suppose my sister looked forward to the arrival with more impatience than the rest of the party; and certainly its male portion were far more interested in hunting the wolf all the morning through the snows, and drinking down the fatigues of the chase in the evening over the fire, than in anything connected with the tender passion.

The wished-for morning arrived at last. Sobieski appeared in the castle of his ancestors amid the acclamations of an admiring peasantry, to be kissed by his mother, shaken hands with by his friends, and looked at, I suppose, by his betrothed. Foreign travel had improved him, and a single year had sufficed to turn the handsome stripling into a fine and noble-looking young man. The Princess was happy, Adelaide was happy, Sobieski was happy, we all were happy: but the happiness was destined to be of short duration; for we had hardly risen from breakfast when a wearied courier arrived, bringing in the melancholy information that my father had been suddenly taken ill in Bohemia, and that our attendance was instantly required, as his life was despaired of. It was of course necessary that we should start on the instant; no time could be lost, and our arrangements for departure were made with the utmost rapidity. Sobieski wished to have gone with us; but how could he leave his mother whom he had only seen for two or three hours after a year's absence? Besides, why expose him to the trouble and inconvenience of the journey? If, as we hoped, we found the alarm exaggerated, it would be easy to send for him, or to return: if the event were what our fears suggested, it was arranged that my sister's future home was to be that of the Princess. Adelaide and Sobieski had a long private interview before we parted. What they said I do not know; but it could not be hard to guess at what was the tenor of their conversation. With much reluctance he gave his consent to remain behind; but, farewell is a word that has been, and must be; it was spoken at last, and we set off in our travelling carriage about six in the morning through the snowy roads of Lithuania leading through the great forest.

We got over the short day without any adventures different from what might be expected. Our carriage sometimes stuck in the snow, sometimes narrowly escaped being upset by the stump of a tree. Relays on the road were few, and the people at the post-houses seemed half frozen, and afraid to open their mouths. We were tolerably independent of them for supplies, as we had been sufficiently stored before we started on our route. We left the last post-house about six in the evening, with a pair of fine, strong young horses, fit to contend with the night difficulties of the forest road. Those difficulties did not appear to be in any degree remarkably formidable. The full moon, just risen, cast a bright light all around, and a strong frost having set in, the path was hard and practicable. Our driver, an old retainer of the Princess, knew the forest well; for forty years, as chasseur or courier, postilion or coachman, he had traversed it at all hours of the day and night, and was as well acquainted with every "dingle and bosky bourne of the wild wood" as with his own stables. I forgot to say that, besides Adelaide and myself, her favourite French maid occupied the interior of the voiture. Heinrich smoked, whistled, and cracked his whip in solitary dignity without. There being nothing in the scenery or its associations to captivate the Parisian soul of Louise, who had done due justice to the contents of our basket while we changed horses, she speedily dropped into a profound slumber, to dream, I suppose, of the glories of the Palais Royal, and to transport herself from the woods and snows of Lithuania to the parterre of some theatre on the Boulevards. She soon gave us audible information that she was far away in the land of dreams, and that, if her slumbers were not melancholy, they were at least musical.

Let it not be imagined that my more delicate companion or myself permitted Louise to enjoy our basket-stored repast without co-operation. Our spirits were severely depressed; the dreaded death of a beloved father filled us both with sorrow and apprehension, and Adelaide in parting with Sobieski had her peculiar sources of grief. But it is a sad truth, that all the most sentimental emotions of the mind give place when the most unsentimental organ of the body makes its demand upon our attention; and the bracing air of the forest had largely contributed to the sharpening of the appetite. The substantial dainties of the Princess, aided by some generous hock, somewhat assisted in my case by a fair proportion of brandy, disposed us also to slumber, and Adelaide fell asleep on my shoulder. Her sleeping thoughts reverted in all probability to a certain Northern castle frowning over the flood, garnished with tower and turret, buttress and bulwark, fosse and rampart, drawbridge and portcullis, and every other adjunct of feudal war; but in which was also the picture-studded corridor, the gay salon, and, above all, the soft boudoir, where sounds more fitted for the ladies' ear than the clashing of arms were uttered; round which were formed trellised gardens, where bouquets, such as the North affords were culled, and where sauntering walks by morning-light or moonbeam made life forgotten; or spreading parks and chases, where some rode together who thought of other joys than those which the sylvan sports afforded. For my part, my mind wandered to the possible change of my mode of life and position in society. I loved my father with an affection which few sons feel: I admired the lustre of his military career; our house had been honoured by the fame he had won and the high repute he enjoyed; and I looked back with mingled love and reverence on the uniform kindness which I had experienced at his hands;—but I confess, I could not keep myself from thinking what I should do with the family estates when they came into my possession, of the mode in which I was to regulate my conduct, of the figure I was to cut at court, of the way I was to spend the next year,—of—of—of something else that it is now not necessary to speak about. In vain I reproached myself with thinking of anything but the impending death of a dear and honoured father. As I dropped into drowsy half-waking, half-sleeping, fits of dreaminess, other visions would occur, and it was only when I roused myself to look out of the voiture to see how we got on, that a sensation of sorrow would take possession of my mind. On my shoulder still slept Adelaide, on the other side snored Louise; outside smoked Heinrich, thinking, I take it for granted, of nothing but his horses, and these he drove steadily along.

On a sudden, however, it seemed as if they afforded him more than ordinary trouble. I was awaked from one of my noddings by hearing him devoting them to the infernal gods, in all the mingled dialects of Poland, Russia, and Germany,—and that for a crime which seldom awakens the indignation of a traveller in these regions. In spite of all his exertions, they had burst into a furious gallop. He cursed, and swore, and pulled, and tugged, but in vain. With alarmed eye and erected ear, the eager horses disregarded the utmost efforts of curb and bridle, and dragged us forward with a velocity I should have thought beyond their powers. As there was no danger of accident, I was rather amused by the unexpected vigour of our steeds, and the indignation of the usually phlegmatic Heinrich at their apostacy from the regulated pace of the road. All on a sudden, however, our driver ceased to swear, and, uttering a hasty ejaculation, something half-way between a prayer and a curse, exclaimed,

"The beasts are right—right, by a thousand devils right! I should have guessed it long ago."

And so saying, he surrendered to them the reins, no longer endeavouring to control their rapidity. I asked him what he meant. Turning cautiously round, and whispering so as not to disturb my sister, he breathed rather than spoke into my ear,

"They are coming."

"Who—who?" said I; "who are coming? There is not a human being in sight."

"I did not say there was," replied Heinrich; "and *they* are scarce in sight. But don't you hear them?"

"I hear nothing," said I, "but the whistling of the wind and the crushing of our own carriage through the snow."

"Hark!" interrupted Heinrich, dropping his pipe: "they *are* coming, by ——" But he suppressed the oath, and crossed himself instead. "Ay, there they are; I see them plain enough now."

"The last glass of brandy is in your head, Heinrich. What do you hear? What do you see? Who are *they?*"

Profoundly inclining his head, he whispered with a thrilling emphasis,

"THE WOLVES!"

II.

I removed Adelaide from my shoulder as gently as I could, so as not to awaken her, and, standing up in the voiture, looked in the direction pointed out by Heinrich. I looked, however, for a while in vain. I saw a dark mass at a distance in the snow, but, as the country was patched in all directions with timber, persisted, as firmly as ever did Bonaparte at Waterloo, that it was only trees. In about ten minutes, however, I was undeceived as completely as was the fated emperor, and by the same means. The dark mass was unquestionably in motion; and after I had ascertained that fact, my eye, sharpened by fear and anxiety, could perceive that the motion was not only rapid but accelerating. The sound, too, which in the distance I had taken to be the whistling of the wind, came more distinctly upon the breeze, and I recognized the dismal howling of the wolf rushing closer and closer every moment. The terrified horses, whose instinct had discovered to them the enemy long before his approach could be detected by any human organ, as if they were aware of their impending fate, galloped on with more desperate energy than ever, and Heinrich aided their exertions by all the skill of which he was master.

They came nearer and nearer. We could hear not only their dreadful howls, issuing from a hundred ravenous throats, but the tramp of their accursed paws pattering over the snow. I had no arms but a blunderbuss, a fowling-piece, and a brace of pistols: Heinrich had a long pistol. These arms, at best but inadequate against the number of our assailants, were rendered comparatively useless by the discovery we made at the very moment, that we had omitted to bring with us more powder and ball than was barely sufficient for another charge in addition to that which they already contained.

"What is to be done, Heinrich?" I asked in a whisper.

"There is no use in whispering now," said the old chasseur,—"they will be upon us in less than five minutes, and it would be better to wake Miss Adelaide and her woman, to inform them of our danger. Poor things! it would be terrible if they were taken out of the world, as we are very likely to be, without some notice!"

I acquiesced in the propriety of the advice, and roused Adelaide. I was about to inform her of the danger, but she had been lately dwelling for too long a time among huntsmen to render it necessary I should speak.

"Gracious heavens!" she exclaimed, starting up, "it is the howl of the wolf! Oh, Herman—Herman! what will become of us? I see them—I see them; they are gaining upon us. We are lost! We have but a few minutes to live! Last year an English party was torn to pieces and devoured by them some leagues beyond our castle! I shall never see my father again!"

Her cries woke her attendant, who, the moment she comprehended the danger, burst into an agony of yelling that almost rivalled in dissonance the cry of the wolves. She cursed herself, her fate, her stars, her folly, that ever drew her from France to this abominable country. She vowed to all the infernal powers she could think of, that if she were to escape this peril, she would never again commit a fault so unpardonable. She raved about herself, and her life, and her dress, and her Alphonse, (a smart *garçon cuisinier* in Paris, with whom she kept up an amatory correspondence, much to the detriment of King Louis-Philippe's French,) and all sorts of matters, horrible or flimsy, that crossed her distracted brain. I remember, particularly, that death itself did not seem to affect her with so much terror as the prospect of being devoured afterwards by a nasty wolf.

Her grotesque lamentations had the good effect of recalling my sister to her natural firmness of mind. She felt that in this trying occasion it became her to set an example of courage and resignation, and in an instant, (the whole scene I have been just describing did not occupy two minutes,) she was herself again. She assured me in a couple of words of her constancy, and pressed my hand to her heart to show that it was not beating with any undue emotion.

"It is no time to agitate you now, Herman," she said; "chances of escape, I know, are but small: but still, people have escaped from dangers as dreadful, and, under God, our hopes principally depend upon your presence of mind. Our defence is in your hands, and there I am content to leave it. With these words, she turned to her shrieking attendant, whom she endeavoured to soothe with all the topics of consolation— they were few enough in all conscience — she could think of, and to engage in some thoughts of religion, but all equally in vain: Louise could hear nothing but the howling of the wolves outside, and the howling of her own fears within.

The chase continued. I stood ready with my blunderbuss to discharge it on the herd the moment they approached within shot. I had too soon an opportunity. The fleetest of the pack in a few minutes approached within four or five paces of the voiture, and I fired. It was impossible to miss, and I saw two or three fall killed or wounded. To those who were hit it was soon matter of little importance whether the wound which brought them down was mortal or not, for they were in an instant surrounded by the rest, who fought for the fallen bodies. This obtained us the respite of a few minutes, which was occupied by the contest among themselves and the devouring of their slain brethren. We made the best of the time; but, the carcasses once demolished, and the bones left to whiten in the snow, the hunt recommenced, and we had not gained a mile when they came up with us again. My blunderbuss had been reloaded in the meanwhile, and on their near approach I again fired, with similar effect. But this time the respite was briefer. The wolves had now tasted blood, and their fury was excited, so that the devouring of their companions did not occupy half the space it did before, and speedily they renewed the chase with howlings far more terrific than ever.

I appealed to Heinrich, who drove his panting horses at their utmost speed.

"I have not," I said, "enough for another charge for the blunderbuss. What is best to be done?"

"It is of no use," said he, "to fire our fowling-pieces among them, for we could not expect to kill more than one, and that, so far from delaying would only spur them on faster. We had better reserve our fire for our last chance."

"Is there any?"

"One, and that but slight. Not far from this, but I do not know how far,—perhaps a mile, perhaps three,—is the old hunting-lodge built for the chasseurs of the forest. If we could reach that,—but what use is there in talking?—you see these poor devils of horses can scarcely hold out—they are almost sinking under the hell of a pace they have been keeping up this half-hour. Have you your pistols about you?"

"I have; why?"

"Do not discharge your last pistol on any account; no, not to save your own life. Keep it until ——"

Something choked the old man's utterance, and passing his hand over his face, he wiped off some moisture, which bore as much resemblance to a tear as anything his eyes could muster, and, applying to his lips his cherry-tree pipe, which was never forgotten in the extremest danger, he discharged a more than usually voluminous effusion of smoke. This done, he beckoned me to put my head out of the voiture, so that whatever he said should reach my ear alone. I complied.

"Keep it until these damned brutes,—God forgive me for using such words now!—until they are completely masters of the day, and we have no further chance, and then," sinking his voice to the lowest possible whisper, "discharge it into the brains of Miss Adelaide; put it to her temple, and be sure you do not miss."

God! how his words thrilled through my heart!—not even the horror of my own impending death, of the hideous manner in which it seemed inevitable that I should be cut off from existence in the flower of my youth, far from my friends, would how perhaps for ever remain ignorant of my untimely fate—not the fierce forms which I saw hurrying to my destruction, and anticipating with savage howl their bloody repast —not all the terrors of my situation so palsied me as this whisper of Heinrich. I looked at my sister. She was eminently beautiful; and if the dreadful scene around her had banished the colour from her cheeks, it had inspired her figure with an air of exalted courage, and filled her eyes with a blended fire of heroism and religion, that rendered her one of the most majestic beings I ever beheld. And this noble creature, I thought,—she, full of all that renders life one scene of happiness—she, qualified to inspire love and admiration into all hearts, the blessing or the ornament of every circle in which she moves—she, who yesterday was wrapped in visions of delight, who this morning woke to welcome the chosen of her heart, and whose present mission, melancholy as it is, was hallowed by filial duty and soothed by the recollection that she has been all that father could pray for,—is she to die—and so to die?—by the hand of me, her brother — her brother, who would gladly lay down his life for her? Alas! alas!

Perhaps I said these last words aloud, perhaps Heinrich divined what was passing in my bosom, for he continued in a whisper,

"To be sure, it is hard enough; but it is better than that she should die many deaths by the mangling of the wolves. You and I will fight the damned brutes,—God pardon me!—with our pistols to the last, and die like men; and it is no great matter how men die. And, indeed, it is little matter how that screaming baggage, who is almost as great a plague as the wolves themselves, comes to an end: she's fit food enough for them. But that dear young lady, just think from what a horrid death you save her! She must not be torn by the jaws of a wolf. I'd shoot her myself, dear master, with pleasure, but it would not become me, as you are here. It is you are to do it, for you are the head of the family. So don't flinch."

This conversation occupied only a few seconds. It was carried on in the most subdued voice, and I thought Adelaide had not heard it. I learned from her afterwards that she had distinctly heard every word. When I looked at her, she was busily endeavouring to soothe Louise. She told me that she had purposely avoided returning my glance, lest it might shake my resolution. "There was but one other hand in the world," she said afterwards, " by which I should have preferred to have died, if such death was inevitable. He was not there in person; he was indeed too vividly present in my heart, though his name escaped not my lips; and to whom, dear brother, could I look for deliverance but to you?" Such was the effect of the whispering on my sister. It had not passed unnoticed by Louise; though, as it was carried on in German, she would not have understood a word of it, even if spoken aloud. She failed not, however, to interpret it in her own manner.

"Ah, Heinrich! ah, dear baron!" she cried with an agony more intense than ever; "ah! do not—do not—do not! I am sure you cannot be so cruel. Ah, dear sweet Heinrich, of whom I was so fond!"

Even at that moment, Heinrich, who hated everything French in general, and Louise in particular for her especial impertinence towards him and his brother Germans in the service of the Princess, could not refrain from giving a most dissentient grunt.

"Dear Heinrich! dear Monsieur le Baron! do not be so cruel. I know what you are whispering about: I know you are going to throw me to the wolves, that you may get off while they are eating me. Oh, mon Dieu! mon Dieu!"

Adelaide endeavoured to edge in a word, but in vain.

"Oh! dear Monsieur le Baron, remember what became of the wicked prince who did the same to his courier: he was torn by his own dogs for it. Remember the wicked woman who threw her children: she was boiled alive for it. Oh! dear Mr. Heinrich, dear Monsieur le Baron,—oh! oh! oh!"

[Louise in her agony remembered two stories, one German and one French. The German story is, that some Polish prince, travelling through a forest, was pursued by wolves; and that a faithful heyduck devoted himself to save his master's life, by descending from the carriage, and making with his sabre a courageous fight against them as long as he could. He knew that he sacrificed himself, but he did it without a second thought, in order that, by delaying them first by whatever opposition he could offer, and then by the time it would take them to devour his body, his master might escape. His devotion was successful, and the grateful master, according to our version, provided for his family, and heaped his memory with honours. A different version is, that the selfish prince who consented to the sacrifice of so faithful a servant, reaped his reward, by being torn to pieces on entering his own gate by his dogs, who did not know him in the absence of his attendant, under whose immediate care they had been placed.—The other story is, I fear, true: it is that of a wretched mother, who with her three children were overtaken by wolves somewhere in the East of France, when, to save her own life, she flung away the children one by one to be eaten. The wolves pursued her to the gates of a neighbouring town, which was opened to save her; but when she told her story, the populace, indignant at the unnatural conduct of this worse than Medea, stoned her to death in the market-place. As a story never loses by the telling, it is currently said that they put her into a cauldron and boiled her alive.]

We had not time to pay any attention to the lament of the unfortunate *suivante*, for the wolves were by this time quite close upon the carriage. Fast they came as a dark cloud, scouring with inconceivable rapidity over the snow. Their dreadful howls reverberated through the forest, waking its every echo. We could see their flaming eyes, their snorting nostrils, their mouths and tongues red and dripping with the fresh blood of their mangled companions. Another moment and they would be upon us. The moment came, and there they were.

"Oh!" cried Heinrich, "keep them off one minute—one single minute, and we are at the hunting lodge. O that the horses may hold out!"

The poor animals exerted their last efforts. If we had been pressed too closely by the wolves, no other chance remained but to sacrifice them, and make our way as best we could to the lodge, while our assailants were fighting around the spoil. But there was no need; one wolf only succeeded in reaching the window of the voiture, and him I instantly shot with my fusil. Another was making the attempt; but I knocked him on the head with the butt end, and at least stunned him. Before a third could come up, the horses had made some desperate plunges forward, and the welcome lodge was gained. Heinrich jumped down at once, loudly calling me to follow him. I did so, and with the help of Adelaide dragging on Louise, who had fainted the moment the first wolf had put his nose into the carriage, in less than a second we found ourselves inside the iron-bound gate of the lodge.

"Thank God," I exclaimed, "WE ARE SAFE!"

III.

"A pretty safety indeed!" said Heinrich, who had lingered behind for a moment, as he firmly secured the gate. "However, here we are at all events. I had just time to take something out of the voiture that we shall find of use, and unharness the poor horses, to whom we all ought to be so much obliged, so as to give them a run for their lives, though there is hardly a run in them, before the brutes were upon me. I could barely say, ' Take that, canaille,' as I slapped my shot among them, which gave me an instant to get in. Ay! there you are, my beauties! howl away as you like, but you shall be baulked of your expected supper to-night."

The lodge in which we had taken refuge, like all such buildings, consisted of four bare walls of rough but uncommonly strong masonry, with stone benches built all round for the purpose of sitting or sleeping upon. It contained a rude fireplace without a chimney; and furniture it had none, except an iron pot, left behind by chance or design by its last tenants. It contained, however, a treasure to us of inestimable value,—the expected legacy of an immense heap of firewood, which the experienced hand of Heinrich speedily discovered in spite of the intense darkness. What he had risked his life to bring from the voiture, was my lamp and tinder-box; and, by their assistance, he soon succeeded in lighting an ample fire. Though the exertions of the preceding half-hour had sufficiently prevented our blood from stagnating, the tomb-like coldness of the lodge chilled us, now that the excitement was over, to the very soul. The genial warmth was, therefore, very acceptable, and even Louise began to revive. She at first uttered a cry of despair, when she saw herself in a gloomy vault beside a roaring fire, enveloped in thick clouds of smoke, through which she could but dimly discern our figures. She fancied she had descended to the other world, and did her old friend Heinrich the compliment of supposing him to be the devil.

"I am in no humour, woman," said he, "to listen to your prate. Thank your master and mistress, there, for saving you from the wolves, for the devil a hand I'd have stirred towards it. However, as you are here, take this drop of brandy; and that may call back your brains again, if you ever had any in your paper skull."

He proffered her the draught of what he considered a panacea for all the ills of life, and which, to do him justice, he did not prescribe without having duly tried its qualities upon himself. While hastily running back for the tinderbox, he could not resist the temptation of carrying off a small basket of provisions, which happened to contain a brandy-bottle, and it was put into immediate requisition. Louise received the glass with unfeigned politeness in spite of the ungallant speech by which it was prefaced, and, cheered by the restorative, and delighted beyond measure with her escape, was beginning a long story of her own courage during the adventure, when she was suddenly interrupted by a piercing shriek from outside.

"Silence!" said Heinrich mournfully. "I thought so. It is the poor horses, sir. They stand a great deal, the dumb beasts, without making cry or moan; but when one comes to be torn to pieces by wolves, it is quite a different thing. Ay, there's the other. There's an end of them both, poor things! I feared they had not a run in them; and the blackguard brutes outside have 'a supper after all,—and little good may it do them!"

"What!" said Louise with a fresh access of terror, "are the wolves outside?"

"Indeed they are," replied the chasseur, beginning to smoke. "You will soon hear them, my dear, and perhaps see them too. Don't be afraid, however, for a while," continued he, as he saw her clinging to her mistress; "all in good time—you are safe for a bit yet."

It was not long, indeed, before we heard them; for, apparently, after they had eaten the horses, they surrounded the building on all sides. We could hear them scraping and pushing against the gates, and endeavouring to climb up the wall. The only exit for the smoke was by an aperture in the roof, through which at first it issued in volumes, and seemed to serve as a sort of guide to the wolves; at least we heard them clambering along the roof, as if in search of an entrance. After a short time the smoke began to clear, and a fresh wind having arisen, it was so far blown away, that, looking up, we could plainly behold the blue sky studded with stars. You may believe me when I tell you that we had no taste for admiring heaven's clear azure, as we saw plainly that the aperture would enable the wolves to come down upon us. Our fears were not without foundation, for in a short time a wolf appeared and looked in. Louise fainted outright; but we lost no time in striking the intruder with our fowling-pieces, and the brute fell through the hole. We speedily knocked him on the head. Heinrich then thrust a large blazing spar through the aperture, and waved it about for a few minutes, uttering the cry used by the chasseurs when they hunt the wolf. We heard what appeared to us to be a general flight from the roof.

"They will not try that way again," said Heinrich, and he was right, "during the darkness; for they are scared off by the fire, and they have sufficient instinct to know that one of their party is killed. We are then safe all night."

"I wish," said I, "it was morning."

"It is a wise wish," said the old man; "for why should you wish for morning? Our horses are killed;

we have near twenty miles to get through snow to the next post-house; and how could Miss Adelaide, to say nothing of this helpless jade here, walk that distance before nightfall, when we should have the wolves on us again, if we had them not before? We must not expect another lodge like this. Nay, though this fire keeps away the wolves during the night, yet when daylight returns it will shine so much more dimly, that it will lose its effect, and daunt them no more."

"I thought," said I, " the wolves retired by day, and prowled only at night."

"Ay, that's generally the case; but when there is so strong a pack as this, and they know that prey is at hand, and see nobody to scare them away, they sometimes take courage, and do not dread the daylight. Besides, it must have been hunger that drove them so early into these parts; and what brought them here will keep them from going back."

" We, then, have no chance of escape ? "

" Nay, I don't say that neither: while there's life, there's hope. Something may fright the brutes off; or some travellers, seeing our carriage, may stop and come to our assistance; or——"

" Or, in short," said I, " some angel in seven-leagued boots may descend from the sky. But no matter, dear

Adelaide, we have at least another day's provision; and if the worst comes to the worst, as we lived together we shall die together. Strangers must close the eyes of our father, and strangers sit in his halls."

"It is the will of God, dear Herman," said Adelaide; "and God's will be done!"

We wrapped ourselves in our cloaks, and tried to sleep during that dismal night. Louise, who had shrieked and moaned away all her powers, did, I believe, at last fall into an exhausted slumber. Heinrich smoked, and sipped brandy, and alternately sung snatches of ballads or mumbled forth fragments of prayers, until he was as soundly asleep as if he was in bed. Adelaide and I were silent, ruminating on our condition, on the blighting of budding hopes and the darkening of brilliant prospects—on the melancholy fate for which we were reserved, and on our father waiting in the sickly suspense of hope deferred for his children, and perhaps sinking down to die chiding us for the unkindness of our delay. In reflections such as these passed the night, undisturbed by any sound but that of the ceaseless howling of the wolves outside, and the crackling of the faggots within.

All things must have an end, and so had this night. The tardy day broke at last, and Heinrich, rousing himself, flung numerous logs on the fire to excite as great a blaze as possible.

"It will be all of no use," muttered the old chasseur as he plied this work; "they will come in spite of us: but one should never give up. In the meantime, let us take whatever we can get for breakfast; for, believe me, we shall want all the strength and spirits we can muster before long."

He prepared breakfast accordingly, as well as his materials allowed, and we partook of it with heavy hearts. The sun soon shone brightly through the aperture, and the logs began to " pale their ineffectual fire." We made ourselves ready for the expected attack; for, as Heinrich anticipated, the wolves had not withdrawn. A sufficient charge for the blunderbuss, which I committed to the chasseur, was scraped together from our united stores, and, except my pistols, one of which, to say the truth, I had reserved for myself, if dire necessity imposed on me that use of the other on which I dreaded to think, we had no other means of defence but the butt-ends of our fusils. Nothing beyond howling occurred until about three hours after sunrise,—and what awful hours were they!—when suddenly our eyes, which were scarcely for a moment diverted from the aperture, saw the object of their fear. Two or three wolves of the largest size had climbed up the roof, and were preparing to jump in. A discharge of the blunderbuss drove them away, and the body of one huge brute dropped dead into the lodge. Short respite!—the way was found, and the sun had deprived the firebrand of its power. Another and fiercer relay was soon on the roof, and we had no means of preventing their descent.

"Now," whispered Heinrich, "may God help us! for there is no help for us in this world. Have you the pistol ready?"

I assented by a glance.

The shaggy wolves, howling incessantly, glared down upon us with ravenous eyes from the top, waiting the moment to spring. Below stood Heinrich and I, illuminated in the blaze of the faggots, our reversed fowling-pieces in our hands ready to strike. Louise lay at our feet prostrate, fainting on the ground; and Adelaide, sunk upon her knees, seemed, as the light from above streamed upon her uplifted countenance, emerging in radiant beauty from the smoke and glare, like an angel about to wing her way back to her native heaven from the darkness and the turmoil of a hapless and uncongenial world.

* * * * *

"And is this all?" said my cousin Lucy.

"I have not time," said I, "to write any more, for I am going out to shoot with your brother Dick."

"But I tell you this will never do: you must put an end to it. How were they saved?"

"Are you sure they were saved?"

"Yes, quite sure; else how could you hear Herman tell the story? And he says, beside, that Adelaide told him how she overheard his whispering."

"Ah! I forgot that; but I must be off."

"Not before you finish the story."

"Finish it yourself."

"I can't—it's not my business."

"Why, you will never thrive in it, if you cannot devise some way of bringing in the lover to the rescue, with his train of huntsmen and wolf-dogs. He must have heard of the bursting down of a pack of wolves, and following on their traces just at the right moment to save the party, to kill the marauders, to put fresh horses to the carriage, to whirl off to papa, and to come in time for his blessing. Then the rest is easy. Herman gets the estate,—Sobieski gets his wife;—they both get back to his mother's; there they get—very happy,—and I get rid of the story."

WAYLAC.

THE TWO BUTLERS OF KILKENNY.

In all countries and all languages we have the story of *Il Bondocani*. May I tell one from Ireland? It is now almost a hundred years ago—certainly eighty—since Tom—I declare to Mnemosyne I forget what his surname was, if I ever knew it, which I doubt,—It is at least eighty years since Tom emerged from his master's kitchen in Clonmell, to make his way on a visit to foreign countries.

If I can well recollect dates, this event must have occurred at the end of the days of George the Second, or very close after the accession of George the Third, because in the course of the narrative it will be disclosed that the tale runs of a Jacobite lord living quietly in Ireland, and that I think must have been some time between 1740 and 1760,—or say '65. Just before the year of the young Pretender's burst, a sharp eye used to be kept upon the "honest men" in all the three kingdoms; and in Ireland, from the peculiar power which the surveillance attendant on the penal laws gave the government, this sharp eye could not be surpassed in sharpness,—that is to say, if it did not choose to wink. Truth, nevertheless, makes us acknowledge that the authorities of Ireland were ever inclined at the bottom of their hearts to countenance lawlessness, if at all recommended by anything like a noble or a romantic name. And no name could be more renowned or more romantic than that of Ormond.

It is to be found in all our histories well recorded. What are the lines of Dryden?—and Dryden was a man who knew how to make verses worth reading.

And the rebel rose stuck to the house of Ormond for many a day;—but it is useless to say more. Even I who would sing, "Lilla bullalero bullen a la,"—if I could, only I can't sing,—and who give "The glorious, pious, and immortal memory," because I can toast,—even I do not think wrong of the house of Ormond for sticking as it did to the house of Stuart. Of that, too, I have a long story to tell some time or another.

Never mind. I was mentioning all this because I have not a "Peerage" by me; and I really do not know who was the Lord Ormond of the day which I take to be the epoch of my tale. If I had a "Peerage" I am sure I could settle it in a minute; but I have none. Those, therefore, who are most interested in the affair ought to examine a "Peerage," to find who was the man of the time;—I can only help them by a hint. My own particular and personal reason for recollecting the matter is this: I am forty, or more—never mind the quantity more; and I was told the story by my uncle at least five-and-twenty years ago. That brings us to the year 1812,—say 1811. My uncle—his name was Jack—told me that he had heard the story from Tom himself fifty years before that. If my uncle Jack, who was a very good fellow, considerably given to potation, was precise in his computation of time, the date of his story must have fallen in 1762—or 1763—no matter which. This brings me near the date I have already assigned; but the reader of my essay has before him the grounds of my chronological conjectures, and he can form his opinions on *data* as sufficiently as myself.

I recur fearlessly to the fact that Tom—whatever his surname may have been—emerged from the kitchen of his master in Clonmell, to make his way to foreign countries.

His master was a very honest fellow—a schoolmaster of the name of Chaytor, a Quaker, round of paunch and red of nose. I believe that some of his progeny are now men of office in Tipperary—and why should they not? Summer school-vacations in

Ireland occur in July; and Chaytor—by the by, I think he was *Tom* Chaytor, but if Quakers have Christian names I am not sure—gave leave to his man Tom to go wandering about the country. He had four, or perhaps five days to himself.

Tom, as he was described to me by my uncle over a jug of punch about a quarter of a century ago, was what in his memory must have been a smart-built fellow. Clean of limb, active of hand, light of leg, clear of eye, bright of hair, white of tooth, and two-and-twenty: in short, he was as handsome a lad as you would wish to look upon in a summer's day. I mention a summer's day merely for its length; for even on a winter's day there were few girls that could cast an eye upon him without forgetting the frost.

So he started for the land of Kilkenny, which is what we used to call in Ireland twenty-four miles from Clonmell. They have stretched it now to thirty; but I do not find it the longer or shorter in walking or chalking. However, why should we grumble at an act of "justice to Ireland?" Tom at all events cared little for the distance; and, going it at a slapping pace, he made Kilkenny in six hours. I pass the itinerary. He started at six in the morning, and arrived somewhat foot-worn, but full not only of bread, but of wine (for wine was to be found on country roadsides in Ireland in those days), in the ancient city of Saint Canice about noon.

Tom refreshed himself at the "Feathers," kept in those days by a man named Jerry Mulvany, who was supposed to be more nearly connected with the family of Ormond than the rights of the church could allow; and having swallowed as much of the substantial food and the pestiferous fluid that mine host of the "Feathers" tendered him, the spirit of inquisitiveness, which, according to the phrenologists, is developed in all mankind, seized paramount hold of Tom. Tom—? ay, Tom, it must be, for I really cannot recollect his other name.

If there be a guide-book to the curiosities of Kilkenny, the work has escaped my researches. Of the city it is recorded, however, that it can boast of fire without smoke, air without fog, and streets paved with marble. And there's the college, and the bridge, and the ruins of St. John's Abbey, and St. Canice, and the Nore itself, and last, not least, the castles of the Ormonds, with its woods, and its walks, and its stables, and its gallery, and all the rest of it, predominating over the river. It is a very fine-looking thing indeed; and, if I mistake not, John Wilson

Croker, in his youth, wrote a poem to its honour, beginning with

"High on the sounding banks of Nore,"

every verse of which ended with "The castle," in the manner of Cowper's "My Mary," or Ben Jonson's "Tom Tosspot." If I had the poem I should publish it here with the greatest pleasure; but I have it not. I forget where I saw it, but I think it was in a Dublin magazine of a good many years ago, when I was a junior sophister of T. C. D.

Let the reader, then, in the absence of this document, imagine that the poem was infinitely fine, and that the subject was worthy of the muse. As the castle is the most particular lion of the city, it of course speedily attracted the attention of Tom, who swaggering in all the independence of an emancipated footman up the street, soon found himself at the gate. "Rearing himself thereat," as the old ballad has it, stood a man basking in the sun. He was somewhat declining towards what they call the vale of years in the language of poetry; but by the twinkle of his eye, and the purple rotundity of his cheek, it was evident that the years of the valley, like the lads of the valley, had gone cheerily-o! The sun shone brightly upon his silver locks, escaping from under a somewhat tarnished cocked-hat guarded with gold lace, the gilding of which had much deteriorated since it departed from the shop of the artificer; and upon a scarlet waistcoat, velvet certainly, but of reduced condition, and in the same situation as to gilding as the hat. His plum-coloured breeches were unbuckled at the knee, and his ungartered stockings were on a downward progress towards his unbuckled shoes. He had his hands—their wrists were garnished with unwashed ruffles—in his breeches pockets; and he diverted himself with whistling "Charley over the water," in a state of *quasi*-ruminant quiescence. Nothing could be plainer than that he was a hanger-on of the castle off duty, waiting his time until called for, when of course he was to appear before his master in a more carefully arranged costume.

Ormond Castle was then, as I believe it is now, a show-house, and the visitors of Kilkenny found little difficulty in the admission; but, as in those days purposes of political intrusion might be suspected, some shadow at least of introduction was considered necessary. Tom, reared in the household of a schoolmaster, where the despotic authority of the chief extends a flavour of its quality to all his ministers,

exhilarated by the walk, and cheered by the eatables and drinkables which he had swallowed, felt that there was no necessity for consulting any of the usual points of etiquette, if indeed he knew that any such things were in existence.

"I say," said he, "old chap! is this castle to be seen? I'm told it's a show; and if it is, let's have a look at it."

"It is to be seen." replied the person addressed, "if you are properly introduced."

"That's all hum!" said Tom. "I know enough of the world, though I've lived all my life in Clonmell, to know that a proper introduction signifies a tester. Come, my old snouty, I'll stand all that's right if you show me over it. Can you do it?"

"Why," said his new friend, "I think I can; because, in fact, I am——"

"Something about the house, I suppose. Well, though you've on a laced jacket, and I only a plain frieze coat, we are both brothers of the shoulder-knot. I'll tell you who I am. Did you ever hear of Chaytor the Quaker, the schoolmaster of Clonmell?"

"Never."

"Well, he's a decent sort of fellow in the *propria*

quæ maribus line, and gives as good a buttock of beef to anybody that gets over the threshold of his door as you'd wish to meet; and I am his man,—his valley de sham, head gentleman ——"

"Gentleman usher?"

"No, not usher," responded Tom indignantly; "I have nothing to do with ushers; they are scabby dogs of poor scholars, sizards, half-pays, and the like; and all the young gentlemen much prefer me: —but I am his *fiddleus Achates,* as Master Jack Toler calls me,—that's a purty pup who will make some fun some of these days,—his whacktotum, head-cook, and dairy-maid, slush, and butler. What are you here?"

"Why," replied the man at the gate, "I am a butler as well as you."

"Oh! then we're both butlers; and you could as well pass us in. By course, the butler must be a great fellow here; and I see you are rigged out in the cast clothes of my lord. Isn't that true?"

"True enough; he never gets a suit of clothes that it does not fall to my lot to wear it; but if you wish to see the castle, I think I can venture to show you all that it contains, even for the sake of our being two butlers."

It was not much sooner said than done. Tom

accompanied his companion over the house and grounds, making sundry critical observations on all he saw therein—on painting, architecture, gardening, the sublime and beautiful, the scientific and picturesque—in a manner which, I doubt not, much resembled the average style of reviewing those matters in what we now call the best public instructors.

"Rum-looking old ruffians!" observed Tom, on casting his eyes along the gallery containing the portraitures of the Ormonds. "Look at that fellow there, all battered up in iron; I wish to God I had as good a church as he would rob."

"He was one of the old earls," replied his guide, "in the days of Henry the Eighth; and I believe he did help in robbing churches!"

"I knew it by his look," said Tom; "and there's a chap there in a wilderness of a wig. Gad! he looks as if he was liked to be hanged."

"He was so," said the cicerone; "for a gentleman of the name of Blood was about to pay him that compliment at Tyburn."

"Serve him right," observed Tom; "and this fellow with the short stick in his hand;—what the deuce is the meaning of that?—was he a constable?"

"No," said his friend, "he was a marshal; but he

had much to do with keeping out of the way of constables for some years. Did you ever hear of Dean Swift?"

"Did I ever hear of the Dane? Why, my master has twenty books of his that he's always reading, and he calls him Old Copper-farthing; and the young gentlemen are quite wild to read them. I read some of them wance (once); but they were all lies, about fairies and giants. Howsoever, they say that the Dane was a larned man."

"Well, he was a great friend of that man with the short stick in his hand."

"By dad!" said Tom, "few of the Dane's friends was friends to the Hanover succession; and I'd bet anything that the flourishing-looking lad there was a friend to the Pretender."

"It is likely that if you laid such a bet you would win it. He was a great friend also of Queen Anne. Have you ever heard of her?"

"Heard of Brandy Nan! To be sure I did—merry be the first of August! But what's the use of looking at those queer old fools?—I wonder who bothered themselves painting them?"

"I do not think you knew the people;—they were Vandyke, Lely, Kneller."

"I never heard of them in Clonmell," remarked Tom. "Have you anything to drink?"

"Plenty."

"But you won't get into a scrape? Honour above all; I'd not like to have you do it unless you were sure, for the glory of the cloth."

The pledge of security being solemnly offered, Tom followed his companion through the intricate passages of the castle until he came into a small apartment, where he found a most plentiful repast before him. He had not failed to observe that, as he was guided through the house, their path had been wholly uncrossed, for, if anybody accidentally appeared, he hastily withdrew. One person only was detained for a moment, and to him the butler spoke a few words in some unknown tongue, which Tom of course set down as part of the Jacobite treason pervading every part of the castle.

"Gad!" said he, while beginning to lay into the round of beef. "I am half inclined to think that the jabber you talked just now to the powder-monkey we met in that corridor was not treason, but beef and mustard: ain't I right?"

"Quite so."

"Fall to, then, yourself. By Gad! you appear to

have those lads under your thumb—for this is great eating. I suppose you often rob my lord?—speak plain, for I myself rob ould Chaytor the schoolmaster; but there's a long difference between robbing a schoolmaster and robbing a lord. I venture to say many a pound of his you have made away with."

"A great many indeed. I am ashamed to say it, that for one pound he has lost by anybody else he has lost a hundred by me."

"Ashamed, indeed! This is beautiful beef. But let us wash it down. By the powers! is it champagne you are giving me? Well, I never drank but one glass of it in my life, and that was from a bottle that I stole out of a dozen which the master had when he was giving a great dinner to the fathers of the boys just before the Christmas holidays the year before last. My service to you. By Gor! if you do not break the Ormonds, I can't tell who should."

"Nor I. Finish your champagne. What else will you have to drink?"

"Have you the run of the cellar?"

"Certainly."

"Why, then, claret is genteel; but the little I drank of it was mortal cold. Could you find us a glass of brandy?"

"Of course:" and on the sounding of a bell there appeared the same valet who had been addressed in the corridor; and in the same language some intimation was communicated, which in a few moments produced a bottle of Nantz, rare and particular, placed before Tom with all the emollient appliances necessary for turning it into punch."

"By all that's bad," said the Clonmellian butler, "but you keep these fellows to their knitting. This is indeed capital stuff. Make for yourself. When you come to Clonmell, ask for me—Tom—at old Chaytor's, the Quaker schoolmaster, a few doors from the Globe. This lord of yours, I am told, is a bloody Jacobite; here's the Hanover succession! but we must not drink that here, for perhaps the old fellow himself might hear us."

"Nothing is more probable."

"Well, then, mum's the word. I'm told he puts white roses in his dog's ears, and drinks a certain person over the water on the tenth of June; but no matter, this is his house, and you and I are drinking his drink,—so why should we wish him bad luck? If he was hanged, of course I'd go to see him, to be sure; would not you?"

"I should certainly be there."

By this time Tom was subdued by the champagne and the brandy, to say nothing of the hot weather; and the spirit of hospitality rose strong upon the spirit of cognac. His new friend gently hinted that a retreat to his *gîte* at the "Feathers" would be prudent; but to such a step Tom would by no means consent unless the butler of the castle accompanied him to take a parting bowl. With some reluctance the wish was complied with, and both the butlers sallied forth on their way through the principal streets of Kilkenny, just as the evening was beginning to assume somewhat of a dusky hue. Tom had, in the course of the three or four hours passed with his new friend, informed him of all the private history of the house of Ormond, with that same regard to veracity which in general characterises the accounts of the births, lives, and educations of persons of the higher classes, to be found in fashionable novels and other works drawn from the communications of such authorities as our friend Tom; and his companion offered as much commentary as is usually done on similar occasions. Proceeding in a twirling motion along, he could not but observe that the principal persons whom they met bowed most respectfully to the gentleman from the castle; and, on being assured that this token of deference was paid because they were tradesmen of the castle, who were indebted to the butler for his good word in their business, Tom's appreciation of his friend's abilities in the art of " improving " his situation was considerably enhanced. He calculated that if they made money by the butler, the butler made money by them; and he determined that, on his return to Clonmell, he too would find tradesfolks ready to take hats off to him in the ratio of pedagogue to peer.

The Kilkenny man steadied the Clonmell man to the " Feathers," where the latter most potentially ordered a bowl of the best punch. The slipshod waiter stared; but a look from Tom's friend was enough. They were ushered into the best apartment of the house,—Tom remarking that it was a different room from that which he occupied on his arrival; and in a few minutes the master of the house, Mr. Mulvany, in his best array, made his appearance with a pair of wax candles in his hands. He bowed to the earth as he said,

" If I had expected you, my ———"

" Leave the room," was the answer.

" Not before I order my bowl of punch," said Tom.

" Shall I, my ———"

" Yes," said the person addressed; whatever he likes."

"Well," said Tom, as Mulvany left the room, "if ever I saw anything to match that. Is he one of the tradespeople of the castle? This does bate everything. And, by dad, he's not unlike you in the face neither! Och! then, what a story I'll have when I get back to Clonmell."

"Well, Tom," said his friend, "I may perhaps see you there; but good-by for a moment. I assure you I have had much pleasure in your company."

"He's a queer fellow that," thought Tom, "and I hope he'll soon be back. It's a pleasant acquaintance I've made the first day I was in Kilkenny. Sit down, Mr. Mulvany," said he, as that functionary entered, bearing a bowl of punch, "and taste your brewing." To which invitation Mr. Mulvany acceded, nothing loth, but still casting an anxious eye towards the door.

"That's a mighty honest man," said Tom.

"I do not know what you mean," replied the cautious Mulvany; for "honest man" was in those days another word for Jacobite.

"I mane what I say," said Tom; "he's just showed me over the castle, and gave me full and plenty of the best of eating and drinking. He tells me he's the butler."

"And so he is, you idiot of a man!" cried Mulvany. "He's the chief Butler of Ireland."

"What?" said Tom.

"Why, him that was with you just now is the Earl of Ormond."

My story is over—

"And James Fitzjames was Scotland's king."

All the potations, pottle-deep, the roadside drinking, the champagne, the cognac, the punch of the "Feathers," vanished at once from Tom's brain, to make room for the recollection of what he had been saying for the last three hours. Waiting for no further explanation, he threw up the window (they were sitting on a ground-floor), and leaving Mr. Mulvany to finish the bowl as he pleased, proceeded at a hand-canter to Clonmell, not freed from the apparition of Lord Ormond before he had left Kilcash to his north; and nothing could ever again induce him to wander in the direction of Kilkenny, there to run the risk of meeting with this fellow-butler, until his lordship was so safely bestowed in the family vault as to render the chance of collision highly improbable. Such is my *Il Bondocani*.

T. C. D.

A LOVE STORY IN THREE CHAPTERS.

CHAPTER I.

" —— Whence springs this deep despair?
From such a cause as fills mine eyes with tears,
And stops my tongue, while heart is drown'd in cares."
Henry the Sixth. Third Part, Act iii. Sc. 3.

I HAD not seen Russell for many years—nearly a dozen. We were contemporaries in college, but many events kept us asunder. I spent a considerable time on the Continent; and when I returned, it so chanced that my visits to London were short and far between. I heard of him occasionally, but with no minute particulars as to his career. It was merely known to me that he had been called to the bar, and that the expected succession to a tolerably handsome inheritance, by the death of an uncle some few years earlier than it had been calculated upon, made him at first indifferent to his profession, and shortly estranged him from it altogether in everything but name. In fact, I knew scarcely anything about him, and for some four or five years had hardly heard his name mentioned.

Business with which it is needless to trouble any one but those immediately concerned, rendered it necessary that I should pass through London, last month, on my way to America. I had only four or five days to remain in town, and these were busily occupied. On the day before my departure, however, it so happened that all I had to do was got over at an early hour, and I lounged somewhat easily through the streets, diverting myself with their various wonders, when I was saluted by a friendly slap on the shoulder. Turning round, I recognised my old friend Russell. He was not much altered during the twelve years I had not seen him,—much less, in fact, than men usually alter,—and his manner and style of address were as good-humoured and good-natured as ever.

After the usual wonderments, and mutual applauses of our marvellous good looks, we fell into such conversation as might be expected between old acquaintances meeting after a long period of absence. Jack This was dead, Tom T'other was married; Will Smith had got on in the world, Joe Brown had been unlucky. Bright-eyed Miss A. was now sober-eyed Mrs. B. with half a dozen daughters, one to come out this season; brighter-eyed Lady C. the reigning belle of our early circle, was still unmarried. Then there was that shocking story of Mrs. D. and the sad fate of poor Sir Richard E. and so on until we got through the alphabet of our old friends chatting in this manner, as we sauntered along, not caring where. The evening began to set in, and Russell asked me if I was engaged to dine. I answered in the negative, and he therefore made it a point that I should dine with him.

"Must I dress?" said I; "For I start for Liverpool in the morning, my luggage is all packed up; so if there be the least ceremony, I must decline."

"Not the least—you may come precisely as you stand, and we are not very far distant from our destination."

I accompanied him, and a few minutes brought us to his house. It is situated in one of the good streets near Cavendish Square, and among the most spacious of its neighbourhood. We arrived there about six o'clock. He apologised for leaving me for a moment, and I found myself alone in an elegantly-furnished drawing-room. It is hard to say what it is that reveals the presence of a lady in a house, and yet you cannot enter one in which she dwells without being at once convinced of female superintendence. It is not merely order and care, for in the well-arranged house of a wealthy bachelor these may be attained with as much scrupulous rigour as in any *ménage* superintended by a lady. Nor is it necessary that the inexplicable array of those matters in which female taste, or what they are pleased to call industry, should be met with on the tiny tables they so much love, for these we do not always meet with; but the *ensemble* of a room inhabited by a lady has an air strikingly different from that which is the result of the carelessness of a master or the anxiety of a servant. Such was the air impressed on me by my first glance round Russell's drawing-room.

Is he married? I thought. Perhaps.—I never heard so. But then we have been so much asunder. —Would he not have said something about it? But then he might have taken for granted that I knew of his marriage, but nothing of his lady.

My doubts were soon resolved. Russell returned with some slight alteration of dress.

"You are a man of the world," he said, "George, —and, in short, have you any objection to meet to-day at dinner a lady to whom I give my name, but who,— who, in fact—never consulted the church about our union? I could not, of course, introduce her to Lady Herbert; but to you—"

"Never mind me," said I, "it is a matter of no consequence—I have seen too many strange things in my travels to start at so ordinary a trifle. Mrs. Russell shall be accepted by me as you introduce her."

His eye gleamed with satisfaction, and murmuring, "Poor Jane!" he diverted the conversation to some common-place topics. In a few minutes dinner was announced; and on proceeding to the dining-room, I found that the lady was there before us.

She was tall and dark, with hair as black as the skies at midnight, and eyes as flashing as the brightest meteors that ever flitted across them. Her features were handsome and lofty, but, I thought, marked by a varying expression of melancholy and sternness. This might be no more than mere fancy, occasioned by my knowledge of the unhappiness of her position. She was dressed in black velvet, which admirably set off her majestic and symmetrical figure. Her gestures and manner were of the highest order of grace and dignity, and the few words of greeting with which she addressed me were marked by a sweetness of tone, and an elegance of style, which acts like a masonic sign to introduce on the instant to each other persons who belong to what Burke calls the Corinthian capital of society. She is indeed a splendid woman. Her age may be about thirty, or, rather, a year or two less.

During dinner, our conversation was of the ordinary kind; her share in it was sufficient, however, to prove that she had mingled in good society, had read much, and had thought more. Russell's conduct towards her appeared to me to be studiously tender—nay, gallant. In her behaviour she seemed anxious to please him in every manner, but without for a moment bending from the stateliness which was evidently her ordinary characteristic. I played my part as if I had no suspicion that Mr. and Mrs. Russell were not united by the most orthodoxal ceremonies of the rubric.

We had talked ourselves into high spirits, when almost immediately after dinner, a servant brought a note to Russell. He evidently knew the writing of the address, for, making me a slight apology, he tore open the envelope with a look of the utmost chagrin. Glancing his eye over the contents with the rapidity of a moment, he looked first at Mrs. Russell, and said, "It is what we expected: it must be attended to at once." She turned deadly pale, and made no reply. "Herbert," said he, "I really must beg your pardon. Here is a cursed law business—a consultation, which I *must* attend. The chambers of the lawyers are not very far off, and I shall drive there as fast as I can. I hope that I need not be absent an hour. Will you excuse me? Take care of the claret on the table, and I am sure Mrs. Russell will entertain you in my absence. But I must go for an hour."

"I am sure," said I, "you leave me in good hands: Mrs. Russell, without the claret, would be a more than sufficient inducement to stay."

He laughed. She looked at me, and I returned the look. I do not know how it was, but the equivocal nature of her situation—or, rather, as it was known to me, its unequivocal nature—confused me under her glance: I suppose I looked somewhat puzzled. She coloured. It was clear the secret was known to us both. In a few minutes the wheels of Russell's cab were heard in rapid whirl bearing him off to his destination.

I began playing with the walnuts before me, thinking of a topic to commence upon; but I was speedily saved the trouble.

"Sir George," said the lady, fixing her dark eyes upon me, "you know what I am here."

I paused.

"You know that I am not the wife of Arthur Russell—say it. Your looks have said so already: it is less sorrow to be stigmatised by the tongue, than pitied or despised by the eye."

"Stigmatised! Mrs. Russell," I exclaimed; "who stigmatises you? I am sure I do not."

"You know it, then, from Arthur? perhaps—but no matter. He had a right to put you on your guard against what you would have heard less kindly from all the world. Yet I know *you* will not judge of me hardly."

"Mrs. Russell ———"

"No! I know *you* will not. There was a kindness and a good-nature in your tone about women to-day at dinner,—alas! was it affected to console me? It may be so. How can I help it, if it were! If that were the only hypocrisy in the world, how little should I have cause to feel so keenly as I do now!"

"I spoke, Mrs. Russell, as I thought, without reference to anything beyond the subject on which we were talking. Do not agitate yourself to no purpose: I am incapable, I hope, of offering the insolence either of affront or patronage to any lady in the world."

"I do not know. You seem kind, at all events. Do not despise me utterly."

"I do not despise you at all. Why, dear Mrs. Russell, ——"

"Give me a glass of wine; the fit is passing. I was almost overpowered just now: but I am calm at present,—calm—calm—quite calm." And she bent her head upon her hand and wept aloud.

CHAPTER II.

"Left her in her tears, and dried not one of them with his comfort; swallowed his vows whole * * * in few bestowed on her, her own lamentation, which yet she wears for his sake,"
"His unjust unkindness,
That in all reason should have quench'd her love,
Hath, like an impediment in the current, made it
More violent and unruly."
Measure for Measure. Act iii. Sc. 1.

"You have known Russell long?" she said recovering herself.

"Almost from his boyhood. Circumstances have separated us, but we were most intimate friends in youth."

"I have heard him mention your name with great affection; and in some things which I have heard of you from others, know you acted like a gentleman and a man of honour. Do you care much about Russell?"

"It is an odd question," I answered. "I have already told you he was a friend of my youth; and though years have elapsed since I last saw him before to-day, I do not think my original feelings towards him are in the slightest degree altered. He was, when I knew him, and I am sure he is still, an honourable, high-minded, noble, and generous fellow, full of kindly dispositions, and possessed of the accomplishments which ornament the solid merits of life."

"He is," she said,—"he is all—all—all that you say. If you knew him as I know him, you would say more. He is the most unselfish of men. He has made sacrifices that few men would make—what no man whom I have ever met would make; and he has made them for me—for me, the degraded woman you see before you!"

"Nay, Mrs. Russell, do not use such ———"

"Mrs. Russell!—God forgive me! Am I Mrs. Russell—I, Mrs. Russell? Oh! Sir George, Sir George! you know that the name is in itself an insult. Nay, do not apologise; I know you meant none. Is it not another mark of kindness I do not deserve, that even the small respect of that thin-veiled covering of disgrace is granted me by him? Good Arthur! honourable Arthur! kind Arthur! dear Arthur! O that to those words of unfeigned affection I could add beloved Arthur!"

"And why not?"

"Why not? Oh, sir, ask me not the question! I know not. There is not a noble quality which I should not as willingly, as truly concede,—though concede is not the word—that I should not blazon forth, as the merit of that man. He is a handsome man, too, and fit to win a lady's love. But how little there is in that!—*he* was not handsome."

"Who?"

"No matter for a name," she said with a shudder. "I was talking of Russell. I was saying that all you, his old friend, could advance in his praise, was nothing to what I know of his goodness; but—I love him not."

I felt it was far too delicate a matter for me to interfere about, and I therefore held my tongue, looking as mysterious as I could. In the dilemma I took another class of claret, and cracked a filbert. She, too, was silent for a short space; but she was again the first to speak.

"It is odd why I should say this—this to a gentleman whom I have never seen before, who tells me that to-morrow is his last day in England, and whom, in all probability, I shall never see again. I say to you, who know nothing of me, who see me only in this melancholy and fallen situation—I say that which must make you despise me for my faithlessness, at least of heart, and my apparent treachery to your old friend who introduced you. But I love another."

Her tears fell fast, and I remained silent and embarrassed.

"I love another, sir," she continued; "as unlike your friend, as darkness to day, as baseness to honour, as falsehood to truth. Bear with me for a moment. I thought nothing more of Russell, some fifteen years ago, than that he was a pretty boy, when I was, as they told me, a pretty girl. We are about the same age—he is but two or three years older; and as our fathers dwelt in the same neighbourhood, we had played together in childhood; but the intercourse between our families was slight. When I first knew him, we had no notion that there were any such things as hearts to lose; and, God knows, I little dreamt of the horrid fate for which I was destined! There was, however, one—a gentleman he was, and he is in the eyes of the world,—he was a cousin of my own——. I must take another glass of wine. Mr. Russell is away, sir, and you are not doing as you would have done if he were here: take some more wine."

"It is no use in dwelling on the story. He persuaded me to leave my father's house: I left it. I am of good family—nay, I may say, I am of high family, Sir George, and I left my father's house with *him*. It is a shameful thing to tell: I was wrong—oh! how wrong! and how was I repaid! Smooth and elegant of manner, cruelty and selfishness alone swayed him: he sought but his own gratification, and for a passing whim would sacrifice all the stock of happiness of another. I do not think he ever seriously cared about me—I once thought he did. But, for some reason—may be he was tired of me, though scarce that, for I was not much more than seventeen, and it was but three months since he had taken me away from my father's house;—maybe he had other ladies in view, and that I *do* think, his present marriage is most unhappy, and, God forgive me! I am not Christian enough at heart to be sorry for it;—for some reason, no matter to me what, he left me one morning in furnished lodgings in London, telling me he would return to dinner. Fifteen years have passed, and, save in one or two casual glimpses, I have not seen him since. He left me ruined of name, exiled from my family, with scarcely a farthing in my pocket, a stranger, a beggar, and a word of scorn!"

"He was a scoundrel!" said I.

"So said my brother—my only brother, and he is no more!"

A still bitterer flood of tears followed these words. I shall not attempt to repeat the broken and scarcely intelligible conversation which immediately succeeded. I learned enough to know that her brother had challenged her seducer, and had been shot dead on the spot in the duel which followed; her father had inexorably resolved on not seeing her; the man who was the cause of all this sorrow shortly after married a somewhat elderly lady of large fortune; and my new confidante was, at the age of less than eighteen, flung upon her own resources in the most pitiable condition of helplessness.

CHAPTER III.

"One eye yet looks on thee;
But with my heart the other eye doth see.
Ah! poor our sex! this fault in us I find,
The error of our eye directs our mind:
What error leads must err."
Troilus and Cressida. Act v. Sc. 2.

AFTER a while, she continued, in a more composed strain—

" I knew not what to do. My brother's death, occasioned by me—and so occasioned, almost drove me mad. I do not know why I should say *almost*—I think I was quite mad. The people of the house in which I was abandoned, were civil—nay, kind; but I felt that I could not remain much longer. Where to go I knew not. The Serpentine was rising every moment in my thoughts; one plunge, and then adieu to my misfortunes for ever. A still more dreadful suggestion arose; for one of the servants, who was not deceived as to my situation, hinted plainly enough that I might live by infamy. Oh, sir! not even in that time of horror and despair, shameful as you may think—as indeed you must feel my present mode of life to be, not even in thought came I to that!

" But as I wandered, one day—destitute of all;

poverty and desperation suggesting the evil thoughts of self-inflicted death, or torturing me with dreaded anticipations of self-inflicted shame—towards the river, mere chance threw your friend Arthur Russell in my way. He knew all my melancholy—all my wicked story, and his heart melted. He brought me back to my apartments, he put an end at once to my pecuniary difficulties. I accepted these favours from him, as from the lad who had been the playfellow of my childhood, without scruple. He interested himself with my angry father, but in vain. He endeavoured to arouse the feelings and sympathies of my false lover, but in vain. He tried everything that the most zealous and the most honourable friend could do to lift me from my sunken position, but in vain. Just then his uncle died. He offered me an asylum in his house. God forgive me! I accepted it. How it is that we are thus living, I hardly know—nor does he. We liked one another's society, and our connexion became daily more and more intimate almost without our observing its progress. I have been a sad impediment to him in his onward course in life; but he loves me. Often and often has he pressed me to marry him. Oh! Arthur, Arthur! I cannot, I cannot!"

"Why not?" I asked: "if he wishes it, it may be easily managed. As for society ——"

"Society!" she said, flashing her dark and fierce eyes upon me,—"Society! do you think I care for that phantom of folly? Let me be in or out of it, it is nothing to me.—But, sir—Sir George, pardon a woman's weakness! your friend Arthur Russell is all that I can praise,—what he has done for me, what he has offered to do for me, shall never be erased from my soul; he— he, my seducer, has deceived me, cheated me, dishonoured me, robbed me, insulted me! by him my father's grey hairs have been, indirectly, brought to the tomb earlier than nature would have demanded; directly by his hand fell my only brother,—but then *he* exposed himself in that, life against life; he has done to me all that can hurt or grieve the heart, all that can humble or crush the feeling of woman; and still I love him; I love him, Sir George, as I loved him the first day I confessed it under the winning lustre of his false, false eyes."

She wept. I could not restrain my tears, though I made a strong effort.

"And yet," she continued, "I tried to check all recollections of my love; and in part I succeeded. I was beginning to be reconciled to my lot, such as it is, and to forget—oh, no! but not to think of what had been. But now the wound is opened afresh, and my heart is torn again from its nest of quietude. I told you *he* was my cousin: it so happened that, in the days of my delusion, I gave him an interest in some estates of which I was to be mistress when I came of age. How I had the right to do so, or how he had the power of converting that right, whatever it might have been, into money, I do not know—I do not care. If it had been my heart's blood, I should then have given it him. Why do I say *then?* I feel I should do it *now:* ay! after all—after all, I should do it again!—But my father died, leaving his property in such a manner as to come into the hands of the lawyers, and it is absolutely necessary that I should appear. Oh! that the estate was sunk at the bottom of the sea! I care nothing about it, I loathe its very name! I have not thought of it for many a long year. And now, I must meet *him*—ay! and alone."

"You distress yourself" I said, "without much reason, dear Mrs. Russell. If you meet this gentleman, it is on business. There will be attorneys, and barristers, and all the regular people of the law."

"No, no! it is quite necessary, on account of one thing in my father's will that no person should be present at first, but ourselves. It is a matter that none out of the pale of the family must know."

"Even so, still it is business. You will talk of

family affairs, deeds, wills, bonds, stamps, obligations, and so forth, with all the technicalities of law! There need not be any reference to other events."

"O, sir, sir, sir! that I could think it! I alone with him—I under the glance, within the influence of the magic of that voice, and talk of nothing else but the technical matters of the law! O that I could!"

"Why, Mrs. Russell, you should muster a lady's pride. Without wishing to speak more harshly of him than you have spoken, I think the gentleman's conduct to you has been such as to call up any other feelings than those of regard or respect, far less love. If a man had behaved to me with so much insolence, putting all other matters out of the question, I should be far more inclined to kick him down stairs than to receive him with even ordinary civility."

"You never loved, Sir George,—you never loved as a woman. I have mustered that lady-pride of which you speak; I have thought of all the wrongs I have suffered,—I have thought of the slight with which he insulted me, the shame he has wrought me,—I have thought of his meanness even in this matter of the money,—I have thought on my dead brother and on my broken family;—I have thought on the unutterable kindness, goodness, gentleness, generosity, the unwearied love, the self-sacrificing devotion, of this dear, dear gentleman with whom I live. I have contrasted it with the cold and calculating selfish heartlessness of the other;—I have summoned pride, anger, contempt, disdain, revenge, remorse, to my assistance;—and, God pity me! I feel assured that all will be defeated by one perjury-breathing accent, one softened look of practised falsehood. Well shall I know that they are perjury and falsehood; but can I resist them, when I know that they are assumed for me?"

"He is unworthy," said I, "of such affection; he is ——"

"Hush!" she said; "that is Russell's knock. I must clear my eyes. Do not say anything to him of my strange discourse. It was on that business he went —to have the papers ready for the lawyers: he is himself, you know, at the bar. It should have been done on the first day of term,—it is now the fifteenth,—but I put it off day by day. Oh! that the morning appointed for my meeting him—it must come soon, perhaps tomorrow,—Oh! that that morning found me dead!"

She left the room. Russell returned in good humour. "It was a troublesome job," said he, "about which I went; but I think I have smoothed it. The matter is not worth talking about, nor would you know anything of the parties if I told you. However, I think you will be glad in general to hear that a great scoundrel, and a most heartless scoundrel to boot, will get a trouncing, if some people's scruples can be got over. And I am pretty sure, too, that even without exposing those feelings to pain, it can be done. He is a ruined man to-morrow, as sure as fate!"

"Who?" I asked.

"A person," said Russell, darkening, "of whom you know nothing; but a scoundrel. A month cannot pass over, without his being driven to the pistol, as an escape from the hangman. But where is Jane?"

"She left the room only as you came in."

"Pardon me—I must see her."

In a few minutes she returned, paler than Carrara marble, in company with Russell. She cast her eyes on me as if to say, "Forget our conversation," and, at Russell's request, sate down to the piano, to sing, with sweet and unfaltering voice, the romantic ballads and melodies of which he is fond, as if there were nothing in the world to agitate or distress but the poetic sorrows sung in the melting notes that thrilled from her melodious tongue.

WAYLAC.

MY SOLDIER-BOY.

VERSES FOR MUSIC BY DR. MAGINN.

I give my soldier-boy a blade,
  In fair Damascus fashioned well;
Who first the glittering falchion swayed,
  Who first beneath its fury fell,
I know not, but I hope to know,
  That for no mean or hireling trade,
To guard no feeling base or low,
  I give my soldier-boy a blade.

Cool, calm, and clear, the lucid flood,
  In which its tempering work was done,
As calm, as clear, as cool of mood,
  Be thou whene'er it sees the sun.
For country's claim, at honour's call,
  For outraged friend, insulted maid,
At mercy's voice to bid it fall,
  I give my soldier-boy a blade.

The eye which marked its peerless edge,
  The hand that weighed its balanced poise,
Anvil and pincers, forge and wedge,
  Are gone, with all their flame and noise—
And still the gleaming sword remains.
  So when in dust I low am laid,
Remember by these heart-felt strains
  I gave my soldier-boy a blade.

FINIS.

Printed in the United Kingdom by
Lightning Source UK Ltd., Milton Keynes
141573UK00002B/23/P